Corporate Financial Analysis

Corporate Financial Analysis

Third Edition

Diana R. Harrington
University of Virginia

Brent D. Wilson
Nexus Consulting Group

1989

Homewood, IL 60430
Boston, MA 02116

© RICHARD D. IRWIN, INC. 1983, 1986 and 1989

A professional edition of this book is available through Dow Jones-Irwin.

Sponsoring editor: Michael W. Junior
Project editor: Suzanne Ivester
Production manager: Carma W. Fazio
Cover design: Diana Yost
Compositor: Carlisle Communications, Ltd.
Typeface: 10/12 Century Schoolbook
Printer: R. R. Donnelley & Sons Company

Library of Congress Cataloging-in-Publication Data
Harrington, Diana R., 1940-
    Corporate financial analysis.
    Includes bibliographies and index.
    1. Corporations—Finance. I. Wilson, Brent D.,
1944-   . II. Title.
HG4026.H34 1989   658.1′5   88–16631
ISBN 0-256-06514-4 (pbk.)

Printed in the United States of America
1 2 3 4 5 6 7 8 9 0 DO 5 4 3 2 1 0 9 8

For Will and Renee

Preface

This book was originally written with the objective of discussing financial analysis as it relates to decision making. For this third edition, although we have updated the examples and significantly changed the presentation of some concepts, the basic objective remains unchanged. We believe that analysis is useful only as it assists the manager in making better decisions and that the goal of decision making is to enhance the value of the firm. We believe that it is possible for managers to create value through the financial decisions they make; and we have used the concept of value-creation as the basic framework of the book, relating techniques of financial analysis to this objective.

As a result of our practical orientation toward value, we have chosen not to present abstract financial theory. Rather than deriving rigorous mathematical proofs, we have explained how the tools, concepts, and theories of finance can be used to improve financial decision making. We have followed this practical approach throughout the book by using current examples of actual business situations to illustrate the application of modern financial theories and techniques.

USING THIS BOOK

The book was written for three different groups of readers. First, the book is intended to be used by students studying finance. Although we wrote the book as a companion reference for students taking finance case courses, the book also has been and will continue to be useful for students who want a basic supplement to a more advanced textbook, or for instructors who wish to discuss the applications or concepts presented in more theoretical finance courses.

Second, we have found that the book has been useful for executive management education in courses where basic techniques of financial analysis are needed or used. Our experience in teaching executives suggests that a straightforward, pragmatic approach is required in such courses, and we wrote and revised the book with this in mind.

Third, the book can serve as a useful reference for the practicing manager who wants a review of current financial concepts and techniques. Thus, we have found that the book can be used effectively as a stand-alone reference.

Since we believe that managers and students of management can best develop the ability to apply techniques and concepts of financial decision making through practice, we have included problems at the end of each chapter. We encourage the reader to work through these problems and refer to the solutions in Appendix C at the end of the book.

The use of computer-based financial modeling can significantly enhance the ability of a manager to analyze financial problems and decisions. We have included explanations of how this can be done. Appendix A is an overview of financial modeling techniques; Appendix B is a primer for using one of the most popular spreadsheet programs—Lotus 1-2-3, Version 2. Managers or students wanting to enhance their modeling skills can do so by modeling the problems at the end of each chapter and comparing their models to the Lotus 1-2-3 solutions contained in Appendix C.

ACKNOWLEDGMENTS

The book is a compilation of ideas and materials developed during the past few years at the Darden Graduate School of Business Administration at the University of Virginia, and Brigham Young University. The material has benefited from the responses of students in undergraduate and MBA classes, and has been refined through the comments of executives attending executive management courses.

We wish to express our thanks to our colleagues at the Darden School and Brigham Young University. We are appreciative of the support provided by numerous students and executives who not only encouraged us to write the book, but provided suggestions for improving the presentation of ideas and concepts. We want to thank the following reviewers for their helpful suggestions for the third edition: Michael D. Atchison, University of Virginia; Chris J. Muscarella, Southern Methodist University; Joseph D. Vinso, University of Southern California; and Paul N. Wilson, The Mader Group, Inc., Narberth, Pennsylvania. As always, the mistakes are my coauthor's.

Diana R. Harrington
Brent D. Wilson

Contents

1 Analyzing Corporate Performance   1

Financial Statements, *1*
Statement of Earnings
Statement of Financial Position
Statement of Changes in Financial Position
Statement of Changes in Shareholders' Equity

Analysis of Financial Statements, *6*
Profitability Ratios
Asset Utilization Ratios
Capitalization Ratios
Sustainable Growth Rate
Market Ratios

Comparative Ratio Analysis, *26*
Historical Comparisons
Comparisons with Other Companies
Comparisons with the Industry

2 Managing Working Capital   35

The Working-Capital Cycle, *35*
The Impact of Inflation
The Impact of Sales Growth
The Impact of Variable Sales Demand

Cash Management, *40*
Managing Receipts
Managing Disbursements
Investing Cash Balances

Managing Other Working-Capital Requirements, *43*
Minimizing Working-Capital Needs
Financing Working-Capital Needs

3 Forecasting Future Needs   51

Cash Budgets, *52*
Projected Financial Statements, *54*

Developing Forecasts from Cash Budgets
Developing Projections Directly

Analyzing Assumptions, *60*
Historical Comparisons
Sensitivity Analysis
Probability Analysis

4 Valuation 1: Capital Budgeting   72

Cost-Benefit Analysis of Proposed Investments, *73*
Cash Benefits
Cash Payments

Evaluating Incremental Costs and Benefits, *76*
The Breakfast Proposal
Salad-Pasta Bar Proposal

Choosing among Investments, *82*
Simple Valuation Methods
Dealing with the Timing of Cash Flow: Discounting Techniques
Ranking Projects
Dealing with Risk

Other Considerations in Creating Value, *95*

5 The Cost of Capital   105

Capital Markets, *106*
Debt Markets
Equity Markets

Determining the Cost of Debt, *116*

Determing the Cost of Equity, *120*
Cash Flow Valuation: The Dividend Discount Method
Capital-Market Estimations: Risk-Premium Methods
Other Concerns in Determing Equity Costs

Calculating the Weighted-Average Cost of Capital, *132*

6 Valuation 2: Acquisitions and Divestitures   138

Present Value Analysis of Cash Flows, *140*
Calculating the Marginal Value of an Acquisition without Synergy
Calculating the Marginal Benefit of an Acquisition with Synergy

Earnings-Valuation Method, *148*

Other Valuation Techniques, *151*
Book Value
Liquidation Value
Replacement Cost
Market Value

7 Obtaining Outside Capital   *156*

The Value of Leverage, *157*
RICHS Analysis, *163*
  Risk to Lenders
  Income
  Control
  Hedging/Speculating
  Greenway's Financing Decision
  Leasing
  Leverage and Corporate Value

Appendix A: Financial Modeling   *192*

Appendix B: Using Lotus 1-2-3   *199*

Appendix C: Solutions to Study Questions   *226*

Index   *311*

Corporate Financial Analysis

CHAPTER 1

Analyzing Corporate Performance

The financial performance of a corporation is of vital interest to many different groups and individuals. Lenders are concerned with the corporation's ability to repay loans as well as whether it is abiding by loan contracts. Purchasing agents for other companies are concerned with its viability as a supplier of goods or services: they want to determine whether the company is a qualified vendor, will be able to fulfill contractual obligations, and will be able to provide future service for its products. Potential investors are interested in determining the financial strength of a company as an element in assessing the company's value.

In addition to these external analysts, managers within the corporation are also concerned with analyzing its financial performance. These internal analysts compare the actual performance of the company and its divisions and lines of business with plans, budgets, or objectives. They also compare the company's performance with that of current and potential competition.

The primary sources of information these analysts use to evaluate a firm's performance are its financial statements, the historical record of its past performance. In this chapter, we will discuss how historical financial performance may be evaluated and interpreted.

While past performance is interesting, many managers and analysts are more interested in what will happen in the future. The past performance of a company, as shown in its financial statements, may be used to help predict future performance. How historical statements and analysis of those statements can be used to help forecast the future will be the subject of Chapter 3. First, let's look at the various financial statements that a company provides to its internal and external analysts.

I. FINANCIAL STATEMENTS

The types of financial information published in financial statements vary among countries, each of which has different requirements for disclosure of information. Regulations in the United States and in the United Kingdom and other Commonwealth countries require the most complete disclosure; however, most industrialized countries require that financial statements disclose sufficient data to allow a meaningful analysis of per-

1

formance. The growing trend of major international companies to raise funds in foreign capital markets necessitates that these multinational companies provide the level of financial information expected by investors in other countries.

In all countries, public disclosure requirements apply only to publicly owned companies. Privately owned corporations may not be required to disclose publicly any financial information. However, certain sources, such as banks, may have access to financial statements from privately owned companies.

In the United States, publicly owned companies are required to prepare four financial statements: statements of earnings, of financial position, of changes in financial position, and of changes in owners' equity. Typically, such statements are prepared quarterly; however, annual statements satisfy the minimum legal requirement.

1. Statement of Earnings

The statement of earnings, also known as the **income statement** or **profit and loss statement,** shows the total revenues earned and the total expenses incurred by a company during a specific period of time. The difference between revenues and expenses is termed **net income** (also known as **earnings** or **profits**) or **net loss** for the period.

This statement reports all revenue or expense transactions during a specified period of time, the reporting period. A quarterly report includes only the transactions made during a three-month reporting period. An annual report includes all income and expense items for a year. Exhibit 1–1 is an example of an annual statement of earnings. It is the 1987 statement for La-Z-Boy Chair Company, the largest manufacturer of reclining chairs in the United States and a major producer of home, office, and health-care furniture.

2. Statement of Financial Position

The statement of financial position is also referred to as the **balance sheet.** This statement reports the corporation's assets, liabilities, and owners' equity at the end of the reporting period. The corporation's assets must balance with the funds used to purchase the assets (hence the term balance sheet). Funds provided by lenders are recorded on the balance sheet as liabilities; funds provided by shareholders are recorded as owners' equity— or, for a publicly held corporation, shareholders' equity.

The balance sheet differs from the statement of earnings in that it reports the firm's status at a point in time, the end of the reporting period. While the earnings statement reports on the flow of transactions or funds, the statement of financial position reports on the resulting status of funds. Thus a quarterly report specifies the status of the assets, liabilities, and

EXHIBIT 1–1

LA-Z-BOY CHAIR COMPANY
Statement of Earnings
(in thousands except per share data)

	Year Ended April 25, 1987
Net sales	$419,991
Cost of sales	(289,779)
Selling, general, and administrative	(85,469)
Total costs and expenses	(375,248)
Income from operations	44,743
Interest expense	(1,877)
Other income	2,081
Income before income taxes	44,947
Provision for income taxes	
Federal—current less investment tax	
credits of $582 in 1986 and $835 in 1985	(19,558)
—deferred taxes	1,175
State	(1,900)
Total taxes	(20,283)
Net income for the year	24,664
Retained earnings at beginning of year	138,932
Less: Cash dividends ($1.55 per share in 1987,	
$1.40 in 1986, and $1.28 in 1985)	7,130
Retained earnings at end of year	$156,466
Weighted-average shares (thousands)	4,600
Net income per share	$5.36

owners' equity at the end of a quarter; an annual report indicates their status at the conclusion of the reporting year. The La-Z-Boy Chair Company's annual statement of financial position, or balance sheet, for 1987 is Exhibit 1–2. Note that La-Z-Boy's fiscal year runs from April to April; most companies' fiscal year is the same as the calendar year.

3. Statement of Changes in Financial Position

Also known as a **funds flow statement** or **sources and uses of funds statement,** this statement reports the amount of funds generated by the company during the period as well as their sources and disposition. The difference between the sum of the sources of funds and the sum of their uses is typically reported as a change in cash or **net working capital.** Sources and uses are determined by comparing the current statement of financial position with that of the previous reporting period. This comparison highlights significant changes that have occurred in the firm's financial position during the period.

EXHIBIT 1–2

LA-Z-BOY CHAIR COMPANY
Statement of Financial Position
April 25, 1987
(in thousands)

Assets

Current assets:

Cash	$ 1,393
Short-term investments	21,172
Receivables, less allowances of $3,118 in 1987 and $2,814 in 1986 for doubtful accounts	113,834
Inventories:	
Raw materials	19,541
Work in process	17,143
Finished goods	8,791
Total inventories	45,475
Other current assets	5,037
Total current assets	186,911
Other assets	9,488
Property, plant, and equipment, at cost:	
Land and land improvements	3,586
Buildings and building fixtures	52,782
Machinery and equipment	66,821
Gross property, plant, and equipment	123,189
Less: Accumulated depreciation and amortization	(49,701)
Net property, plant, and equipment	73,488
Total assets	$269,887

A company generates new financial resources in several ways: by borrowing additional funds, by increasing owners' equity, by retaining the period's earnings, or by decreasing assets (for instance, selling excess equipment). The resources thus generated can be used to increase assets through the purchase of new equipment, to decrease liabilities by paying off loans, or to decrease owners' equity by paying a dividend or repurchasing shares.

The statement of changes in financial position from the 1987 annual report of the La-Z-Boy Chair Company is shown in Exhibit 1–3.

4. Statement of Changes in Shareholders' Equity

This report may also be called the **statement of retained earnings.** It provides additional detail on the composition of the owners' equity accounts for the company. Its purpose is to highlight changes in owners' equity or retained earnings that have occurred during the reporting period.

EXHIBIT 1–2   (*concluded*)

Liabilities and shareholders' equity

Current liabilities:

Notes payable to bank	$ 6,099
Current portion of long-term debt	979
Accounts payable	20,134
Payrolls and other compensation	15,941
Other accrued liabilities	10,014
Estimated income taxes	7,168
Deferred income taxes	11,241
Total current liabilities	71,576
Long-term debt	23,270
Deferred income taxes	9,697

Shareholders' equity:

Common shares, $1.00 par value—20,000,000 authorized,	
4,660,185 issued	4,660
Capital in excess of par value	6,054
Retained earnings	156,466
Currency translation adjustments	(499)
Gross shareholders' equity	166,731
Less: Treasury shares, at cost (54,146 in 1987 and 67,608 in	
1986)	(1,387)
Net shareholders' equity	165,344
Total liabilities and shareholders' equity	$269,887

This statement is similar to the statement of changes in financial position; however, it focuses specifically on changes within the owners' equity segment of the balance sheet. The statement of changes in shareholders' equity is frequently combined with the statement of earnings because the way in which earnings are used has a major impact on the owners' equity account. Exhibit 1–4 shows the statement of changes in shareholders' equity for La-Z-Boy from the 1987 annual report.

In addition to the data contained in these statements, companies also include significant financial information in notes to the statements. These footnotes typically contain information about taxes, the composition of debt, contingent liabilities, and nonconsolidated subsidiaries as well as depreciation schedules for property, plant, and equipment.

Since specific accounting conventions and policies can have a significant impact on the performance reported in financial statements, companies usually include in the notes an explanation of major accounting procedures used in preparing the statements. For instance, recent changes in accounting policies require that U.S. companies report inflation-adjusted earnings data

EXHIBIT 1–3

LA-Z-BOY CHAIR COMPANY
Statement of Changes in Financial Position
For the Year Ended April 25, 1987
(in thousands)

Cash provided by:	
Net income for the year	$24,664
Noncash items:	
Depreciation and amortization	9,033
Deferred income taxes	(220)
Changes in working capital related to operations:	
Receivables	(10,010)
Inventories	(10,242)
Current liabilities and other current assets	16,447
Cash provided by operations	29,672
Proceeds from sale of stock under stock option plans	645
Disposal of property, plant, and equipment	43
Decrease in unexpended IRB* funds	7,944
Decrease in other assets	663
Short-term debt borrowings	7,380
Total cash provided	46,347
Cash used for:	
Additions to property, plant, and equipment	25,675
Retirement of debt	6,894
Payment of cash dividends	7,130
Foreign currency translation adjustments	(210)
Purchase of treasury stock	17
Total cash used	39,506
Change in cash and short-term investments	6,841
Cash and short-term investments at beginning of year	15,724
Cash and short-term investments at end of year	$22,565

*IRB = industrial revenue bond.

---

and that U.S. firms with operations in different industries or different countries detail income and assets by industry or country. This and other information is included in the notes to financial statements. For purposes of brevity, the notes to the La-Z-Boy Chair Company annual report have not been reproduced here.

II. ANALYSIS OF FINANCIAL STATEMENTS

When analyzing financial statements, one must keep in mind the purpose of the analysis. Since different analysts are interested in different

EXHIBIT 1–4

LA-Z-BOY CHAIR COMPANY
Statement of Changes in Shareholders' Equity
(in thousands except per share data)

	Common Shares	Capital in Excess of Par Value	Retained Earnings	Currency Translation Adjustments	Less: Treasury Shares	Total
Balance at April 28, 1984	$4,660	$5,540	$106,843	$(271)	$ 154	$116,618
Purchase of treasury shares					2,717	(2,717)
Currency translation adjustments				(383)		(383)
Exercise of stock options		(26)			(510)	484
Dividends paid			(5,867)			(5,867)
Net income			21,359			21,359
Balance at April 27, 1985	4,660	5,514	122,335	(654)	2,361	129,494
Currency translation adjustments				(5)		(5)
Exercise of stock options		269			(617)	886
Dividends paid			(6,413)			(6,413)
Net income			23,010			23,010
Balance at April 26, 1986	4,660	5,783	138,932	(659)	1,744	146,972
Purchase of treasury shares					17	(17)
Currency translation adjustments				210		210
Exercise of stock options		271			(374)	645
Dividends paid			(7,130)			(7,130)
Net income			24,664			24,664
Balance at April 25, 1987	$4,660	$6,054	$156,466	$(449)	$1,387	$165,344

aspects of a corporation's performance, no single analytical technique or type of analysis is appropriate for all situations. However, there are several general things the analyst should bear in mind in reviewing data on financial statements.

First, all financial statement data are historical. Although one may make projections based on such data, the accuracy of these projections depends both on the forecaster's ability and the continued pertinence of the historical relationships to current or future operations and industry and economic conditions.

Second, historical data are collected and reported on the basis of particular accounting conventions. These accounting principles and rules vary among countries. Even within a country, several approaches to specific issues may be allowed at one time, and these approaches may change over time. Although notes to financial statements summarize some of the significant accounting policies, the analyst should be aware of the impact that accounting policies, and changes in these policies, have on the reported performance of a company.

Third, because of the variability of seasonal funds flows and requirements for some businesses, the timing of the reporting period should be considered. For companies in highly seasonal or cyclical industries, comparisons of different reporting periods should be approached cautiously.

Despite these concerns, an analyst can develop an insightful examination of a corporation's financial performance. The most common method of analyzing financial statements is the use of ratios. These ratios are simple mathematical relationships between various items on financial statements. The analytical skill lies not in computing the ratios but in determining which ratios to use in each case and interpreting the results. The ratios by themselves are relatively meaningless. Only by comparing ratios over time and between companies—and by determining the underlying causes of the differences among them—does ratio analysis help the analyst or manager gain insight into corporate performance.

The primary ratios used for analyzing the internal performance of a company can be categorized into three groups: (1) profitability ratios, (2) asset utilization or efficiency ratios, and (3) capitalization or leverage ratios. These primary ratios can be combined to determine the **rate of return** for a company and its owners and the rate at which the company can grow— the sustainable rate of growth. By adding data about the company's stock market performance, the analyst can gain insight into how financial markets view the company's performance.

1. Profitability Ratios

Analysts use a number of methods to determine the relative profitability of a company. The primary figure is called the **return on sales** (ROS), which relates a company's net income to its sales. This ratio is also referred to as the **net profit** or **profit margin.** Using data from the 1987 La-Z-Boy Chair Company's annual financial statements, this ratio is calculated as follows.[1] Note that because the financial statements report performance in thousands of dollars, the calculations are done in thousands; thus La-Z-Boy's net income was $24,664 thousand, or over $24 million, in 1987.

$$\text{Return on sales} = \frac{\text{Net income}}{\text{Net sales}}$$

$$= \frac{\$24{,}664}{\$419{,}991}$$

$$= .059 \text{ or } 5.9\%.$$

Profitability of companies differs among industry groups and their competitive situations. For example, grocery stores operate on very low profit margins because competition in this industry tends to be based on low prices and high volumes. On the other hand, profit margins in industries with highly differentiated products, such as cosmetics, are generally much higher.

In addition to differences in ROS among industries, profitability can change for a company or an industry over time. Cyclical companies usually have much lower returns on sales at the bottom of a business cycle than at the top. At the bottom of a cycle, costs tend to be high, but prices have been kept low to lure the few buyers. At the top of a cycle, companies are able to raise or maintain their prices; and since they are operating close to capacity, fixed costs tend to be low. Thus it is important for the analyst to know and understand the nature of a company's business for proper interpretation of the ratios.

Companies make and sell products in many ways. Companies with low profit margins may have high costs of production, or they may have high marketing, selling, or research expenses. Thus, to understand the sources of profitability, many analysts look at the profit a company earns after direct costs of production. This ratio is called the **gross margin.**

$$\text{Gross margin} = \frac{\text{Net sales} - \text{Cost of sales}}{\text{Net sales}}$$

$$= \frac{\$419{,}991 - \$289{,}779}{\$419{,}991}$$

$$= .31 \text{ or } 31\%.$$

For La-Z-Boy, the gross margin was 31 percent; that is, 69 percent of every dollar of revenue was used to cover the direct costs of producing the com-

---

[1] The 1987 La-Z-Boy Chair Company financial data will be used in the remainder of the chapter to illustrate calculation of ratios.

pany's products. Because the net profit margin was 5.9 percent, the rest of the company's profits, 25.1 percent, went to cover other expenses.

In addition to production costs, companies must sell their products and pay the general costs of administration (including interest on debt) and research and development. To determine the relative profitability of a company after all costs except taxes, analysts use the **operating margin.**

$$\text{Operating margin} = \frac{\text{Income before taxes}}{\text{Net sales}}$$

$$= \frac{\$44,947}{\$419,991}$$

$$= .107 \text{ or } 10.7\%.$$

Analysts who want to know how profitably a company produces and markets its goods—not how inexpensively it finances itself—may calculate yet another ratio, called **EBIT/sales.** EBIT stands for earnings before interest and taxes.

$$\text{EBIT/sales} = \frac{\text{Earnings before interest and taxes}}{\text{Net sales}}$$

$$= \frac{\$46,824}{\$419,991}$$

$$= .111 \text{ or } 11.1\%.$$

Because the difference between the operating margin and the EBIT/sales ratio is small, one might conclude that La-Z-Boy either has little interest-bearing debt or that its debt is quite inexpensive. We will look at how much debt the company has after we have looked at how efficiently the company has produced its goods.

There is one other way in which analysts often examine the statement of earnings or income statement, the statement from which all these profitability ratios were derived. That analysis is called a **component percentage** analysis. To calculate component percentages, the analyst simply relates each item on the income statement to revenues or sales. This form of analysis is used to examine the composition of various items on financial statements. A percentage breakdown of the statement of earnings is frequently used and facilitates a comparison of trends over time. The 1987 component percentage analysis for La-Z-Boy, Exhibit 1–5, shows in detail the cost-revenue relationships for the company.

2. Asset Utilization Ratios

A company typically acquires assets for use in producing sales revenues and, ultimately, profits. The ratios that indicate the effectiveness of asset

EXHIBIT 1–5

LA-Z-BOY CHAIR COMPANY
Percentage Components for Statement of Earnings
For the Year Ended April 25, 1987
(dollars in thousands)

	Dollars	Percentage
Net sales	$ 419,991	100.0%
Cost of sales	(289,779)	(69.0)
Selling, general, and administrative expense	(76,436)	(18.2)
Depreciation and amortization	(9,033)	(2.2)
Interest expense	(1,877)	(0.4)
Other income	2,081	0.5
Income taxes	(20,283)	(4.8)
Profit after taxes	$ 24,664	5.9%

utilization are often called **efficiency** or **turnover** ratios. The information needed to calculate these ratios is taken from both the income statement and the balance sheet.

The first ratio an analyst turns to in evaluating the efficiency of any company is **total asset turnover (TATO)**.

$$\text{Total asset turnover} = \frac{\text{Net sales}}{\text{Total assets}}$$

$$= \frac{\$419,991}{\$269,887}$$

$$= 1.55 \text{ or } 155\%.$$

The figure for average assets is more representative than total assets if a company has had a large increase or decrease in assets during the prior year. For La-Z-Boy, the change in assets was not large, and thus either average or year-end assets could be used in calculating the ratio. Whichever method is used, it should be used consistently throughout the analysis to avoid any distortions.

As you can see, La-Z-Boy's sales were less than twice its assets in 1987. The nature of the company's business dictates the firm's need for fixed assets like property, plant, and equipment. Service businesses with relatively small investments in fixed assets, such as advertising and consulting, are able to achieve higher asset turnover ratios than are manufacturing companies like La-Z-Boy. A company with older, more fully depreciated plant and equipment will have a lower asset base, and will therefore be able to achieve a higher asset turnover ratio, than will a comparable company utilizing newer facilities. Once again, the ratio alone does not lead to any easy conclusions.

However, when the information is joined with information about the nature of the business, the industry, and economic conditions, the skilled analyst can gain insight. Later in this chapter we will compare La-Z-Boy's financial performance across time and with others in its industry.

Combined with the return on sales (ROS), the total asset turnover (TATO) ratio has a very useful property: by multiplying these two ratios, one can calculate the **return on assets** (ROA).

$$\text{Return on assets} = \text{Return on sales} \times \text{Total asset turnover}$$

$$= \frac{\text{Net income}}{\text{Net sales}} \times \frac{\text{Net sales}}{\text{Total assets}}$$

$$= \frac{\text{Net income}}{\text{Average assets}}$$

Using this relationship for La-Z-Boy, the ROA is:

$$\text{ROA} = \text{ROS} \times \text{TATO}$$
$$= .059 \times 1.55$$
$$= .091 \text{ or } 9.1\%.$$

By understanding this relationship, you can easily see why capital-intensive companies have lower returns on assets, all other things being equal, than do low-asset service companies.

One can, of course, calculate the ROA directly:

$$\text{ROA} = \frac{\text{Net income}}{\text{Assets}}$$

$$= \frac{\$24,664}{\$269,887}$$

$$= .091 \text{ or } 9.1\%.$$

After examining the overall asset efficiency of a company, the analyst may want to delve into the way the company uses some or all of its assets. This is particularly true if the analyst finds the asset efficiency to be different from what was expected. Since inventory is a very large asset for many companies, the analyst may want to know how efficiently the company has used its investment in inventory. To estimate that, the analyst might calculate the **inventory turnover** ratio.

$$\text{Inventory turnover} = \frac{\text{Cost of sales}}{\text{Average inventory}}$$

$$= \frac{\$289,779}{(\$45,475 + \$35,233)/2}$$

$$= 7.18 \text{ or } 718\%.$$

This ratio indicates the number of times La-Z-Boy's inventory was sold and replaced during the reporting period of one year. Note that the numerator is the cost of sales, not net sales. The effect is to factor out the profit portion of sales, leaving only the production costs contained in cost of sales. If the net sales figure were used and the company had high prices relative to costs, the ratio would be higher than the actual inventory turnover. It is important to note, however, that this relationship assumes that inventories are valued at cost, the normal accounting practice. If inventories are carried on the financial statements at market value, then net sales should be used as the numerator in the ratio.

A high inventory turnover ratio indicates that the company is using financial resources efficiently by maintaining low inventories. La-Z-Boy has a relatively rapid turnover of its inventory. The nature of some companies' production processes—for instance, aircraft manufacturers—makes achieving a high inventory turnover ratio difficult.

Since La-Z-Boy has a relatively low total asset turnover ratio and a high inventory turnover, the analyst will no doubt wonder how efficiently other assets are being utilized by the company—for instance, what quantity of the company's sales has not been paid for? The ratio of **accounts receivable to net sales** indicates the relative proportion of the company's sales made on credit and still outstanding at the end of the reporting period.

$$\text{Accounts receivable/Sales} = \frac{\text{Accounts receivable}}{\text{Net sales}}$$

$$= \frac{\$113,834}{\$419,991}$$

$$= .271 \text{ or } 27.1\%.$$

As you can see, of the sales made by La-Z-Boy in 1987, over 27 percent remained unpaid at the end of 1987. If we had wanted to know the average outstanding over the year, we could have used average accounts receivable in the ratio.

We can also use this ratio to determine the **days' sales outstanding** or the **receivables collection period.** Companies that sell their products on credit, such as furniture manufacturers, will have long collection periods.

$$\text{Days' sales outstanding} = \frac{\text{Accounts receivable}}{\text{Net sales}} \times 360 \text{ days}$$

$$= 27.1 \times 360 \text{ days}$$

$$= 97.6 \text{ days.}$$

For convenience in calculation, most analysts use 360 days for annual data rather than the actual 365 days. This custom allows for five annual holidays and 12 months of 30 days each. La-Z-Boy's customers paid their bills in an average of about 98 days. If the company's credit terms were net 30 (that is, payment was due within 30 days after the goods were received), its customers were taking advantage of La-Z-Boy.

Other analysts may want to look at the efficiency with which the company manages its short-term liabilities. For instance, the company's suppliers may wonder how much the company owes in relation to its income. To determine this, the ratio of **accounts payable to cost of sales** is analyzed.

$$\text{Accounts payable/Sales} = \frac{\text{Accounts payable}}{\text{Cost of sales}}$$

$$= \frac{\$20,134}{\$289,779}$$

$$= .069 \text{ or } 6.9\%.$$

Another way to see how promptly the company is paying its obligations is to measure the **payables payment period**.

$$\text{Payables payment period} = \frac{\text{Accounts payable}}{\text{Cost of sales}} \times 360 \text{ days}$$

$$= 6.95\% \times 360 \text{ days}$$

$$= 25.0 \text{ days}.$$

La-Z-Boy pays its suppliers more promptly than its customers pay La-Z-Boy. Companies that use their accounts payable as a major source of funding will take longer to pay suppliers, and thus have longer payables payment periods.

In measuring the length of time a firm takes to pay for its purchases, it is more appropriate to use the value of purchases the company has made, rather than sales or cost of sales, as the denominator in this ratio. However, because purchase data are normally not available to external analysts, the cost of sales (also called cost of goods sold) is typically used as an approximation.

For companies with seasonal sales, care must be taken in calculating this ratio, as well as days' sales outstanding and inventory turnover. Using the annual cost of sales may inflate or deflate the ratio. Therefore, some analysts calculate a monthly ratio based on the cost of sales for that month, or an average for several months during the same season, rather than using annual cost of sales.

In addition to, or in place of, these ratios, the analyst may perform a **component percentage** analysis of the company's balance sheet. In this analysis each asset, liability, and equity account balance is compared with the total asset figure. This analysis is especially useful for comparing changes over time. Such a component analysis is shown in Exhibit 1–6.

After the analyst has fully investigated the profitability, return on sales, and asset efficiency of the company, the next concern is to see how the company has financed itself. Earlier we deduced from the income statement

EXHIBIT 1–6

LA-Z-BOY CHAIR COMPANY
Component Analysis of Balance Sheet Items
Year Ended April 25, 1987
(dollars in thousands)

	Dollars	Percentage
Assets		
Cash	$ 1,393	0.5%
Short-term investments	21,172	7.8
Receivables	113,834	42.2
Inventories	45,475	16.9
Other current assets	5,037	1.9
Total current assets	186,911	69.3
Other assets	9,488	3.5
Property, plant, and equipment	123,189	45.6
Accumulated depreciation	(49,701)	(18.4)
Net property, plant, and equipment	73,488	27.2
Total assets	$269,887	100.0%
Liabilities and owners' equity		
Notes payable	$ 6,099	2.2%
Current portion of long-term debt	979	0.4
Accounts payable	20,134	7.5
Payrolls and other compensation	15,941	5.9
Other accrued liabilities	10,014	3.7
Estimated taxes	7,168	2.6
Deferred taxes	11,241	4.2
Total current liabilities	71,576	26.5
Long-term debt	23,270	8.6
Deferred taxes	9,697	3.6
Shareholders equity:		
Common shares ($1.00 par value)	4,660	1.7
Capital in excess of par	6,054	2.3
Retained earnings	156,466	58.0
Currency translation adjustments	(449)	(0.2)
Treasury shares at cost	(1,387)	(0.5)
Total shareholders' equity	165,344	61.3
Total liabilities and shareholders' equity	$269,887	100.0%

that La-Z-Boy either had little debt or debt that was very inexpensive. Let's see which is the case.

3. Capitalization Ratios

Capitalization or **leverage** ratios provide information about the sources the company has used to finance its investment in assets. The term **leverage**

is used to indicate the impact debt financing has on the returns of the company to its owners: if the income generated by investment in assets is greater than the cost of the debt, the equity holders will benefit from financing an increased amount of assets through borrowing. The term **gearing** is also used in referring to this concept. Later we will see how leverage or gearing affects return on equity.

Leverage ratios are based on information from the balance sheet. The primary leverage ratio of interest to a company's owners is the **asset to equity ratio.** For La-Z-Boy, this ratio is:

$$\text{Assets to equity} = \frac{\text{Total assets}}{\text{Shareholders' equity}}$$

$$= \frac{\$269,887}{\$165,344}$$

$$= 1.632 \text{ or } 163.2\%.$$

A company with a high ratio of assets to equity finances a high proportion of its assets with debt and therefore is highly leveraged. If the ratio were 100 percent, the company would be totally financed by its owners.

Because this ratio shows the proportion of the firm financed by its owners, when it is combined with return on assets (ROA), we can find the return that shareholders earned on the book value of their investment in the company, the **return on equity (ROE).**

$$\text{Return on equity} = \text{ROS} \times \text{TATO} \times \text{Leverage}$$

$$= \text{ROA} \times \text{Leverage}$$

$$= \frac{\text{Net income}}{\text{Net sales}} \times \frac{\text{Net sales}}{\text{Total assets}} \times \frac{\text{Average assets}}{\text{Equity}}$$

$$= \frac{\text{Net income}}{\text{Total assets}} \times \frac{\text{Assets}}{\text{Equity}}$$

$$= \frac{\text{Net income}}{\text{Equity}}$$

For La-Z-Boy, the return on equity is:

$$\text{ROE} = \text{ROS} \times \text{TATO} \times \text{Leverage}$$
$$= .059 \times 1.55 \times 1.63$$
$$= .091 \times 1.63$$
$$= .149 \text{ or } 14.9\%.$$

Looking at this relationship, you can see that debt financing has the effect of increasing, leveraging or gearing, the return that shareholders in La-Z-Boy earned. If the company had been financed with more debt—for instance, an asset-to-equity ratio of 200 percent—the ROE would have been almost

20 percent. If it had been financed by shareholders alone, the return on equity would have been 9.1 percent, exactly the same as the return the company earned on its assets. If, in addition, the total asset turnover (TATO) were 100 percent, the ROS, ROA, and ROE would be the same. The fewer assets a company uses to generate sales, and the more debt it uses to finance those assets, the higher the return shareholders earn.

Constituents other than shareholders are interested in the way a company finances itself. Lenders, who may provide a large portion of the company's capital resources, are especially interested in the way the company is capitalized. While they could certainly deduce their position from the ratio of assets to equity, they have developed ratios that show their position directly. Two lender-perspective ratios are commonly used: **long-term debt to equity** and **long-term debt to total assets.** For our La-Z-Boy example, the first is:

$$\text{Long-term debt to equity} = \frac{\text{Long-term debt}}{\text{Shareholders' equity}}$$

$$= \frac{\$23,270}{\$165,344}$$

$$= .141 \text{ or } 14.1\%.$$

And the second is:

$$\text{Long-term debt to assets} = \frac{\text{Long-term debt}}{\text{Total assets}}$$

$$= \frac{\$23,270}{\$269,887}$$

$$= .086 \text{ or } 8.6\%.$$

In determining the long-term debt of a company, there is some disagreement over which items to include. If the decision is made to include deferred taxes, long-term contingent liabilities, or other long-term liabilities, these items should be included consistently throughout the analysis.

The appropriate size of a capitalization ratio depends on the perspective of the analyst, the nature of the company, and its situation. Lenders such as bondholders and bankers typically prefer low debt ratios, which provide greater security for their loans. Equity investors generally prefer more leverage, which provides a higher return on equity if the company is profitable. Issues involved in determining the appropriate amount of debt—the appropriate capital structure—are discussed in Chapter 7.

Lenders and other sources of short-term capital—for instance, suppliers—also want to know how the company will meet its obligations in the short run. Since some companies use significant amounts of short-term debt to finance their operations, three ratios have been found to be useful for examining the situation: **total liabilities to assets, current ratio,** and **acid-test** ratio. For La-Z-Boy, the first of these is:

$$\text{Total liabilities to assets} = \frac{\text{Total liabilities}}{\text{Total assets}}$$

$$= \frac{\$104,543}{\$269,887}$$

$$= .387 \text{ or } 38.7\%.$$

Over 38 percent of La-Z-Boy's assets have been financed by long-term borrowing.

The current and acid-test ratios both measure the company's ability to pay current liabilities only. These ratios, also called **liquidity** ratios, reflect the size of short-term obligations. La-Z-Boy's current ratio is:

$$\text{Current} = \frac{\text{Current assets}}{\text{Current liabilities}}$$

$$= \frac{\$186,911}{\$71,576}$$

$$= 2.611 \text{ or } 261.1\%.$$

Companies with high liquidity ratios are considered more liquid than those with low ratios: their short-term assets are greater than their short-term liabilities. Being more liquid generally means that the company is better able to pay off short-term obligations. There is one catch, however: some current assets may not be easy to turn into the cash needed to pay current liabilities. The current asset that is often hardest to turn into cash, at least quickly, is inventory. By deducting inventory from current assets, the analyst can determine whether the company would be able to pay its current liabilities without resorting to selling off inventory. La-Z-Boy's acid-test or **quick** ratio is:

$$\text{Acid-test} = \frac{\text{Cash} + \text{Short-term investments} + \text{Accounts receivable}}{\text{Current liabilities}}$$

$$= \frac{\$1,393 + \$21,172 + \$113,834}{\$71,576}$$

$$= 1.906 \text{ or } 190.6\%.$$

You can see that La-Z-Boy is less liquid when inventory is removed from current liabilities. But is this a problem? Determining what constitutes a good or bad level of liquidity depends on who is analyzing the current or acid-test ratio. A banker who has made a short-term loan would like both ratios to be high, because the banker believes they indicate that the company has sufficient current assets to pay all current liabilities, including the bank's loan. On the other hand, the company's manager might prefer lower ratios, in the belief that it shows the company has minimized the funds invested in current assets—assets that may yield low returns.

All these capitalization ratios show the relative ability of a company to repay the principal of its short- and long-term debt obligations. However, the ability to repay principal is only one of the concerns lenders have. In fact, it may be the lesser of two concerns: whether the company can repay the principal, and whether the company can pay the interest on the debt. Because the lender's product is debt, and to make a profit the product must be sold, lenders are concerned less with actual repayment of the principal than with the company's ability to repay it if requested. Companies that have the ability to repay the debt make good candidates for loans, if they can pay the interest on the debt. Lenders have developed several ratios to test the company's ability to pay interest. These are called **coverage** ratios. They test the company's ability to pay interest; interest and principal; or interest, principal, and other contractual obligations. They are also called **debt-service** ratios.

Over the long term, interest must be paid out of funds generated by company operations. Since earnings are usually the primary source of funds to service debt obligations, a frequently calculated coverage ratio is **EBIT coverage.**

$$\text{EBIT coverage} = \frac{\text{Earnings before interest and taxes}}{\text{Interest expense}}$$

$$= \frac{\$46,824}{\$1,877}$$

$$= 24.95 \text{ or } 2,495\%.$$

Note that we used La-Z-Boy's EBIT, not net income, in calculating this ratio, since both interest and its tax effect are deducted in calculating net income. EBIT is the amount available to cover interest expense.

While La-Z-Boy appears quite able to pay its interest, analysts use a number of other coverage ratios to determine the ability of a company to meet its interest obligations. For instance, the analyst might add depreciation to EBIT in estimating the coverage ratio to show the cash available for paying interest. Cash is important because debt payments must be made with cash, not with earnings. To calculate the ratio of **cash flow coverage,** we add to EBIT the amount shown for depreciation in Exhibit 1–3.

$$\text{Cash flow coverage} = \frac{\text{EBIT} + \text{Depreciation}}{\text{Interest}}$$

$$= \frac{(\$46,824 + \$9,033)}{\$1,877}$$

$$= 29.76 \text{ or } 2,976\%.$$

If a company has depreciation, the ratio for cash flow coverage will always be larger than that for EBIT coverage.

While interest coverage is of first concern, lenders also require principal payments. Principal payments are sometimes called **sinking fund** payments. These payments are not deductible for tax purposes, so they must be paid with after-tax funds. To determine the ability of the company to meet both interest and principal payments, the ratio of **debt-service coverage** is used. In this ratio, debt repayments are adjusted to a before-tax basis to compensate for their lack of tax deductibility. (The principal obligations and marginal tax rates for a company can be found in the notes to financial statements.)

$$\text{Debt-service coverage} = \frac{\text{Earnings before interest and taxes}}{\text{Interest} + [\text{Principal payment}/(1 - \text{Tax rate})]}$$

$$= \frac{\$46,824}{\$1,877 + [\$2,219/(1 - .34)]}$$

$$= 8.937 \text{ or } 893.7\%.$$

Note that for La-Z-Boy, both the interest and debt-service coverage ratios are well above their minimums, 100 percent. In fact, even when principal payments are included, the company can easily cover its obligations, at least its debt obligations, more than seven times.

There are really two basic ratios, interest coverage and debt-service coverage, that can be adapted for other contractual or noncontractual obligations such as lease payments and dividends, and one can use EBIT or cash flow in the denominator. Each variety of these two basic ratios gives a somewhat different view of the company's ability to meet its contractual and perceived obligations. It is up to the analyst to determine which ratio gives a better view.

Lenders and lessors like coverage ratios to be high. Shareholders, seeking to maximize their returns, prefer the ratios to be as low as possible without dropping below 100 percent. The best level for each of the ratios depends on the nature of the business, the economic situation, and the willingness of the owners or managers to take risk.

4. Sustainable Growth Rate

By combining return on sales, total asset turnover, and leverage, we determined shareholders' return on equity. While shareholders may earn that return on equity, they may not receive all the returns immediately. As illustrated in Exhibit 1–7, some of the returns may be provided to the shareholders in the form of cash dividends while the rest are retained by the company to fund future growth.

One measure of the proportion of the earnings paid out to shareholders is the ratio of **dividend payout** (DPO). La-Z-Boy's payment of cash dividends is shown in Exhibit 1–3.

$$\text{Dividend payout} = \frac{\text{Dividends paid}}{\text{Net income}}$$

$$= \frac{\$7,130}{\$24,664}$$

$$= .289 \text{ or } 28.9\%.$$

The proportion of earnings retained for use by the firm, the **earnings retention** ratio, is simply the opposite of the payout ratio:

$$\text{Earnings retention} = 1 - \text{Dividend payout ratio}$$
$$= 1 - .289$$
$$= .711 \text{ or } 71.1\%.$$

La-Z-Boy retains over 71 percent of its net income to finance future growth.

This ratio yields a useful result when combined with the ROS, TATO, and leverage ratios. By multiplying them, we can determine the maximum rate at which the company can grow using internally generated funds, which is called the **sustainable growth rate** (SGR). Note that this approach assumes that the ratios all stay the same; that is, as earnings are retained, they are matched with enough new debt to keep the ratio of assets to equity the same, and the TATO and ROS ratios do not change. An example of the SGR is calculated as follows:

SGR	= ROS	× TATO	× Leverage	× Retention
	$= \dfrac{\text{Profit}}{\text{Sales}}$	$\times \dfrac{\text{Sales}}{\text{Total Assets}}$	$\times \dfrac{\text{Assets}}{\text{Equity}}$	$\times \dfrac{\text{Earnings retained}}{\text{Net Income}}$
	$= \dfrac{\$24,664}{\$419,991}$	$\times \dfrac{\$419,991}{\$269,887}$	$\times \dfrac{\$269,887}{\$165,344}$	$\times \dfrac{\$17,534}{\$24,664}$
	$= .059$	$\times 1.55$	$\times 1.63$	$\times .711$
	$= .106 \text{ or } 10.6\%.$			

This ratio may also be calculated using the following shortcut.

$$\text{SGR} = \text{ROE} \times (1 - \text{DPO})$$
$$= .149 \times (1 - .289)$$
$$= .106 \text{ or } 10.6\%.$$

Based on 1987 performance, La-Z-Boy Chair Company can grow in the future at a sustainable rate of 10.6 percent a year. That is, La-Z-Boy can have an increase in assets, sales, and profits of 10.6 percent per year without having to issue additional common stock to finance the growth, if all the ratios stay the same. The additional assets required for the growth at this rate can be financed through retained earnings and new debt which maintains a constant capitalization ratio. If the company wants to grow more rapidly than the SGR yet not sell additional equity, management must

EXHIBIT 1–7   Disposition of Net Income to Shareholders

increase the profit margin, increase the asset turnover, use higher leverage, or reduce the dividend payout.

The segmentation of the sustainable growth rate into the four sources of growth—profit, asset efficiency, leverage, and profit retention—allows the analyst to examine the individual factors that affect the growth rate. This approach provides for a clear diagnosis of past financial performance. In addition, understanding of this concept and an analysis of the SGR components can allow an analyst or management to determine what would have happened if the company had followed a different strategy for any component. And if the sustainable growth rate turns out to be lower than expected or desired, management can review the various components to determine in which areas the company is underperforming. Exhibit 1–8 shows the components and sustainable growth rates for several different industries.

5. Market Ratios

In addition to ratios that are calculated using only data from the company's financial statements, for publicly owned companies analysts often calculate ratios using information from the stock market. These ratios facilitate analyzing the company's financial market performance because the company's internal performance should and will be reflected in the capital market's evaluation. Since the return on investment for an equity owner may come primarily from changes in the market price of the equity, these ratios are of particular interest to the shareholders of a company. Because equity investors purchase shares of common stock in the company, most market ratios are calculated on a per share basis rather than on totals. A typical starting point for market analysis is **earnings per share** (EPS). That figure is shown in Exhibit 1–4 as $5.36. However, in September 1987, La-Z-Boy had a 4-for-1 stock split. For the resulting 18,640 shares, earnings were $1.32 per share.

EXHIBIT 1–8 Industry Average Sustainable Growth Rates, 1986

Industry	Return on Sales	Sales/ Assets	Assets/ Equity	Retention Ratio	Sustainable Growth Rate
Automotive	3%	140%	286%	88%	11%
Bank holding companies	7	82	196	42	5
Beverage/brewers	5	160	162	67	9
Broadcasting	14	112	214	81	27
Building materials/cement	8	87	423	27	8
Chemicals	6	140	213	69	12
Coal	3	135	213	63	5
Containers	4	178	218	61	9
Cosmetics	4	135	256	53	7
Electric equipment	3	158	417	87	17
Forest products	9	121	163	69	12
Metal/aluminum	4	115	203	78	7
Paper	5	138	198	67	9
Retail stores	2	235	360	90	15
Soaps	4	152	270	36	6

SOURCE: Data derived from Standard and Poor's *Stock Pack II*, February 1988.

$$\text{Earnings per share} = \frac{\text{Net income}}{\text{Number of common shares outstanding}}$$

$$= \frac{\$24{,}664}{18{,}640}$$

$$= \$1.32$$

Other ratios are based on the market price for a share of common stock. In January 1988, the share price for La-Z-Boy Chair Company was $14.50. Using this price, several useful ratios can be calculated. The first is the **price/earnings** or P/E ratio.

$$\text{Price/Earnings} = \frac{\text{Market price per share}}{\text{Earnings per share}}$$

$$= \frac{\$14.50}{\$1.32}$$

$$= 10.98 \times$$

Note that the P/E ratio is not usually used as a percentage but as a multiple: here, price is nearly eleven times earnings. This ratio can be used to evaluate the relative financial performance of the stock. Most analysts believe that it gives an indication of how much investors are willing to pay for a dollar of the company's earnings, and it provides a scaled measure that allows market-value comparisons of companies with different earnings levels.

Another ratio is often used as a rough measure of whether management has created and is expected to create value for its shareholders. This ratio relates the market value per share of common stock to the book value or net worth per share. A ratio of **market-to-book value** greater than 100 percent indicates that shareholders are willing to pay a premium over the book value of the stock. The book value per share of a company is calculated by dividing retained earnings on the financial statements by the number of shares outstanding.

$$\text{Market-to-book value} = \frac{\text{Market value per share}}{\text{Book value per share}}$$

$$= \frac{\$14.50}{\$165{,}344/18{,}640}$$

$$= 1.63 \text{ or } 163\%.$$

The analyst should keep in mind that book values result from specific accounting conventions that require the use of historical values for assets. When historical values do not reflect the underlying economic value or earning potential of these assets, the use of replacement cost or inflation-adjusted valuations may result in a more meaningful ratio of market-to-book value. Market-to-book values, price/earnings ratios, and sustainable rates of growth for a number of industries are shown in Exhibit 1–9.

Typically, investors expect companies with high P/E ratios to grow—to have more rapid increases in dividends in the future (earnings retained now will feed the company's growth) than companies with low P/E ratios. Additionally, companies with higher sustainable growth rates are expected to have higher P/E ratios. Looking at Exhibit 1–9, you can see for yourself whether there is a relationship.

Another ratio, **dividend yield,** indicates the return on a stock investment provided by the current dividend payment.

$$\text{Dividend yield} = \frac{\text{Dividends per share}}{\text{Market price per share}}$$

$$= \frac{\$0.39}{\$14.50}$$

$$= .027 \text{ or } 2.7\%.$$

La-Z-Boy's shareholders received a 2.7 percent return on the market price from the dividends the company paid.

Of course, dividends are only part of the return investors expect from their investment in common stock; the remainder comes from the potential growth in future dividends that results from wise investment of the profits retained by the company. Usually companies with higher dividend yields are expected to have lower growth in future dividends. Since they are paying more of their earnings out in the form of current dividends, these companies typically have lower sustainable growth rates. Companies with lower cur-

EXHIBIT 1–9 Industry Average Market-to-Book Values, Price/Earnings Ratios, and Sustainable Growth Rates, 1987

Industry	Market Value/ Book Value	Price/ Earnings	Sustainable Growth Rate
Broadcasting	445%	23.8	27%
Electric equipment	316	11.9	17
Retail stores	180	14.4	15
Chemicals	238	12.6	12
Containers	193	14.1	9
Paper	176	12.5	9
Beverage/brewers	256	19.9	9
Building materials/cement . . .	112	5.3	8
Metal/aluminum	106	9.1	7
Coal	104	9.1	5
Bank holding companies	107	58.2	5

SOURCE: Data derived from Standard and Poor's *Stock Pack II*, February 1988.

rent dividends usually are retaining more of their profits for future growth, which their sustainable growth rates tend to reflect (see Exhibit 1–8).

This discussion of ratios is not intended to be all-inclusive. Rather, these ratios are only illustrations of the types that may be calculated to provide the analyst or manager with insights into the performance of the corporation. Any number of ratios can be computed; the important considerations are to determine what information is relevant to the problem at hand and then to undertake the appropriate ratio analysis.

III. COMPARATIVE RATIO ANALYSIS

Calculating the ratios or percentages is relatively simple. The critical ingredient in a useful analysis is the analyst's interpretation of these figures. To interpret the ratios, analysts generally compare performance (1) from various time periods, (2) with that of one or more companies in the same industry, and (3) with the average performance of the industry. To ensure comparability of the results, the financial statements used to prepare the various ratios must be based on comparable accounting procedures or properly adjusted statements. Furthermore, the analyst must thoroughly understand the firm and the industry—its products, marketing techniques, and organization—if she or he is to explain the differences in performance among various time periods or companies.

Using the La-Z-Boy Chair Company as an example, we can see how much more we can discover about the company by such comparisons.

1. Historical Comparisons

The easiest first step in making historical comparisons is to do a full analysis of the components in the sustainable growth rate. This analysis, showing the five relevant ratios for La-Z-Boy from 1983 to 1987, is given in Exhibit 1–10.

EXHIBIT 1–10

LA-Z-BOY CHAIR COMPANY
Sustainable Growth Rate Component Analysis

Ratio	1983	1984	1985	1986	1987
Return on sales	6.5%	9.1%	7.5%	6.3%	5.9%
Total asset turnover	152	163	155	160	155
Assets to equity	145	147	149	159	163
Earnings retention	71	81	73	72	71
Sustainable growth rate . . .	10.2	17.7	12.8	11.5	10.6

Exhibit 1–11

LA-Z-BOY CHAIR COMPANY
Component Percentages for Statements of Earnings

	1983	1984	1985	1986	1987
Net sales	100.0%	100.0%	100.0%	100.0%	100.0%
Cost of sales	(69.5)	(65.7)	(67.7)	(68.9)	(69.0)
Selling, general, and administrative expense ...	(19.6)	(18.0)	(19.4)	(19.2)	(20.4)
Interest expense	(0.5)	(0.4)	(0.4)	(0.5)	(0.4)
Other income	1.0	1.2	1.1	0.8	0.5
Income taxes	(4.9)	(8.0)	(6.1)	(5.5)	(4.8)
Net income	6.5	9.1	7.5	6.7	5.9

As you can see, 1984 was a very profitable year for La-Z-Boy and 1987 was not. That was the major notable difference in performance for the company over these five years. That extra profitability in 1984 was clearly reflected in the ROE and SGR. What caused the higher return on sales?

Exhibit 1–11 makes a historical comparison of component percentages drawn from La-Z-Boy's statements of earnings over a five-year period. The purpose of this comparison is to determine whether any significant changes occurred during those years. The analysis shows that cost of sales was the largest component of the company's expenses. Over the five-year period, the cost of sales decreased slightly; year-by-year analysis indicates, however, that this cost dropped significantly in 1984 and increased in each subsequent year. Similarly, selling and administrative expenses increased each year after 1984. The combination of these two expense items caused net income to decline following the increase in 1984.

If you looked further into 1984 results, the decreased earnings from then on appear to have resulted from two factors. La-Z-Boy acquired three other companies during 1985 and 1986 and was attempting to assimilate these acquisitions. In addition, the company invested in purchasing, warehousing, distribution, and internal information and control systems. Both the new investments and the three acquisitions hurt profitability in 1985– 1987 but hopefully will result in improved future profits.

In addition to component analysis, the analyst can examine the growth in various accounts over the same periods. **Percentage change** analysis can be used to determine the relative change in an item (expense, income, asset, or liability) over time, since the magnitude of raw data can mask the changes. The analyst can then compare these percentage changes with the changes in related items over the same time period. Exhibit 1–12 shows this analysis for La-Z-Boy. As you can see, this analysis gives you the change in each account each year.

EXHIBIT 1–12

LA-Z-BOY CHAIR COMPANY
Year-to-Year Statement of Earnings Percentage Change

	1984	1985	1986	1987
Net sales	29.39%	10.94%	20.84%	22.93%
Cost of sales	22.22	14.29	23.11	23.04
Gross margin	45.75	4.52	16.08	22.69
Selling, general, and				
administrative expense	19.27	18.60	18.53	30.07
Depreciation and amortization	17.33	23.48	33.31	32.00
Income before interest and taxes				
	89.68	(10.59)	8.78	8.07
Net interest	(6.60)	19.00	37.00	19.55
Income from operations	82.33	(8.27)	7.73	7.19
Taxes	109.63	(14.66)	8.20	8.18
Net income	82.33	(8.27)	7.73	7.19

2. Comparisons with Other Companies

Another type of analysis that is useful for analyzing a particular company's performance is to contrast two or more companies. Because financial requirements and uses of funds differ among industries, it is important that companies chosen for comparison first be limited to those within the same industry. Such an analysis is shown in Exhibit 1–13. Data for Bassett Furniture Industries, Inc., another company in the furniture industry, are compared with La-Z-Boy data.[2]

The differences between the two companies lies largely in their returns on sales and leverage. The first, which we can discover with further knowledge of the companies' business, comes as a result of Bassett's customers: Bassett sells about 16 percent of its production directly to the J. C. Penney Co. This type of buyer-supplier relationship usually results in low gross margins (Bassett's are 20 percent and La-Z-Boy's 31 percent) and low selling expenses. Bassett does have lower selling and administrative expenses than La-Z-Boy as a proportion of net sales.

As to the issue of leverage (as measured by the ratio of assets to equity), much more would have to be known about the company, its history, and its management to understand why Bassett finances itself almost entirely with equity. Often firms with such little debt held have managers with personal

---

[2] The La-Z-Boy Chair Company 1987 annual report covers the period from April 27, 1986, to April 25, 1987. The Basset Furniture Industries, Inc., 1986 annual report is for the 1986 calendar year. There do not appear to be seasonal differences that make the statements uncomparable.

EXHIBIT 1–13   Comparison of 1987 La-Z-Boy Chair Company and Bassett
Furniture Industries, Inc.

	La-Z-Boy	Bassett
Return on sales	5.9%	4.5%
Total asset turnover	155.0	155.8
Return on assets	9.2	7.0
Assets to equity	163.2	110.8
Return on equity	14.9	7.8
Dividend payout	28.9	51.6
Sustainable growth rate	10.6	3.8

knowledge of the Great Depression, who are thus averse to debt; are in very
risky businesses; or have been very profitable and are growing slowly.

While further information and knowledge about these companies is
needed to understand the differences between their ratios, the sustainable
growth rates point us in the right direction. The most interesting result of
the analysis is that Bassett, as a result of its strategy (its high proportion
of sales to one customer), can grow much more slowly than La-Z-Boy. If it
does not expect much growth, there is no cause for concern. However, if
Bassett management wants the company to grow much faster, it must bring
about major changes in one or more of its ratios: profitability, asset efficiency,
leverage, or earnings retention.

3. Comparisons with the Industry

Comparisons can be expanded to include several companies or all of the
relevant industry. Typically, industrywide comparisons are based on industry averages. These averages are available from several sources that collect
and publish the data. Exhibit 1–14 compares the 1986–87 La-Z-Boy data
with 1986 industry averages.[3] Because of financial differences in companies
of differing sizes, analysts commonly select from the industry a sample of
companies that correspond in size with the target company. Such a selection
was made in preparing Exhibit 1–14.

An analysis of the data indicates that La-Z-Boy's performance compares
very favorably with that of the industry. La-Z-Boy's cost of goods sold was
lower than that of the industry, which gave La-Z-Boy a higher before-tax
profit margin—10.7 percent as compared with 5.8 percent for the industry.

In addition, La-Z-Boy had a much higher sustainable growth rate than
the average for the industry. That resulted from La-Z-Boy's higher ROS and
lower dividend payout, in spite of its lower asset efficiency (TATO).

---

[3] These are the most recent data available. Because of the delay in collecting and compiling
the data, industry data usually lag behind individual companies' reported information.

EXHIBIT 1–14   Comparison of La-Z-Boy Chair Company with the Industry, 1986

	La-Z-Boy	Furniture Industry Average
Return on sales	5.9%	3.1%
Total asset turnover	155.0	254.0
Return on assets	9.2	7.9
Return on equity	14.9	16.1
Dividend payout	28.9	45.0
Sustainable growth rate	10.6	8.9

SOURCE: Data on the industry are for medium-sized companies, as reported in *Industry Norms and Key Business Ratios, 1987,* Dun & Bradstreet, 1987.

There are a number of other things an analyst should assess in looking at a company. If the performance being analyzed occurred over a period during which there was a significant change in industry or economic conditions (for instance, inflation), the analyst might want to look at the company's relative performance. Factoring out inflation-driven growth might give the analyst quite a different view of a company's real growth over a period. For example, from 1983 to 1987, La-Z-Boy's net sales grew by 20.8 percent. Over the same period, inflation was less than 3.5 percent. Thus, in real terms, the company's sales grew by over 17 percent. The extensiveness of an analysis depends, in part, on how the analyst will use the results.

IV. SUMMARY

Using the major external sources of financial information, the financial statements, an analyst can learn a great deal about the financial performance of a company through comparative ratio analysis. Calculating a ratio is not a difficult skill. It is in the assessment of which ratios to use and the interpretation of the results that analytical skills are required.

Proper interpretation requires an understanding of the company as well as the environment. Critical issues that need to be considered are general economic conditions, the competitive situation, and the business and financial strategy of the company. All of these factors, individually and in combination, affect the financial results for the company and the value that will be earned by the company's owners, its shareholders.

SELECTED REFERENCES

Sources of industry data and financial ratios are found in current issues of:
Dun & Bradstreet, *Industry Norms and Key Business Ratios.*

Robert Morris Associates, Annual Statement Studies.

Troy, Leo. *Almanac of Business and Industrial Financial Ratios.* Englewood Cliffs, N.J.: Prentice-Hall, 1985.

An in-depth example of the use of financial ratios is found in:

Backer, Morton, and Martin L. Gosman. "The Use of Financial Ratios in Credit Downgrade Decisions." *Financial Management,* Spring 1980, pp. 53–56.

The concept of sustainable growth is discussed in:

Higgins, Robert C. "How Much Growth Can a Firm Afford?" *Financial Management,* Fall 1977, pp. 7–16.

Lewellen, Wilbur G., and William A. Kracaw. "Inflation, Corporate Growth, and Corporate Leverage." *Financial Management,* Winter 1987, pp. 29–36.

Van Horne, James C. "Sustainable Growth Modeling." *Journal of Corporate Finance,* Winter 1987, pp. 19–25.

For further discussion on using financial ratios, see:

Brealey, Richard, and Stuart Myers. *Principles of Corporate Finance.* 3d ed. New York: McGraw-Hill, 1988, chap. 25.

Fraser, Lyn M. *Understanding Financial Statements: Through the Maze of a Corporate Annual Report.* Reston, Va.: Reston Publishing, 1985.

Pringle, John J., and Robert S. Harris. *Essentials of Managerial Finance.* 2d. ed. Glenview, Ill.: Scott, Foresman, 1987, chap. 7.

Ross, Steven and Randolf Westerfield. *Corporate Finance.* St. Louis, Mo.: Times Mirror/Mosby, 1988, chap. 2.

Van Horne, James C. *Financial Management and Policy.* 7th ed. Englewood Cliffs, N.J.: Prentice-Hall, 1986, chaps. 27–28.

Weston, J. Fred, and Eugene F. Brigham. *Essentials of Managerial Finance.* 8th ed. Hinsdale, Ill.: Dryden Press, 1988, chap. 7.

STUDY QUESTIONS

1. Melissa Hampton was reviewing the recent performance of CSX Corporation. Once primarily a railroad company, CSX had diversified into oil and gas exploration and transportation and ocean shipping. Her expectation was that the nature of the company had changed and that the sustainable growth had changed as well. To determine what effect the diversification moves had on the sustainable growth rate, she collected the following data for the company.

	1982	1983	1984	1985	1986
Sales	$4,409	$ 5,787	$ 7,934	$ 7,320	$ 6,345
Net income	$ 338	$ 272	$ 465	$ (118)	$ 418
Dividend payout	35%	48%	33%	(145)%	43%
Total assets	$8,109	$10,835	$11,636	$11,494	$12,661
Total equity	$3,398	$ 4,526	$ 4,909	$ 4,595	$ 4,873

    a. How has the sustainable growth rate changed over the time period? What has caused the changes?

    b. The railroad industry in 1986 had a dividend payout of 75 percent and a return on equity of 3.4 percent. How did CSX compare with the industry?

2. Mark Phillips has just been promoted to vice president of New Tech, which has two divisions. To assess the divisions' historical performance, he has asked you to compute component and percentage changes for the statements shown below. Are there any positive or negative trends?

New Tech
Income Statement
(in millions)

	Manufacturing Division			Chemical Products Division		
	1986	1987	1988	1986	1987	1988
Sales	$2,384	$2,500	$2,600	$1,562	$1,623	$1,687
Cost of goods sold	(1,058)	(1,075)	(1,300)	(950)	(967)	(980)
Gross profits	1,326	1,425	1,300	612	656	707
Operating expense	(159)	(178)	(185)	(88)	(97)	(100)
EBIT	1,167	1,247	1,115	524	559	607
Interest	(350)	(325)	(322)	(180)	(174)	(168)
Taxes	(302)	(341)	(357)	(130)	(142)	(66)
Net income	$ 515	$ 581	$ 436	$ 214	$ 243	$ 373

3. Complete the balance sheet and income statement below from the following data: (a) Dividend payout is 40 percent on shares with a market price of $75; (b) Dividend yield on 10 million shares outstanding is 20 percent; (c) Return on equity is 15 percent; (d) Ratio of long-term debt to equity is 2.3; (e) Current ratio is 2.67; (f) Acid-test ratio is 1.34; (g)

Income Statement	
Sales	
Cost of sales	____
Gross profit	
Operating expense	____
Operating profit	
Interest	
Taxes	____
Net income	____

Balance Sheet

Cash	Accounts payable
Accounts receivable	
Inventory	Other current ____
Other current	
Other current ____	
Current assets	Current liabilities
Net property, plant, ____	Long-term debt
and equipment	Owner's equity ____
	Total liabilities
Total assets	and owners' equity
═══	═══

Profit margin is 5 percent; (h) Gross margin is 20 percent; (i) Return on assets is 4 percent; (j) Inventory turnover is six times; (k) Operating profit is 90 percent of gross profit; (l) Accounts receivable collection period is 24 days (360-day basis); (m) Accounts payable payment period is 61 days; (n) Tax rate is 50 percent.

4. As the new financial analyst for Peterson's Chemicals, you have been asked to analyze the profitability problems encountered in the last two years. Current financial statements and selected industry averages are as follows:

Peterson's Chemicals
Income Statement
(in millions)

	1985	1986	Industry Average (% of sales) 1985	1986
Sales	$1,435	$1,478	100%	100%
Cost of goods sold	(1,076)	(1,182)	(67)	(68)
Gross profit	$ 359	$ 296	33	32
Selling and administrative expenses	(445)	(443)	(27)	(26)
Operating profit	$ (86)	$ (147)	6	6
Interest expense	(29)	(27)	(1)	(2)
Net income	$ (115)	$ (174)	5%	4%

Comparative industry ratios for both 1985 and 1986 are: current ratio 1.5; acid-test ratio .9; receivables collection period 65 days; payables payment period 60 days; debt-to-equity ratio 1.1; return on equity 19 percent; return on assets 7 percent.

Peterson's Chemicals
Balance Sheet
(in millions)

	1985	1986		1985	1986
Cash and equivalent	$ 76	$ 120	Accounts payable	$ 412	$ 500
Accounts receivable (net)	437	432	Other current	98	309
Inventory	284	324	Total current	$ 510	$ 809
Other current	38	37	Long-term debt	300	178
Total current	$ 835	$ 913	Total liabilities	$ 810	$ 987
Plant, property,			Owners' equity	400	226
and equipment	375	300			
			Total liabilities		
Total assets	$1,210	$1,213	and owners' equity	$1,210	$1,213

a. Calculate the appropriate ratios needed for this analysis. How does Peterson's Chemicals compare with the industry?

b. Management has decided to reexamine the company's short-term credit policies. The chief financial officer estimates that reducing the receivables collection period to 78 days will result in a sales decrease of 3 percent. The purchasing department reports that by reducing the payables period to 69 days, discounts would be available that would reduce the cost of goods by 9 percent. Initially the cash required to finance these changes will come from additional long-term debt, resulting in a debt-to-equity ratio of 1.0. If management had made these changes at the beginning of 1986, would Peterson's Chemicals have been profitable? How would ROE and ROA have been affected? Prepare new financial statements to reflect these changes.

CHAPTER 2

Managing Working Capital

Most financial managers find that a significant amount of their time is spent dealing with "brush fires"—short-term problems or opportunities. There is no doubt that the development of a long-term financial strategy in conjunction with a corporate business strategy is important for the long-term growth of the company. However, the financial manager must ensure that the corporation can successfully cope with short-term contingencies; otherwise, the long-term plan will have no value.

One of the major problems facing managers is the company's need for working capital. Working capital refers to the current assets of the corporation and therefore includes inventories, accounts receivable, cash, and marketable securities. These are resources directly involved in the company's production and sales. Successful management of corporate working capital will create value for the shareholders.

I. THE WORKING-CAPITAL CYCLE

The term **working-capital cycle,** or **production-sales cycle,** refers to the ebb and flow of funds through the company in response to changes in the level of activity in manufacturing and sales. When the company decides to manufacture a product, funds are needed to purchase raw materials, pay for the production process, and maintain the inventory. If the product is sold on credit, the company also requires funds to support the accounts receivable until customers ultimately reimburse the company for the products.

The term **cycle** refers to the difference between the time payment is due for production expenses and the time the customer pays for the product. If the company received payment for the product at the same time it was required to pay the expenses of producing the product, there would be no working-capital cycle, nor would firms have difficulty managing working capital.

This timing difference can be illustrated with a simple graph, Exhibit 2–1. In this highly simplified, hypothetical cycle, the company orders the raw materials required for production at Day 0. The materials arrive and production begins. As production proceeds, the company begins to pay for

EXHIBIT 2–1   Graph of Working-Capital Cycle

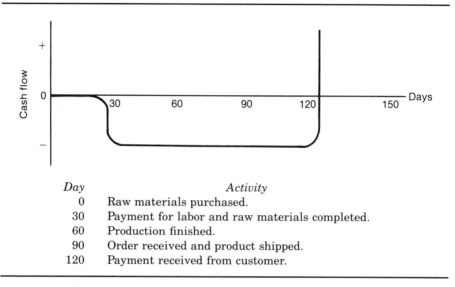

Day	Activity
0	Raw materials purchased.
30	Payment for labor and raw materials completed.
60	Production finished.
90	Order received and product shipped.
120	Payment received from customer.

the labor, and by Day 30 has paid for all labor involved in the production process as well as for materials. The product is completed on Day 60 and is put into finished goods inventory. A customer order is received on Day 90, and the product is sold. Payment is received from the customer on Day 120. In this example, the working-capital cycle is a total of 120 days or four months.

From a cash flow standpoint, the company has made all of the cash payments for labor and raw material costs by Day 30 but receives no cash payment from the customer until Day 120. Consequently, the company requires some type of financing for more than 90 days.

The working-capital cycle can vary significantly among different companies. Two extreme examples are wine producers and grocery retailers. The wine producer typically must store wine for several years to attain proper aging. There may be several years between the cash outflows for production and the receipt of cash from sales to customers. The grocery retailer usually has a very rapid inventory turnover and makes mostly cash sales. In such a case, the working-capital cycle is very short.

Most companies do not produce one unit at a time. Many units are produced, and all are at various stages in the production-sales cycle at any given time. Thus, once a company is able to complete the start-up phase of operations successfully, it will be able to rely on a continuous flow of products through the cycle to provide funds for its needs. The company can use the cash from previous sales to pay for the expenses of producing current units. If the company were in a stable environment with no inflation, no sales growth, and no changes in customer demand, it would be able to deal with the working-capital cycle without difficulty. All of these factors exist, however, and combine to cause an increased need for working capital.

1. The Impact of Inflation

In an inflationary environment, the cost of producing each unit increases over time. Thus, by the time the company has collected the cash from its previous sales, the production costs on subsequent units have increased. Unless the company is able to price units with sufficient profit margins, it may not be able to meet subsequent production costs with revenues from prior production.

To illustrate this problem, we will examine a simplified production cycle for a steel company with a $1,000 beginning cash balance, as shown in Exhibit 2–2. Assume that the company can produce a ton of steel for $400 and charges the customer $430 per ton to allow for a profit. If the working-capital cycle is about four months, the company will not receive any cash payment for the first ton of steel until four months after production begins. In the interim, production of the second ton of steel commences.

If the inflation rate is 20 percent annually, the cost of producing the second ton of steel six months later will have increased to $440. Thus, when

EXHIBIT 2–2 Impact of Inflation on the Working-Capital Cycle

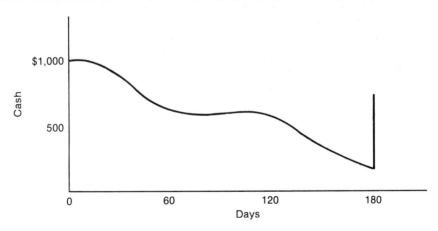

Day	Activity	Cash Balance
0	Production of first ton commences	$1,000
90	Production of first ton completed at $400 cost	600
90	Production of second ton commences	600
120	Sale of first ton at $430 with 60-day collection terms	600
180	Production of second ton completed at $440 cost	160
180	Payment for first ton received	590

the company receives cash payment for the steel billed at $430 per ton, its current production costs will be $440 per ton. The company will require some additional financing to allow it to meet the increased production costs, which, in this example, exceed the revenues received from the previous sales. Without financing, the cash balance will continually be reduced until it reaches zero.

Of course, the company will probably increase the price of the steel to maintain the profit margin. In this example, the price would probably be about $473 per ton. However, by the time the steel company collects this amount, inflation will have continued to increase the cost of the next ton produced.

This example is obviously highly simplified. Continual production, and multiple products with varying working-capital cycles and exposures to inflation, complicate the analysis. Nevertheless, the conceptual framework for analyzing the increased working-capital requirements caused by inflation is the same. The net effect of inflation is to increase the working capital required by the company.

2. The Impact of Sales Growth

The effect of sales growth on working-capital needs is similar to that of inflation. In the case of sales growth, the problem is not caused by an increasing per-unit cost but by an increasing number of units. Although the cost per unit may be stable, total costs increase because of the increased volume.

For example, a microcomputer producer may have been very successful in developing a market for its products. Assume that the company can produce microcomputers for a cost of $700 each. The company produces 500 units and sells each for $800 during a particular month. The company extends credit for 30 days to buyers of the microcomputers. During the ensuing month, the demand for microcomputers is such that the company produces 600 units. At production costs of $700 per unit, the company incurs a total production cost of $420,000. However, the sales revenue collected from the sales of the previous month will be only $400,000 (500 × $800).

Thus, even if the company continues to charge $800 per unit, a price that allows a profit margin of 12.5 percent, the sales growth alone will require new working capital; the company will have insufficient cash inflow each month to meet the expenses incurred for the production of the next units.

In this situation, the problem is not that the company has priced its products inappropriately. The company's prices allow an adequate profit margin above the costs of production. The problem stems from the timing differences between the payment of production expenses and the receipt of payment from sales.

This illustrates a problem that growing companies face. In order to grow, companies require funds to support that growth. The inability to provide the required funding may restrict the potential growth of the company. The maximum growth rate a company can fund with its existing financing policies is termed the sustainable growth rate (discussed in Chapter 1). Sustainable growth depends on the profitability of the company, the need for assets to support sales growth (as measured by the asset turnover ratio), and the financing of the company (as indicated by the dividend payout and the ratio of equity to assets). In general, the more rapid the growth rate, the greater the need for funds to support the growth.

3. The Impact of Variable Sales Demand

The other major factor that can cause working-capital problems is a varying level of sales. Changes in sales activity are of three types:

1. *Seasonal:* Peak demand occurs during particular periods of the year; snow-skiing equipment is a seasonal product.
2. *Cyclical:* Peak demand occurs during different phases of the business cycle; the demand for building materials is cyclical.
3. *Secular:* Demand fluctuates over a long period of time; radio broadcasting revenues have been secular.

All three cycles differ in duration but have similar effects on the company's working capital. For simplicity's sake, we will focus on the seasonal cycle; because it is of shorter duration, its impact on working-capital needs is easier to trace.

In a seasonal industry, the company may not have sold the completed units before it is necessary to incur the costs of producing additional units. To illustrate the problem, we will use the example of the snow-skiing equipment manufacturer. This business is highly seasonal; peak consumer demand occurs during fall and winter. The producer's peak sales period, however, occurs in late summer and early fall, when retailers place their orders to have the equipment for sale during the peak snow-skiing months.

The peak sales period for the manufacturer is not, however, the peak production period. It would be very inefficient to attempt to produce skiing equipment as orders from retailers are received. To do so, the manufacturer would need a large production capacity which would be idle for most of the year. New workers would have to be hired and trained for each production season. During the peak production period, the work force would be required to work overtime; at the conclusion of the period, workers would be laid off. All in all, this would be a very inefficient and expensive production method.

To avoid these problems, the ski-equipment manufacturer may utilize a level production approach. During the slack sales months, in the late winter and spring, production is continued but little equipment is actually sold to retailers. The manufactured equipment is stored in inventory. The growing inventory will be used by the company to fill sales orders as they arrive in the late summer and early fall. During this period of inventory buildup, the company still incurs the costs of raw materials and labor associated with the production of the skiing equipment.

As retailers begin to place orders in the late summer, the manufacturer ships equipment from the inventory. During this period, the manufacturer starts to draw on the finished goods inventory if orders exceed the continuing production level. However, the manufacturer still has not received payment for any of the equipment. The retailers buy from the manufacturer on credit, with perhaps 30 or 60 days in which to pay for the equipment. During this period of high but decreasing inventories, continuing production, and increasing accounts receivable, most seasonal companies experience the greatest working-capital needs.

As the selling season progresses, additional orders will be received by the manufacturer. As these orders are filled, the large finished goods inventory is drawn down much more rapidly than it is being replenished from continuing production. While receivables increase from the credit sales, the company begins to receive some payment for shipments made in the late summer.

By the end of the fall selling season, the company's inventory is depleted, and all of its receivables should have been collected. At this point, the company should have a large amount of cash ready to begin the next cycle of inventory buildup, receipt of orders, increase in accounts receivable, and collection of funds.

The seasonal cycle requires cash to begin the cycle. Once the cycle starts, funds cycle through different balance sheet accounts. Initially cash is invested in inventory in anticipation of future sales. Then, as orders are placed and goods shipped, inventories are reduced and capital is transferred to accounts receivable. As payments for accounts receivable are received, the working capital is returned as cash, which is invested in production for inventory in preparation for the next selling season. This cycle is shown in Exhibit 2–3.

Even though the total amount of funds invested in working capital does not change over the cycle, the company must have the funds required at the beginning of the working-capital cycle. This pattern of inflow and outflow of funds might occur for several seasonal peaks during a year, over a business cycle, or over a long-term secular trend. In any of these situations, the pattern of working-capital needs would be similar. The primary difference among these situations is the duration of the cycle. The working-capital pattern in many businesses is determined by industry practice. When there is a choice (e.g., level versus seasonal production), the analytical techniques discussed in Chapter 4 can be used to determine which choice will create more shareholder value.

II. CASH MANAGEMENT

Because financial obligations must be paid in cash, the most important resource in the working-capital cycle is cash. Corporate managers need to

EXHIBIT 2–3   Seasonal Inventory and Accounts Receivable Investment

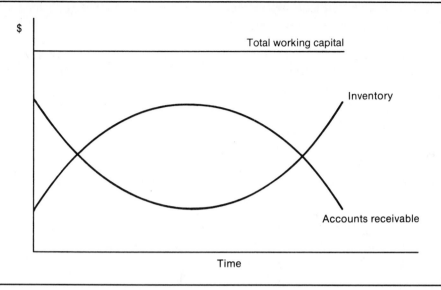

ensure that sufficient cash is available to meet their obligations. This need has led to the development of sophisticated techniques to manage the cash in companies. These techniques have three objectives: accelerate the speed of cash receipts, decelerate the speed of cash disbursements, and maximize the return on investment of cash balances. In recent years, high interest rates have emphasized the importance of managing cash, while the development of computers has allowed managers access to the information needed for close monitoring of cash balances.

1. Managing Receipts

The process of managing cash receipts involves collecting funds as quickly as possible and concentrating them in accounts so that the financial manager can control them.

Lockboxes.   The use of lockboxes speeds the collecting, processing, depositing, and reporting of payments received through the mail. A lockbox is a special post office box to which the company's customers are instructed to mail payments. The box is checked several times daily in the processing operation, which is usually operated by a bank. Checks are immediately entered into the check-clearing process to be converted into funds for the company.

Electronic funds transfer.   A faster method of collecting funds is to require that payment be made electronically rather than with a paper check.

In this system, payment is made by transferring funds directly from the payer's bank account to the recipient's account. This makes the funds immediately available and also eliminates the cost of handling paper checks.

Preauthorized checks.   Preauthorized checks (PACs) are preprinted, unsigned checks. For fixed, repetitive payments, companies authorize their creditors to draw checks on their accounts. The creditor sends the PAC to the bank, which then deposits the funds into the creditor's account.

Deposit concentration.   Because it is difficult to control funds in many different banks, most receipt management systems provide for transferring funds through electronic or wire transfers into a few or even one large account. Central accounts can be more closely managed.

2. Managing Disbursements

The goal in managing disbursements is to delay payments in order to keep funds in use as long as possible.

Managed balance account.   A managed balance account is a special checking account that has a zero balance. As checks are presented to this account, a negative balance is created. Funds are then automatically transferred from a control or master account to bring the account back to zero or another predetermined balance. In this way, all funds are centralized and no idle balances remain in the disbursing account.

Controlled disbursement system.   The purpose of this system is to maximize the time it takes for checks to clear a corporation's account. By making payments through geographically remote banks, the clearing time or "float" is increased. This postpones the date when the company must provide funds to cover checks. It allows funds to remain in interest-earning assets or delays the need to borrow.

3. Investing Cash Balances

By carefully managing cash accounts, a financial manager can minimize the cash the corporation must maintain. This increases the amount of funds available for investment in productive assets, such as inventories or plant and equipment, and reduces the need to raise additional capital. By maximizing the amount of funds available to invest in productive or working assets, the manager is operating more efficiently and creating value.

The ultimate success in minimizing cash would be to have a zero balance in all cash accounts. Despite the efforts to control and predict disbursements, there may be some unforeseen need for disbursements or a slow-down in receipts. Therefore, corporations typically maintain a balance for transaction liquidity. Having these balances sitting idly, as cash or in checking accounts, is an unproductive use of funds. Managers attempt to maximize the return on these fund balances by investing them in the money market.

The money market consists of borrowers and lenders of short-term funds. Although technically money market instruments can have a maturity of up to one year, most have much shorter maturities. The money market is highly liquid in that there are many buyers and sellers. Furthermore, borrowers in this market are institutions with high credit ratings. These factors allow any investment to be quickly converted into cash if needed. Money market investments include Treasury bills (T-bills), short-term notes issued by the U.S. government; commercial paper, short-term notes issued by corporations; and certificates of deposit, short-term notes issued by banks. Although the returns from these short-term investments may be relatively low compared to longer-term, less liquid investments, it is still better than having no earnings from idle cash balances.

In order to invest in these instruments, the financial manager must know how much cash is available to invest. Cash management systems are designed to provide daily information about the amount of funds available. Managers can use this information to decide how much to invest in money market instruments. In many cases, investments will be made for periods as short as overnight to maximize the return available from cash balances.

III. MANAGING OTHER WORKING-CAPITAL REQUIREMENTS

Cash by itself is not a productive asset. Most corporations are in business to make and sell a product. In order to be successful, companies need to invest their cash in the other elements of working capital—inventories and accounts receivable. Just as cash must be managed, the other working-capital investments must be managed as well. Similarly, managing these accounts is based on minimizing the working-capital investment while still providing the resources required.

1. Minimizing Working-Capital Needs

The two components of working-capital needs are accounts receivable and inventories. The task of minimizing working capital, then, is one of reducing the company's investments in these two accounts.

The size of a company's accounts receivable is, to a large extent, determined by its competitive environment. If competitors are selling goods on credit, the company may be forced to follow that practice to remain competitive. The company has little control over the magnitude of credit sales. The only method of reducing accounts receivable is to ensure that credit collections are prompt. If goods are sold on 30-day terms, management should vigorously attempt to ensure that payment is received within the 30-day period. Any extension represents a noninterest-bearing credit by the manufacturer to the customer. Some companies charge overdue-account penalties or interest to encourage timely payment.

A method of monitoring accounts receivable based on the due date is called **accounts receivable aging.** In this process, receivables are categorized according to the number of days they are overdue. For example, they might be categorized as 30, 60, and 90 days overdue. Collection efforts can then be focused on those accounts that are most overdue. The intent is to minimize the number of accounts not collected punctually. Because of the costs associated with the company's financing of its working-capital needs, any unnecessary increases in accounts receivable due to lax collection of overdue accounts must be recognized as an extraneous expense for the company.

In an environment in which a company can independently determine its accounts receivable policy, the critical factor to be considered is the relationship between sales and accounts receivable. By reducing the financing it is willing to offer buyers, a company may be eliminating some potential buyers. Thus accounts receivable may be reduced, but only at the cost of reducing total revenues.

On the other hand, extending more credit to customers may have the effect of reducing the inventory the company must keep. With easier credit terms, buyers may be willing to purchase more goods, thereby assuming some of the costs of inventory maintenance from the manufacturer. However, while the company's investment in inventory would decline, the investment in accounts receivable would increase.

An increased volume of credit sales also exposes the company to additional risk of uncollectible accounts. The potential cost of bad debts must be weighed against the potential incremental profits resulting from sales generated by the easier credit terms.

Like accounts receivable, inventory is directly related to sales volume. While maintaining too much inventory is expensive, it will have no impact on sales volume; too little inventory may cause stock-outs and lost sales. Maintenance of an appropriate inventory level has become so significant that sophisticated inventory models have been developed. The aim of these models is to determine the relationship between inventory levels and sales levels, so the company can determine the optimum inventory level.

In sum, from the standpoint of reducing the need for working capital, the company should attempt to reduce its investment in accounts receivable and inventories. However, the company risks the loss of sales revenues if these accounts are reduced inordinately. The managerial task is to ascertain the appropriate level for each of these accounts.

2. Financing Working-Capital Needs

Having determined the minimum level of working capital needed to carry out the production and sales cycle, the manager must then select the most appropriate method of financing the needs. Not surprisingly, an important consideration is the cost of various sources of financing.

An immediate source of funds are the assets of the company—in most cases, the cash and marketable securities. To minimize cash holdings, companies use the cash-management techniques previously described.

Cash and marketable securities come from several sources. The most significant source of internal funding is the profit margin on sales. If the competitive environment allows, the company may be able to price its products so that there is sufficient profit to fund working-capital requirements. For example, in an inflationary environment, the company might attempt to increase its prices in excess of the inflation rate in order to finance the working-capital needs caused by inflating production costs. The company's ability to adjust its prices in this manner naturally depends on the competitive situation. In a highly competitive environment, the company may not have much latitude in its pricing and will need to turn to other sources.

One of the most readily available external sources is the company's suppliers. Unfortunately, there is a limit to supplier-supplied credit: The company's suppliers may refuse to ship materials needed for production. Such refusals might force the company to stop production. This is usually the last course of action a supplier will take, because it results in the loss of a customer.

More often, suppliers encourage prompt payment: Vendors often allow the purchaser to take a discount from the sales price if the payment is made within a specified time period. For example, suppliers may indicate payment terms of 2/10, net 30. This means that if the purchaser pays within ten days, a discount of 2 percent from the sales price is allowed; otherwise, the full sales price is due in 30 days. If the purchaser decides to wait 30 days to pay rather than paying within 10 days and taking the 2 percent discount, the cost of holding the funds for the additional 20 days is 43.5 percent on a compounded annualized basis.[1] Even if the purchaser decides to pay after 60 days rather than the 30 days specified by the terms of the sale, the effective cost is 15.6 percent. This suggests that, when a supplier offers a discount, stretching the payables period is an expensive source of funds, unless payment is delayed for a very long time.

The other major nonfinancial-institution creditor for most corporations is the government. While government taxing authorities may allow a temporary deferral of taxes, nonpayment of amounts due is a punishable offense—which limits the usefulness of this as a source of funds.

A typically less expensive source of short-term financing is bank debt. A standard borrowing arrangement for creditworthy companies is a **line of credit** with a bank. This is an agreement that the bank will lend up to a

---

[1] If the discount is not taken, and the bill is paid on the due date in 30 days, the customer has paid 2 percent for the use of the funds for 20 days—an annualized rate of 43.5 percent. (Compounding is explained in Chapter 4.)

specified amount during a specified period of time. The borrower can borrow or draw down against the credit line as the need arises. In situations where the borrower may not be considered a good credit risk, the bank may extend a secured line of credit. In this case, the bank has a claim on specific assets of the company if the borrowed funds are not repaid as agreed. Typically, the bank requires the company to pledge its accounts receivable and inventory in such situations. A standard practice is for secured lines not to exceed 75 percent of the value of receivables and 50 percent of inventory.

Some companies have found it advantageous to sell their accounts receivable to financial institutions. This process is called **factoring.** The company receives immediate payment for the receivables and does not have to wait until accounts are collected to have usable funds. The factoring company buys the receivables at a discount from their stated or face value, so the company incurs a cost in selling its receivables. The advantage of factoring is that it reduces the firm's need for working capital. In addition, for a somewhat higher discount, the receivables may be sold **without recourse.** This means that if an account is not collectible, the financial institution rather than the company must absorb the loss.

In recent years, companies considered to be good credit risks have developed direct access to short-term financial markets without using commercial banks as intermediaries. These high-quality companies have issued short-term notes, called **commercial paper,** at interest rates slightly below the rates banks would have charged. Companies are using increasingly sophisticated and innovative methods of raising short-term funds. The objective obviously is to obtain funds at the lowest cost.

The focus is on short-term financial sources because for companies with seasonal financing needs, the expected cash flows will provide funds to retire the debt. Since the financing needs are short-term, short-term debt is considered appropriate. For this reason, a company's **net working capital** is often defined as current assets minus current liabilities. It is often suggested that long-term debt or equity is a more appropriate way to fund working-capital needs caused by inflation, sales growth, and cyclical or secular trends. In these situations, financing requirements are longer term, and a reliance on short-term debt might be inappropriate. It is, of course, possible for a company to utilize short-term debt to fund these needs. The risk is that the company will continually need to refinance its debt, exposing itself to continuing interest-rate fluctuations as well as potential unavailability of funds. If the company is willing to accept these risks, it might benefit from the lower interest costs normally associated with short-term debt. Equity is the most expensive source but has an advantage: There are no restrictions or contractual obligations associated with it.

All of these sources of financing will be discussed in greater detail in Chapters 5 and 6.

IV. SUMMARY

Through the normal course of business operations, companies require current assets or working capital. These assets—inventories, accounts receivable, and cash—are needed to allow the company to manufacture and sell its products. However, because of the timing differences between the cash outflow for costs of production and the cash inflow from sale of products, companies usually require some financing for these working-capital needs.

Because of the magnitude of the amounts required, skillful management can make a significant impact on profitability by reducing the needed working capital by shortening the working-capital cycle or eliminating unneeded assets. In assessing working-capital needs, managers must balance reducing working capital and reducing sales. Having achieved an appropriate working-capital level, management's remaining responsibility is to finance it in the least costly manner.

SELECTED REFERENCES

For further discussion of cash-management systems, see:

Kamath, Ravindra R.; Shahriar Khaksari; Heidi Hylton Meier; and John Winkle-pleck. "Management of Excess Cash: Practices and Developments." *Financial Management,* Autumn 1985, pp. 70–77.

Serraino, William J.; Surrendra S. Singhvi; and Robert M. Soldofsky. *Frontiers of Financial Management.* 4th ed. Cincinnati: South-Western Publishing, 1984, part VI.

Stone, Bernell K., and Ned C. Hill. "Cash Transfer Scheduling for Efficient Cash Concentration." *Financial Management,* Autumn 1980, pp. 35–43.

Stone, Bernell K., and Tom W. Miller. "Daily Cash Forecasting with Multiplicative Models of Cash Flow Patterns." *Financial Management,* Winter 1987, pp. 45–54.

For discussion of inventory and accounts receivable management, see:

Gentry, James A., and Jesus M. DeLa Garza. "A Generalized Model for Monitoring Accounts Receivable." *Financial Management,* Winter 1985, pp. 28–38.

Halloran, John A., and Howard P. Lanser. "The Credit Policy Decision in an Inflationary Environment." *Financial Management,* Winter 1981, pp. 31–38.

Scott, David., Jr.; Arthur J. Keown; John D. Martin; and J. William Petty III. *Readings in Financial Management.* New York: Academic Press, 1982, sec. 2.

For additional information on money markets, see:

Brick, John R., ed. *Financial Markets: Instruments and Concepts.* Richmond, Va.: Robert F. Dame, 1981, sec. I.

For a more detailed explanation of working-capital management in general, see:

Brealey, Richard, and Stewart Myers. *Principles of Corporate Finance.* 3d ed. New York: McGraw-Hill, 1988, chaps. 27–30.

Ross, Steven, and Randolf Westerfield. *Corporate Finance.* St. Louis, Mo.: Times Mirror/Mosby, 1988, chaps. 23–25.

Seitz, Neil. *Financial Analysis: A Programmed Approach.* 3d ed. Reston, Va.: Reston Publishing, 1984, chap. 4.

VanHorne, James C. *Financial Management and Policy.* 7th ed. Englewood Cliffs, N.J.: Prentice-Hall, 1988, chaps. 13–16.

Weston, J. Fred, and Eugene F. Brigham. *Essentials of Managerial Finance.* 8th ed. Hinsdale, Ill.: Dryden Press, 1988, chap. 10.

STUDY QUESTIONS

1. Chateau Royale International is anticipating explosive sales growth for 1989. As their account manager at Bank & Trust, you are concerned about the amount of short-term borrowing that will be required under current working-capital policies. Forecast a balance sheet and income statement for 1989, as well as the change in net working capital and the current ratio, to assist management in understanding the effects of this increase in sales volume. Financial statements for 1988, and your assumptions, are indicated below.

Chateau Royale International
Income Statement
(in millions)

Sales	$375,000
Cost of goods sold	(276,150)
Gross profit	98,850
Operating expenses	(75,000)
Depreciation	(5,100)
Operating profit	18,750
Taxes	(7,500)
Net profit	$ 11,250

Balance Sheet
(in millions)

Cash	$ 75,000	Accounts payable	$ 23,116
Accounts receivable	46,233	Short-term debt	51,867
Inventory	93,750		
Current assets	214,983	Current liabilities	74,983
		Long-term debt	125,000
Net property, plant,		Common stock	100,000
and equipment	115,000	Retained earnings	30,000
		Total liabilities and	
Total assets	$329,983	owners' equity	$329,983

Based on your knowledge of the company and the industry, you have made the following assumptions: (a) Sales will increase 60 percent; (b) Cost of goods sold is 75 percent of sales; (c) Operating expenses will grow 10 percent; (d) Depreciation will be $8,000; (e) For this analysis, common stock and long-term debt remain constant from 1988; (f) Sales are outstanding 45 days; (g) Payables payment period is 30 days; (h) Inventory turnover is three times; (i) Management requires a minimum cash balance of 20 percent of sales; (j) There are no purchases or disposals of property, plant, or equipment; (k) The tax rate is 40 percent; (l) No dividends will be issued in 1989; (m) Additional funding will be in the form of short-term debt.

2. After reviewing your analysis, Chateau Royale management suggests the following working-capital policy changes: (a) Reduce minimum cash balance to 15 percent of sales; (b) Increase payables payment period to 45 days; and (c) Increase inventory turnover to four. Recompute the balance sheet and net working capital to reflect these changes. Is the current ratio in line with the industry average of 3.2? What are the implications of these policy changes?

3. Cindy Brittain, chief financial officer of the Kurz Corporation, is meeting with her two top analysts regarding working-capital management. Tony Triano has suggested that a more lenient accounts receivable collection policy would result in higher sales. He has estimated that, by increasing the receivables collection period to 60 days, sales growth would be 50 percent, inventory turnover would be increased to seven times, and bad debt would only be 2 percent of net sales. Furthermore, an increase in the minimum cash balance to 20 percent of net sales would offset any liquidity problems. Jim Dine, however, has advised against an aggressive working-capital policy—citing, among other issues—the expectation of slower economic growth. He has estimated that by reducing the receivables collection period to 30 days, there would be no bad debt expense and sales growth would still be 20 percent. Although inventory turnover would decrease to five times, the minimum cash balance could be reduced to 15 percent. All additional financing would be in the form of short-term debt. The tax rate will remain at 35 percent, cost of goods sold at 75 percent of gross sales, accounts payable at 30 days, and operating expenses will be constant.

   a. Compute an income statement, balance sheet, net working capital, and current ratio under each alternative. To assist in your analysis, the current financial statements are shown on the next page.

   b. Which policy changes should Ms. Brittain implement?

Kurz Corporation
Income Statement
(in thousands)

Sales	$505,000
Bad debt	5,000
Net sales	500,000
Cost of goods sold	375,000
Gross profit	125,000
Operating expense	90,900
Operating profit	34,100
Taxes	11,935
Net profit	$ 22,165

Balance Sheet
(in thousands)

Cash	$ 90,000	Accounts payable	$ 30,822
Accounts receivable	61,644	Short-term debt	86,322
Inventory	62,500	Current liabilities	117,144
Current assets	214,144	Long-term debt	110,000
Net property, plant, and		Common stock	75,000
equipment	130,000	Retained earnings	42,000
		Total liabilities and	
Total assets	$344,144	owners' equity	$344,144

CHAPTER 3

Forecasting Future Needs

Most analysts are more concerned about a company's future performance than its past. Although an analysis of past performance can provide useful insights into the operation of a company, historical data are most valuable for providing perspective in developing forecasts for the company's future. Sophisticated techniques, most of which are beyond the scope of this book, have been developed to forecast a company's future. Despite the level of quantitative and statistical sophistication involved, however, all forecasting techniques are essentially projections of historical relationships and results. The accuracy of forecasts is therefore contingent on proper interpretation of historical data as well as extrapolation of identified relationships. The manager must bear in mind that the application of sophisticated quantitative analysis should not give such forecasts an unwarranted aura of veracity.

All forecasts are necessarily based on certain assumptions—assumptions about relationships between past and future performance and about relationships among the variables that are being forecast. These assumptions are critical and therefore should be explicit. The fact that forecasts are based on assumptions will not invalidate the results: rather, inability to recognize that assumptions have been made and failure to test them will result in tenuous forecasts.

Although technically similar, basic approaches to forecasting vary depending on the planned use of the results. The purpose of the forecast suggests the appropriate methods and variables to be used. External analysts typically make forecasts to determine a company's expected performance. For example, they may try to determine the returns from an equity investment in a company or whether a company will generate sufficient cash to remain solvent and repay its obligations. Internal analysts, on the other hand, are concerned with forecasting needs for financial resources so that managers can plan future operations and investments. The remainder of this chapter will focus on the types of analyses typically used by internal corporate managers.

In forecasting funding needs, analysts usually use two methods of analysis. For short time periods, a method known as cash budgeting is most often employed. For longer periods of time, projected financial statements are typically developed. We will discuss each of these methods in turn. We will then describe the means of testing the assumptions used to prepare the forecasts.

I. CASH BUDGETS

The cash-budget approach to forecasting financial needs focuses specifically on the cash account of the company. This approach differs significantly from the more common method of accounting in corporations, the accrual method. Accrual accounting attempts to match the revenues earned during a specific period with the expenses incurred without regard to actual cash receipts or disbursements. In cash budgeting, the manager focuses on the actual cash account balances. The objective is to identify whether sufficient cash will be available to meet financial needs as they occur. This is done by comparing cash receipts with cash disbursements. The difference between cash receipts and disbursements reveals either an excess of or a need for additional cash.

The cash-budget cycle is similar in many respects to the working-capital cycle discussed in Chapter 2. Like working-capital problems, a company's cash problems are typically caused by timing differences between receipts and payments. Assuming that the company is adequately pricing its products, it will have no cash problems if cash payments for its sales are received at the same time payments for its production costs are required. However, credit sales, seasonal demand, and other factors combine to cause delays between receipts and disbursements.

In drawing up a cash budget, the analyst's first step is to choose an appropriate time period for analysis. Usually, cash budgets are developed by analyzing monthly cash flows. In industries with highly volatile cash flows or during times of high interest rates, cash budgets may be based on weekly or daily cash flows. In some highly inflationary environments, companies have been known to prepare cash budgets for hourly cash flows. The analyst's second step is to choose a suitable forecast horizon date. The forecast horizon for the cash budget also depends on the firm's situation. If monthly cash budgets are used, the company typically prepares a 12- or perhaps a 24-month forecast. Cash budgets based on shorter time periods are usually developed for correspondingly nearer forecast horizons.

After the appropriate time period and forecast horizon have been chosen, the next step is to determine which variables will be used as the bases for the forecast's critical underlying assumptions. Most forecasts begin with an assumption about sales volume during the period. Predictions for all other variables are based on the forecasted level of sales. The assumed relationships between sales and the other variables are, of course, important and need to be explicitly stated.

Cash budgets developed for Murphy's Apparel, a wholesale distributor of tennis and swimming clothing and accessories will serve as examples for forecasting the cash position. Although Murphy's Apparel sustained some losses during its initial operations, management expects that continuing operations will be profitable. The company has only been in existence for two years, and the owner has relied on a bank loan of $50,000 to offset the financial drain caused by the early losses. Although sales are expected to increase annually by 10 percent, the necessity of extending long credit during the peak summer sales season causes severe cash problems. To determine the severity of these problems, a monthly cash budget, commencing on September 1, 1989, and extending through mid-1990 has been prepared.

Starting with the assumed sales growth of 10 percent, analysts prepared a set of assumptions for the cash budget. These are listed in Exhibit 3–1. Using these assumptions, the analysts forecast the expected sales volume, cash sales, accounts receivable collections, and purchases of merchandise for each of the 12 months of the cash-budget period. These forecasts are shown in Exhibit 3–2.

To determine the effect of delays in receiving cash from sales and in paying cash for purchases, the accounts receivable and payable schedules in Exhibits 3–3 and 3–4 were prepared. On the basis of these data, monthly cash receipts and cash disbursements were calculated. The results are shown in Exhibit 3–5. For each month, cash payments for expenses and merchandise were subtracted from the cash generated by cash sales and collections of previous credit sales. On a cumulative basis, an excess of receipts over disbursements increases the cash balance, while a shortfall reduces it.

Using the cash budget, managers determined that the firm would need cash in June and July of 1990. The cash need of $3,000 in June and $28,000 in July is less than the $50,000 credit line already arranged with the bank. Even though Murphy's will need to draw on the credit line, the cash-budget

EXHIBIT 3–1   Assumptions for Murphy's Apparel, Cash Budget 1989–90

1. Sales will be seasonal, peaking in the summer. In general, sales will increase by 10% annually.
2. About 10% of sales will be for cash. Credit terms during summer peak months will be about eight weeks, off-season collections average four weeks.
3. Suppliers will require payment within 30 days.
4. The bank will not allow more than the current $50,000 credit line.
5. The expected purchase of new equipment will require a $15,000 payment in May 1990.
6. Cost of sales will be 79% of sales.
7. Selling and administrative expenses will be 9% of sales.
8. Fixed operating costs will be $5,400 a month, including $500 depreciation expense.
9. The monthly lease and interest payments will total $3,000. This is a simplifying assumption, since interest costs will depend on the actual amount borrowed.
10. No taxes will be paid because of a tax loss carryforward.

EXHIBIT 3-2   Forecast of Net Sales, Purchases, and Collections, Murphy's
Apparel, 1989-90 (in thousands)

	Net Sales	Cash Sales (10%)	Credit Sales	Collections from Accounts Receivable	Purchases of Merchandise*
1989:					
September	$ 95	$10	$ 85	$111	$ 67
October	75	8	67	144	51
November	55	6	49	137	40
December	45	5	40	51	32
1990:					
January	35	4	31	41	32
February	45	5	40	32	45
March	70	7	63	39	69
April	105	11	94	61	99
May	145	15	130	16	128
June	180	18	162	85	136
July	165	17	148	117	119
August	135	14	121	159	95

forecast indicates no significant cash problems because of the large cash amounts accumulated early in the year. With these cash reserves, Murphy's will be able to fund most of its cash needs without resorting to additional borrowing from the bank.

Of course, a company's need for cash also depends on its need for liquidity. This, in turn, is determined by the company's environment. Companies in a more volatile environment, with greater uncertainty about sales, collections, costs, etc., need to maintain a higher cash balance than those operating in a more stable environment. The more difficult it is to forecast future events, the greater the need to maintain a high cash reserve to provide for unforeseen needs. The cash reserve need not be maintained as an actual cash balance. Establishing a line of credit with a bank may provide adequate protection for a cash shortfall.

The cash budget also provides a benchmark that may be used to measure the company's performance. If the cash account falls below the level forecasted for a particular month, the company has an early warning of potential cash problems. Therefore, the cash budget is not only a planning tool but a control device as well.

II. PROJECTED FINANCIAL STATEMENTS

The cash budget describes the flow of cash during the forecast period: forecasted financial statements, like normal financial statements, provide

EXHIBIT 3–3 Monthly Accounts Receivable 1989–90, Murphy's Apparel (in thousands)

	1989				1990							
	Sept.	Oct.	Nov.	Dec.	Jan.	Feb.	Mar.	Apr.	May	June	July	Aug.
Beginning accounts receivable	$246	$220	$143	$55	$44	$34	$42	$66	$ 99	$213	$290	$321
Credit sales	85	67	49	40	31	40	63	94	130	162	148	121
Collections	(111)	(144)	(137)	(51)	(41)	(32)	(39)	(61)	(16)	(85)	(117)	(159)
Ending accounts receivable	$220	$143	$ 55	$44	$34	$42	$66	$99	$213	$290	$321	$283

EXHIBIT 3–4 Monthly Accounts Payable 1989–90, Murphy's Apparel (in thousands)

	1989				1990							
	Sept.	Oct.	Nov.	Dec.	Jan.	Feb.	Mar.	Apr.	May	June	July	Aug.
Beginning accounts payable	$84	$67	$51	$40	$32	$32	$45	$69	$ 99	$128	$136	$119
Purchases	67	51	40	32	32	45	69	99	128	136	119	95
Payments	(84)	(67)	(51)	(40)	(32)	(32)	(45)	(69)	(99)	(128)	(136)	(119)
Ending accounts payable	$67	$51	$40	$32	$45	$69	$99	$128	$136	$119	$ 95	

EXHIBIT 3–5 Monthly Cash Budget 1989–90, Murphy's Apparel (in thousands)

	1989				1990							
	Sept.	Oct.	Nov.	Dec.	Jan.	Feb.	Mar.	Apr.	May	June	July	Aug.
Receipts:												
Cash sales	$ 10	$ 8	$ 6	$ 5	$ 4	$ 5	$ 7	$ 11	$ 15	$ 18	$ 17	$ 14
Collections	111	144	137	51	41	32	39	61	16	85	117	159
Total receipts	$121	$152	$143	$ 56	$ 45	$ 37	$ 46	$ 72	$ 31	$103	$134	$173
Disbursements:												
Accounts payable payments	$ 84	$ 67	$ 51	$ 40	$ 32	$ 32	$ 45	$ 69	$ 99	$128	$136	$119
Administrative and selling expenses	9	7	5	4	3	4	6	9	13	16	15	12
Fixed costs*	5	5	5	5	5	5	5	5	5	5	5	5
Lease and interest	3	3	3	3	3	3	3	3	3	3	3	3
New equipment	0	0	0	0	0	0	0	0	15	0	0	0
Total disbursements	$101	$ 82	$ 64	$ 52	$ 43	$ 44	$ 59	$ 86	$135	$152	$159	$139
Receipts less disbursements	$ 20	$ 70	$ 79	$ 4	$ 2	$ (7)	$ (13)	$ (14)	$(104)	$ (49)	$ (25)	$ 34
Cumulative cash flow	20	90	169	173	175	168	155	141	37	(12)	(37)	(3)
Monthly cash change:												
Beginning cash	$ 9	$ 29	$ 99	$178	$182	$184	$177	$164	$150	$ 46	$ (3)	$ (28)
Change in cash	20	70	79	4	2	(7)	(13)	(14)	(104)	(49)	(25)	34
Ending cash	$ 29	$ 99	$178	$182	$184	$177	$164	$150	$ 46	$ (3)	$ (28)	$ 6

*Not including depreciation.

56

aggregate information for the forecast period. Projected financial statements are essentially summaries of the information provided by the cash budget. Cash budgets provide the details while forecasts provide summaries in the more familiar financial statement format. Projected income statements forecast earnings and expenses for the period; projected balance sheets forecast assets and liabilities at the conclusion of the period; and projected sources and uses of funds statements forecast funds availability during the period. Although financial statement forecasts could be prepared weekly or monthly, as are cash budgets, they are usually developed as annual forecasts. A typical five-year forecast consists of a series of annual forecasted financial statements.

Like cash budgets, forecasts require definition of one or more critical variables (again, usually the sales forecast) and definition of the relationships of other variables to the basic independent variable. These assumed relationships should be explicitly stated.

1. Developing Forecasts from Cash Budgets

Since cash budget forecasts require the same information as forecasted financial statements, it is possible to develop a set of forecasts using the cash budget. The only additional information needed is the balance sheet as of the beginning of the forecast period. Using data from the cash budget, one can calculate an income statement. Then, using the income statement forecast, the cash budget, and the beginning balance sheet, the analyst can develop a projected balance sheet and a sources and uses of funds statement.

The data from the cash budget for Murphy's Apparel have been used to develop a projected income statement for the period from September 1, 1989, to August 31, 1990. This income statement is shown in Exhibit 3–6.

EXHIBIT 3–6

Murphy's Apparel
Projected Income Statement
September 1, 1989 to August 31, 1990
(in thousands)

Net sales	$1,150
Cost of goods sold	(909)
Gross profit	241
Expenses:	
Selling and administrative expense	(103)
Fixed operating costs	(60)
Depreciation	(6)
Lease and interest expense	(36)
Net profit*	$ 36

*As noted in Exhibit 3–1, Murphy's Apparel has a tax loss carryforward which exceeds the expected profit and, therefore, has no tax liability.

The balance sheet for August 31, 1989, the beginning of the forecast period, and the projected balance sheet for August 31, 1990, are included in Exhibit 3–7. The exhibit also details the changes that are expected to occur in the various accounts during the forecast period. These changes are also included in Exhibit 3–8, the sources and uses of funds forecast.

Although projections do not provide the detail about ebbs and flows in the cash account given in the cash budget, they do show the cash balance at the end of the forecast period. Thus, they do indicate the company's financing needs at the end of the period. For companies that do not experience a significant change in cash during a year, this approach to forecasting funds

EXHIBIT 3–7

Murphy's Apparel
Balance Sheet
(in thousands)

	August 31, 1989 Actual		August 31, 1990 Pro Forma
Assets		**Changes**	
Cash	$ 9	From cash budget	$ 6
Accounts receivable	246	From accounts receivable schedule	283
Inventories	89	+913 (Purchases, from accounts payable schedule) −909 (Cost of goods sold, from income statement)	93
Total current assets	344		382
Equipment	42	+15 (New equipment, from cash budget) −6 (Depreciation, from income statement)	51
Total assets	$386		$433
Liabilities and Equity			
Notes payable	$ 10		$ 10
Accounts payable	84	From accounts payable schedule	95
Total current liabilities	94		105
Long-term debt	100		100
Equity	192	+36 (From income statement)	228
Total liabilities and equity	$386		$433

EXHIBIT 3–8

___

Murphy's Apparel
Projected Sources and Uses of Funds Statement
September 1, 1989 to August 31, 1990
(in thousands)

Sources:

Decrease in cash	$ 3
Increase in accounts payable	11
Net profits	36
Depreciation	6
Total sources	$ 56

Uses:

Increase in accounts receivable	$ 37
Increase in inventories	4
Increase in working capital	41
Increase in equipment	15
Total uses	$ 56

___

needs is usually adequate. Since cash budgets are more time-consuming to prepare, managers of most companies elect to develop financial statement projections directly rather than on the basis of cash budgets.

2. Developing Projections Directly

To develop forecasts directly, analysts use an extension of ratio analysis. First, historic relationships among financial statement accounts for previous years are determined. These relationships, expressed as ratios, are then adjusted to account for expected future events and trends. Finally, pro forma accounts are forecast on the basis of adjusted ratios. As is the case with cash budgets, the first projection made is usually sales. Balances in the other accounts are then forecast on the basis of their expected relationships with sales. Forecasts are made for each account, with the exception of a balancing or "plug" account on the balance sheet.

An easy way to calculate the required balancing amount is to include a "net financing need" liability account in the projected statement. If the balancing amount in this account is positive, it means that assets exceed liabilities and equity and additional financing will be needed. If the net financing need is negative, liabilities and equity are greater than assets. In this case, funds are available for additional investment in assets.

Since these forecasts are derived directly from specified relationships among the various accounts, the assumptions embedded in the analysis may be more obvious than those used in cash budgets. Nevertheless, it is critical to realize that the reliability of the forecasts depends on the validity of the assumptions.

Projected financial statements for the Monson Company, a distributor of surveying, drafting, and architectural supplies, appear in Exhibits 3–9, 3–10, and 3–11. The company was organized as a partnership. The majority equity investment was provided by a silent partner. The minority equity investor is the manager of the company; the silent partner is not involved in any of the company's operations. The silent partner considers his equity position in Monson strictly an investment. He is willing to have the minority partner buy out his equity position at a price that will provide an adequate return on his investment. The minority owner and manager of the company hopes that the Monson Company will provide sufficient funds to allow him to buy out his silent partner in the near future.

To determine whether adequate funds are available to do this, the minority owner developed a five-year forecast. Exhibit 3–9 shows the income statements for the previous three years, the projected five-year income statements, and the assumptions used in developing them. Exhibit 3–10 provides similar information for the balance sheets and Exhibit 3–11 for the sources and uses of funds statement.

From the forecasts, it does not appear that the company will generate sufficient funds during the five years to allow the manager to buy out the silent partner. However, the projections do indicate that the company will accumulate significant excess funds during the forecast period, as indicated by the negative net financing need account. These funds could be paid out in dividends, and the manager could use his portion to purchase some of the equity from the majority owner. Alternatively, he might be able to borrow the required funds from a lending institution, using future proceeds from company operations to repay the loan.

III. ANALYZING ASSUMPTIONS

As has been stated repeatedly, any projection requires underlying assumptions. If the assumptions are not valid, then the subsequent forecasts are valueless. Since the true validity of an assumption is recognizable only after the fact, several procedures have been developed to assist in analyzing the reasonableness of assumptions beforehand.

1. Historical Comparisons

An obvious place to begin examining assumptions is to compare them to recent actual relationships. If an assumption differs significantly from actual results, additional analysis of that assumption is warranted.

Since the relationships are typically stated as ratios, this evaluation of the assumptions is another use of the ratio analysis described in Chapter 1. Just as ratios are used to examine the historical performance of a company,

EXHIBIT 3-9

THE MONSON COMPANY
Income Statements
(in thousands)

| | Actual | | | | | Forecast | | |
	1986	1987	1988	1989	1990	1991	1992	1993
Sales	$1,094	$1,360	$1,402	$1,612	$1,854	$2,132	$2,452	$2,820
Cost of goods sold	(792)	(980)	(984)	(1,128)	(1,298)	(1,492)	(1,716)	(1,974)
Gross profit	302	380	418	484	556	640	736	846
Operating expenses	(244)	(290)	(351)	(376)	(402)	(430)	(460)	(492)
Profit before tax	58	90	67	108	154	210	276	354
Taxes	(15)	(30)	(14)	(36)	(51)	(69)	(91)	(117)
Net income	$ 43	$ 60	$ 53	$ 72	$ 103	$ 141	$ 185	$ 237

Assumptions:
Sales will grow at 15%.
Gross margin will be 30% of sales.
Operating expenses will grow at the expected 7% inflation rate.
Taxes will be 33% of profit before tax.

EXHIBIT 3–10

THE MONSON COMPANY
Balance Sheets
(in thousands)

	Actual					Forecast		
	1986	1987	1988	1989	1990	1991	1992	1993
Assets								
Cash	$ 45	$ 54	$ 60	$ 64	$ 68	$ 73	$ 78	$ 83
Accounts receivable	118	168	165	177	204	235	270	310
Inventory	309	320	365	403	464	533	613	705
Other current assets	46	52	75	80	86	92	98	105
Total current assets	518	594	665	724	822	933	1,059	1,203
Fixed assets (net)	13	19	14	14	14	14	14	14
Total assets	$531	$613	$679	$738	$836	$947	$1,073	$1,217
Liabilities and Equity								
Accounts payable	$ 41	$ 61	$ 73	$ 81	$ 93	$107	$ 123	$ 141
Other current liabilities	3	5	6	6	6	6	6	6
Total current liabilities . . .	44	66	79	87	99	113	129	147
Common stock	350	350	350	350	350	350	350	350
Retained earnings	137	197	250	322	425	566	751	988
Net financing need	0	0	0	(21)	(38)	(82)	(157)	(268)
Total liabilities and equity	$531	$613	$679	$738	$836	$947	$1,073	$1,217

Assumptions:
Receivables will be 11% of sales.
Inventory will be 25% of sales.
Cash, other current assets, and liabilities will increase at the expected 7% inflation rate.
New fixed asset investment will equal depreciation expense.
Accounts payable will be 5% of sales.

EXHIBIT 3–11

THE MONSON COMPANY
Sources and Uses of Funds Statement
(in thousands)

	Actual		Forecast				
	1987	1988	1989	1990	1991	1992	1993
Sources:							
Increase in accounts payable	$20	$12	$ 8	$ 12	$ 14	$ 16	$ 18
Increase in other current liabilities	2	1	0	0	0	0	0
Net income	60	53	72	103	141	185	237
	82	66	80	115	155	201	255
Net financing need	0	0	(21)	(17)	(44)	(75)	(111)
Total sources	$82	$66	$59	$ 98	$111	$126	$144
Uses:							
Increase in cash	$ 9	$ 6	$ 4	$ 4	$ 5	$ 5	$ 5
Increase in accounts receivable	50	(3)	12	27	31	35	40
Increase in inventory	11	45	38	61	69	80	92
Increase in other current assets	6	23	5	6	6	6	7
Increase in working capital	76	71	59	98	111	126	144
Increase in fixed assets	6	(5)	0	0	0	0	0
Total uses	$82	$66	$59	$ 98	$111	$126	$144

Note: A negative entry in "uses" is a source of funds. A negative entry in "sources" of funds is a use.

they can be used to test whether assumptions about future performance are reasonable.

Comparisons of the assumed relationships with those that exist for other companies will also provide a check on the appropriateness of the assumptions. As with any ratio analysis, the companies to be compared should be similar; that is, they should be in the same industry and have similar operating and marketing strategies. If such strictly comparable companies cannot be found for evaluation, then the analyst should adjust the comparison companies' ratios as needed.

Another way of using historical data to forecast future relationships is regression analysis. This statistical technique allows the analyst to mathematically project relationships based on several past periods of data. While this method provides the security of quantitative rigor, it may be a false security if the analyst has good reason to expect future relationships between various accounts to differ from their historical patterns.

Using the Monson Company's forecasts as examples, Exhibit 3–12 is a simple comparison of some of the assumptions used in developing the projected financial statements with actual relationships for the prior years.

Two of the assumptions may be cause for concern. The actual sales growth rate from 1986 to 1987 exceeds the forecast rate, but the growth in sales from 1987 to 1988 is significantly below the forecast. A greater departure from past experience is shown by the operating expense forecast. The forecast is based on operating expenses increasing at a 7 percent inflation rate. Since sales are increasing at 15 percent, operating expenses would decrease as a percentage of sales. The historical data suggest that operating expenses have been between 20 and 25 percent of sales for the past three years. It appears that the forecast may be overly optimistic.

To examine the effects of an increase in operating expenses, the forecasts were recalculated with operating expenses at 25 percent of sales. This provided a 15 percent annual increase in operating expenses, the same growth rate as sales. The revised results are shown in Exhibits 3–13, 3–14, and 3–15.

Using the revised operating expense forecast, the Monson Company's outlook is much different. Profits continue to grow, although at a slower rate. However, instead of excess funds being generated, the revised forecasts indicate an increasing need for additional funding each year. This illustrates how a changed assumption may greatly affect projected results.

2. Sensitivity Analysis

A second means of analyzing the assumptions is called **sensitivity analysis.** This process examines the forecast's sensitivity to changes in the assumptions. If changing a particular assumption has little impact on the forecasts, then the assumption is not considered critical. If changing an assumption causes a major change in the projected statements, then it is

EXHIBIT 3–12   Comparison of Forecast Assumptions to 1987 and 1988 Actual Results, The Monson Company

Relationships	Actual 1987	Actual 1988	Assumptions for Forecast
Sales growth	24%	3%	15%
Receivables as a percentage of sales	12	12	11
Inventory as a percentage of sales	24	26	25
Payables as a percentage of sales	4	5	5
Gross margin	28	30	30
Operating expense as a percentage of sales . . .	21	25	decreasing
Operating expense increase over previous year	25	21	7

EXHIBIT 3–13

THE MONSON COMPANY
Projected Income Statements with Changed Assumptions
(in thousands)

	Actual		Forecast			
	1988	1989	1990	1991	1992	1993
Sales	$1,402	$1,612	$1,854	$2,132	$2,452	$2,820
Cost of goods sold	(984)	(1,128)	(1,298)	(1,492)	(1,716)	(1,974)
Gross profit	418	484	556	640	736	846
Operating expenses	(351)	(403)	(464)	(533)	(613)	(705)
Profit before tax	67	81	92	107	123	141
Taxes	(14)	(27)	(30)	(35)	(41)	(47)
Net income	$ 53	$ 54	$ 62	$ 72	$ 82	$ 94

Assumptions:
Sales will grow at 15%.
Gross margin will be 30% of sales.
Operating expenses will be 25% of sales.
Taxes will be 33% of profit before tax.

EXHIBIT 3–14

THE MONSON COMPANY
Projected Balance Sheets with Changed Assumptions
(in thousands)

	Actual			Forecast		
	1988	1989	1990	1991	1992	1993
Assets						
Cash	$ 60	$ 64	$ 68	$ 73	$ 78	$ 83
Accounts receivable	165	177	204	235	270	310
Inventory	365	403	464	533	613	705
Other current assets	75	80	88	92	98	105
Total current assets	665	724	822	933	1,059	1,203
Fixed assets (net)	14	14	14	14	14	14
Total assets	$679	$738	$836	$947	$1,073	$1,217
Liabilities and Equity						
Accounts payable	$ 73	$ 81	$ 93	$107	$ 123	$ 141
Other current liabilities	6	6	6	6	6	6
Total current liabilities	79	87	99	113	129	147
Common stock	350	350	350	350	350	350
Retained earnings	250	304	366	438	520	614
Net financing need		(3)	21	46	74	106
Total liabilities and equity	$679	$738	$836	$947	$1,073	$1,217

Assumptions:
  Receivables will be 11% of sales.
  Inventory will be 25% of sales.
  Cash, other current assets, and liabilities will increase at the expected 7% inflation rate.
  New fixed asset investment will equal depreciation expense.
  Accounts payable will be 5% of sales.

EXHIBIT 3–15

THE MONSON COMPANY
Projected Sources and Uses of Funds Statement with Changed Assumptions
(in thousands)

	Actual		Forecast			
	1988	1989	1990	1991	1992	1993
Sources						
Increase in accounts payable	$12	$ 8	$12	$ 14	$ 16	$ 18
Increase in other current liabilities	1	0	0	0	0	0
Net income	53	54	62	72	82	94
	66	62	74	86	98	112
Net financing need		(3)	24	25	28	32
Total sources	$66	$59	$98	$111	$126	$144
Uses:						
Increase in cash	$ 6	$ 4	$ 4	$ 5	$ 5	$ 5
Increase in accounts receivable	(3)	12	27	31	35	40
Increase in inventory	45	38	61	69	80	92
Increase in other current assets	23	5	6	6	6	7
Increase in working capital	71	59	98	111	126	144
Increase in fixed assets	(5)	0	0	0	0	0
Total uses	$66	$59	$98	$111	$126	$144

Note: A negative entry as a "use" is a source of funds. A negative entry as a "source" of funds is a use.

considered a critical variable that warrants further analysis and careful monitoring.

It should be obvious that although sensitivity analysis is a fairly simple concept, it is rather time-consuming to execute properly. If the forecasts incorporate many assumptions, a considerable number of them would need to be calculated to adequately examine the sensitivity of the results to changes in each variable. To ease this process, analysts attempt to simplify the assumptions and to estimate which factors will have a critical impact on the results. The sensitivity analysis is then confined to these limited factors.

A frequently used technique is to use three different values for the assumption: the most likely, an optimistic, and a pessimistic value. Since the original projection is usually based on the most likely relationship, the analyst should then project the other two outcomes. These alternative scenarios should be based on different economic forecasts. It is important to understand that the optimistic and pessimistic forecasts are not the same as the absolute best and worst cases. The likelihood of an extremely favorable or undesirable outcome is probably remote. Therefore, it makes more sense to focus on outcomes with a greater likelihood of occurring.

Some analysts only analyze negative outcomes. Their reasoning is that while optimistic relationships may occur and create problems, those problems are easier to deal with than the problems pessimistic outcomes create. By focusing only on the "downside" risks, they forecast a range of potential negative results. In some cases, however, negative results arise from "upside" factors. For example, a large increase in sales may appear positive, but it could also mean an increased need for working-capital financing.

The risk of this simplification is that some critical assumptions might be ignored. Computer-based financial modeling systems have been developed that greatly increase the analyst's ability to undertake sensitivity analysis. Not only can the modeling systems do the calculations rapidly, they also facilitate the use of probability analysis.[1]

3. Probability Analysis

Probability analysis is an extension of sensitivity analysis. The analyst first forecasts a range of possible values for any given variable and then estimates the likelihood that each of the values may occur. For example, the analyst may estimate that a 7 percent sales growth has a probability of 15 percent; a 10 percent sales growth, 70 percent; and a 15 percent sales growth, 15 percent. By combining these probabilities with those estimated for other variables—such as cost of goods sold and rates of inflation—the computer can calculate the overall probabilities of all possible net financial outcomes. This series of calculations, called a **simulation,** provides more

---

[1] The use of these modeling systems is explained in Appendix A.

useful information than do projections relying on a single or "point" estimate for each variable.

IV SUMMARY

Using historic relationships, analysts can project the future performance of a company. The historic pattern must be adjusted for changes in the environment, changes in the company, or both. Based on these assumptions, managers can estimate future cash needs using cash budgets and projected financial statements. The appropriate method depends on the needs of the analyst.

Any projections are only as useful as the validity or reasonableness of the underlying assumptions. An important part of any forecast is testing the assumptions through sensitivity analysis. In so doing, the manager becomes aware of the critical assumptions and is forewarned about areas needing additional analysis and special monitoring.

SELECTED REFERENCES

For discussions on the impact of inflation on funds forecasting, see:

Seed, Allen H., III. "Measuring Financial Performance in an Inflationary Environment." *Financial Executive,* January 1982, pp. 40–50.

Vancil, Richard F. "Funds Flow Analysis During Inflation." *Financial Analysts Journal,* March–April 1976, pp. 43–56.

For an examination of various quantitative forecasting techniques, see:

Vatter, Paul A.; Stephen P. Bradley; Sherwood Frey, Jr.; and Barbara B. Jackson, *Quantitative Methods in Management.* Homewood, Ill.: Richard D. Irwin, 1978, chaps. 7–9.

For additional discussions of forecasting financial needs, see:

Pringle, John J., and Robert S. Harris. *Essentials of Managerial Finance.* Glenview, Ill.: Scott, Foresman, 1984, chap. 8.

Ross, Steven and Randolf Westerfield. *Corporate Finance.* St. Louis, Mo.: Times Mirror/Mosby, 1988, chap. 22.

VanHorne, James C. *Financial Management and Policy.* 7th ed. Englewood Cliffs, N.J.: Prentice-Hall, 1987, chap. 28.

Weston, J. Fred, and Eugene F. Brigham. *Essentials of Managerial Finance.* 8th ed. Hinsdale, Ill.: Dryden Press, 1988, chap. 8.

For a discussion of simulation, see:

Hertz, David B. "Risk-Analysis in Capital Investment." *Harvard Business Review,* September–October 1979, pp. 169–81.

For additional information on the differences between cash and accrual accounting, see:

Kroll, Yoram. "On the Differences Between Accrual Accounting Figures and Cash Flows: The Case of Working Capital." *Financial Management,* Spring 1985, pp. 75–82.

STUDY QUESTIONS

1. Mary Turnbull, of Mary's Ski Chalet, is attempting to plan a monthly cash budget for the coming year but is having difficulty determining her expected cash balance due to the seasonality of her sales. She has been able to accumulate the following data for 1989.

Mary's Ski Chalet

Projected Sales (in thousands)				Beginning Balances (in thousands)	
Jan.	$210	July	$ 30	Accounts receivable . . .	$184
Feb.	175	Aug.	75	Accounts payable	173
Mar.	160	Sept.	90	Cash	65
Apr.	140	Oct.	125	Inventory	50
May	50	Nov.	165	Equity	471
June	30	Dec.	230	PPE (net)	345

- All collections and payments are made on a 30-day basis.
- 25 percent of all sales are paid for in cash.
- Cost of goods sold is 75 percent of sales.
- Selling, general, and administrative expenses are 19 percent of sales.
- Purchases are 100 percent of cost of goods sold plus 6 percent of sales for a cushion against stockouts (safety stock).
- Interest and lease expense is $24,000 for the year.
- Depreciation expense is $12,000 for the year.

Will Ms. Turnbull need additional financing to cover a monthly cash deficit?

2. Prepare a 1989 forecasted income statement and balance sheet for Ms. Turnbull using the information provided above.

3. Aries Corporation has entered a new market in 1988. They have asked you to prepare a five-year projected balance sheet and income statement based on the following projections:

a) Sales growth in 1988 will be the same as in 1987. In 1989, sales growth will dip to 10 percent, and then will increase 1 percent for each year thereafter. b) Negotiations with suppliers have reduced prices 12 percent if the payment period is decreased to 60 days. Purchases made at the higher rate and included in raw materials inventory will result in an average decrease of only 10 percent in 1988. c) There will be no change in the percent-of-sales historical relationship for selling, general, and administrative (SG&A) expenses and cash balance. d) Legislation has been passed that will reduce the tax rate to 38 percent in 1990. e) Inventory turnover has been historically high. Management plans to increase the turnover in 1988 to eight times and level it out in 1991 to six times. f) Management does not expect any change in days' sales outstanding. g) Property, plant, and equipment—net of acquisitions, disposals, and depreciation (which is included in the cost of goods sold allocation)—will be $265,000, $291,000, $323,000, $403,000, $513,000 for 1988 through 1992, respectively. h) Any additional financing required will be short-term (notes payable) financing.

To assist in your analysis, financial statements for 1986 and 1987 are shown below.

Aries Corporation
Income Statement
For the Years 1987 and 1988
(in thousands)

	1987	1988
Sales	$221	$266
Cost of goods sold	145	166
Gross profit	76	100
SG&A expenses	38	35
Operating profit	38	65
Taxes	19	33
Net income	$ 19	$ 32

Aries Corporation
Balance Sheet
For the Years 1987 and 1988
(in thousands)

	1987	1988
Assets		
Cash	$ 22	$ 37
Accounts receivable	49	$ 31
Inventory	47	45
Current assets	$118	$113
Fixed assets	70	122
Total assets	$188	$235
Liabilities and equity		
Notes payable	$ 0	$ 0
Accounts payable	19	34
Current liabilities	$ 19	$ 34
Equity	169	201
Total liabilities and equity	$188	$235

CHAPTER 4

Valuation 1: Capital Budgeting

In the last chapter, we discussed some simple methods of forecasting future financing needs. Most of these techniques used the history of the business to create forecasts for the future, and while most of these techniques are useful for examining the financial effects of corporate strategy and policy, they assume that a specific strategy has been decided on and will be undertaken. What we did not discuss in Chapter 3 is how managers choose among different investments and strategies. In this chapter, we will examine the process by which managers allocate capital among different courses of action. Because we are allocating a usually scarce resource, capital, this process of making investment decisions is called **capital budgeting.**

There are two kinds of corporate investments. Chapter 3 discussed the increases and decreases in current assets that can occur in businesses whose sales are seasonal or cyclical. Most of these changes could be called **spontaneous,** since they do not occur as a consequence of managers' actions but are instead the normal results of changing sales levels. For instance, during a cyclical upturn, a manufacturing firm whose sales are made on credit needs funds for both increased inventories and larger accounts receivable. Both of these increases are investments—that is, they are outlays of funds on which management expects a return. The return, of course, comes from the profit on the expected sales increase.

Spontaneous investments often have short-term benefits and are usually transient changes in working capital (inventory or accounts receivable) rather than capital investments. Typically, a **capital investment** is thought of as having potential benefits extending over a longer period of time, usually more than one year. Investments characterized by these longer-term benefits are called capital investments. They include such things as permanent additions to working capital (such as an increase in accounts receivable as a result of a change in the company's credit policy); purchase of land, buildings, or equipment to expand capacity; and costs associated with advertising campaigns or research and development programs. Because capital investments are often irreversible, or the redeployment of assets comes only at considerable loss of time, money, and managerial effort, capital investments should be and are evaluated more formally than are spontaneous investments.

In most firms, the capital-budgeting process consists of six steps:

1. Generating and gathering investment ideas.
2. Analyzing the costs and benefits of proposed investments.
   a. Forecasting costs and benefits for each investment.
   b. Evaluating the costs and benefits.
3. Ranking the relative attractiveness of each proposed investment and choosing among investment alternatives.
4. Implementing the investments chosen.
5. Evaluating the implemented investments.

Of course, firms continuously repeat these five steps. In this chapter, we will concentrate on steps 2 and 3, the steps in which financial analysts are most involved: estimating and evaluating the costs and benefits and choosing among the alternative investments.

I. COST-BENEFIT ANALYSIS OF PROPOSED INVESTMENTS

The goal of investing is to create value for the owners of the firm. If an investment is to do that, the expected returns from the investment must exceed its costs. In economic terms, we say that the marginal or incremental benefits—the benefits deriving solely from the investment—must exceed the marginal or incremental costs. There are several hidden difficulties with this first step. First, when we say incremental, we must ask, incremental to what? The second difficulty is how to measure costs and benefits.

In estimating the value of an investment, we are measuring costs and benefits that would not have occurred if the firm had not undertaken this particular project. In some instances, the project may be charged with a portion of the ongoing expenses of the firm—the overhead. This is an accounting allocation of costs, and if this investment neither increases nor decreases these expenses, they are neither costs nor benefits for the purposes of the investment analysis. Only incremental, new expenses or benefits are relevant. To estimate the investment's benefits and costs, the analyst forecasts the cash associated with the investment at the time it will be received or disbursed. The analyst does not measure income and expenses as they are recorded by the firm's accountants.

The benefits and costs of an investment are measured by the receipt and disbursement of cash, as discussed in Chapters 2 and 3. Most U.S. corporations use the accrual method of accounting: sales are recorded when an order is received and obligations recorded when incurred. Accrual accounting can trick the investment analyst. For instance, many firms record sales before payment is received. In some industries, payment for purchased products typically lags behind shipment of the order by several months. Thus the real benefit the firm derives, the cash, also lags by several months.

It is the receipt or disbursement of cash that affects the firm, and cash is what concerns the investment analyst.

1. Cash Benefits

Four sources of cash benefits or receipts may be derived from an investment:

1. Cost reductions when a more efficient process is substituted for a more costly one.
2. Profits or revenues from increased sales.
3. Cash received when replaced equipment is sold.
4. Cash received from the salvage value of the new plant or equipment at the end of its useful life.

Let's illustrate these benefits by analyzing a shipping company's investment in a sail-assisted tanker. The shipping firm's managers are considering replacing one of their diesel-fueled, oceangoing tankers with a tanker that has auxiliary metal sails to take advantage of the wind. The firm might benefit from this investment in several ways. First, the wind-assisted ship will use less fuel and thus be less expensive to operate than the diesel-powered vessel. This cost reduction will lower the operating costs for every year the ship is in operation. Furthermore, because the new ship has a larger cargo space, the tonnage carried by the ship will exceed that carried by the old tanker. This increase in tonnage will yield increased yearly revenues. In addition to the benefits from reduced operating expenses and increased sales, the firm will sell the old diesel-powered ship for cash and gain favorable tax treatment as a result of the sale. Finally, at the end of its useful life, the salvage value of the sail-assisted ship as well as any favorable tax effects will also be benefits.

This simple example shows that most investments offer a variety of benefits at various times throughout their useful lives. The analyst's responsibility is to identify the magnitude and timing of all benefits.

2. Cash Payments

The cash payments or costs associated with any investment fall into three categories:

1. The initial cost (capital cost) of the investment.
2. Capital improvements made during the life of the project.
3. Operating costs.

Capital costs include the initial price of making an investment as well as any subsequent major outlays of cash required to extend the life of the project or equipment. In the example of the shipping company, capital costs include the cost of obtaining the new ship and the costs of subsequent major engine replacements and other major repairs needed to extend the life of the vessel. Operating costs are those recurring annual cash outlays that are required once the investment becomes a part of the firm's operations. With the purchase of the tanker, cash will be needed to cover such annual operating costs as wages, fuel, taxes, and maintenance.

Any cash already expended on the investment, such as research done to develop the new tanker's sails, is not a relevant cost in this investment analysis. Instead, this type of expense is considered a **sunk cost:** it represents a past outlay of funds that has no bearing on this decision. The manager's concern is not to recover sunk or irreversible costs but to create value from subsequent new investments. In other words, any investment being considered must have a positive *marginal* return.

Tax benefits and costs also will be incurred by the company as a result of making an investment. Unfortunately, the exact effect tax laws will have over the life of a given project may not be known at the time an investment is made. If current tax laws were to continue in effect during the life of the project, the impact of taxes on the costs and benefits could be determined. However, over the last decade in the United States, we have had three major changes in the tax code that affected the tax treatment of capital investments. From 1981 to 1986, the Accelerated Cost Recovery System (ACRS) was in use. In 1986, a new tax code was enacted that lowered tax rates, removed the investment tax credit, and lengthened depreciation schedules.

Under the tax law adopted in 1986, assets are assigned to different depreciable categories depending on their expected life. For personal property there are six different categories (expected lives of 3, 5, 7, 10, 15, and 20 years); and for real property (real estate) there are two groups with expected lives of 27.5 and 31.5 years.

Costs in the 3-year to 10-year classes are depreciated using an accelerated kind of depreciation called double-declining balance, with a switch to the straight-line method permitted near the end of the life. The switch is allowed to optimize deductions. Costs in the 15- and 20-year categories are depreciated using a 150 percent declining balance rate, switching later to straight-line. Real estate, on the other hand, must be depreciated using the straight-line method.

The straight-line and double-declining balance methods of depreciation will be most used under the new tax code. With straight-line depreciation, the annual depreciation is calculated by simply dividing the investment cost by the allowed depreciable life. For example, if a company were to purchase a piece of equipment for $150,000 that had a depreciable life of five years, the annual depreciation expense would be $30,000:

$$\text{Annual depreciation expense} = \frac{\text{Cost of asset}}{\text{Depreciable life}}$$

$$= \frac{\$150,000}{5 \text{ years}}$$

$$= \$30,000$$

Double-declining balance depreciation is a little more difficult to calculate. However, this method allows a higher deduction from taxes in earlier
years than in straight-line. To calculate double-declining balance depreciation, double the straight-line rate of depreciation is multiplied by the undepreciated investment value.

For our example, the straight-line rate of depreciation is 20 percent,
based on a five-year life. Thus the first year's depreciation using the double-
declining balance method would be twice 20 or 40 percent. Depreciation
expense would be:

$$\text{First year's depreciation} = 2(.20) \times \$150,000$$
$$= \$60,000$$

The depreciation expense is double the amount that would be expensed using
the straight-line method. Thus, the company's taxes would be lower during
the first year when using the double-declining balance method. That is why
a method like this one is called **accelerated depreciation.**

Exhibit 4–1 shows the differences in depreciation using three methods:
straight-line; Accelerated Cost Recovery System (ACRS), the method under
the tax code in force in 1981 to 1986; and double-declining balance, the
method under the 1986 tax code revision. Exhibit 4–1 shows the depreciation
expense allowed under the two recent tax codes compared to straight-line
depreciation, one method favored by many corporations for their public
reporting. As you can see, the depreciation schedule used can affect the
company's profitability. Because depreciation expense is much larger in the
early years under the double-declining-balance method, the company's taxes
will be lower and its cash flow larger. Thus accelerated depreciation methods
are believed to encourage greater investment in capital projects. However,
accelerated methods decrease profits.

In addition to changes in the method of depreciation, the 1986 tax code
stipulated a lower maximum tax rate for corporations of 34 percent (the
ACRS marginal rate was 48 percent). For corporations with taxable incomes
of less than \$75,000, the rate drops to 25 percent, and below \$50,000 the
rate is 15 percent. Investment tax credits, amounting to 8 to 10 percent
under ACRS, were abolished.

Since the tax code and its effect on a project's costs and benefits are
sources of uncertainty, the impact of changes in the code should be assessed.
Later in the chapter, we will describe methods for incorporating uncertainty
into the analysis. To identify and estimate the costs and benefits associated
with any investment, the analyst will call on experts in marketing, engi-
neering, accounting, and operations to provide needed forecasts.

II. EVALUATING INCREMENTAL COSTS
AND BENEFITS

Once costs and benefits have been itemized, the analyst's major task is
to determine the marginal or incremental effect the investment will have

EXHIBIT 4–1   Depreciation Expense under Three Methods of Depreciation

Year	Straight-Line	ACRS*	Double-declining Balance†
1	$ 30,000	$ 22,500	$ 60,000
2	30,000	33,000	36,000
3	30,000	31,500	21,600
4	30,000	31,500	16,200
5	30,000	31,500	16,200
Total	$150,000	$150,000	$150,000

*Most machinery and equipment was depreciated over five years under ACRS rules. For those five years, depreciation was 15, 22, 21, 21, and 21 percent, respectively. An investment tax credit was allowed in the first year, generally amounting to 8 percent of the investment's cost, and the marginal tax rate was 48 percent.
†A switch to straight-line depreciation is allowed, when it is advantageous—in this case, in the fourth and fifth years; in the fourth year the remaining balance is $32,400, to be depreciated over the remaining two years' expected life.

on the firm as a whole. An incremental cost or benefit is one derived exclusively from the investment and one that would not otherwise occur. To evaluate incremental costs and benefits, many analysts group investment proposals into categories that help them examine each proposal in terms of its relation to the firm's business as a whole.

The most useful scheme is to group projects according to the degree of independence of their costs and benefits from the costs and benefits of the firm and its other investments and projects. **Independent investments** are projects that can be accepted or rejected, regardless of the action taken on any other investment, now or later. **Mutually exclusive investments** are projects that preclude one another; once one project is accepted, the others become unavailable or inappropriate. Often mutually exclusive projects are designed to solve the same problem or to serve the same function. For example, managers often must choose among alternate means of adding plant capacity, or among advertising programs, or among several new product lines.

There are two types of mutually exclusive and independent investments—replacements and investments in new products and processes. Replacement investments are made to modernize an existing process or to revitalize an old product line. Because estimating the net effect on the company of replacing a process or product can be especially difficult, analysts often place these investments in a separate category. They are, however, just an especially troublesome type of mutually exclusive or independent investment.

To show the advantages of these categories, we will use them to estimate the incremental costs and benefits of two investment proposals being considered by the management of Consumer, Inc., one of the largest franchisers of fast foods in the West. Consumer, Inc., sells a variety of hamburgers, soft drinks, and french fries through its 500 restaurants. Management has capitalized on the public's health concerns by offering whole-grain hamburger buns, french fries with potato skins, and tofu shakes, as well as the regular fare. Consumer, Inc., managers are considering two investments—opening their restaurants for breakfast or adding salad-and-pasta bars to their existing lunch and dinner menus. Because of the management effort needed to implement either project, management considers these investments mutually exclusive: they may choose one or the other but not both projects.

1. The Breakfast Proposal

Consumer, Inc., restaurants are open from 11 AM to 11 PM. Since many of Consumer's competitors have begun to serve breakfast, Consumer's managers are considering opening from 6:30 to 11:00 AM to serve breakfast. They believe Consumer, Inc., has an edge over its competition because it pioneered the "healthy burger" concept. They would emphasize tasty and nutritious breakfast offerings. While the same buildings and equipment could be used, the longer serving hours would increase overhead expenses. There would be added costs for ingredients, salaries of managers and employees, and advertising. Together, incremental overhead and operating expenses for all 500 restaurants are expected to total $14.25 million per year. In addition, since breakfast would be a new product, management is planning an extensive employee-training program. The program, to be completed before the company started offering breakfast, would cost $1.75 million. Consumer, Inc., would benefit from an estimated $15 million increase in sales per year to be made from the breakfast service. The estimated costs and benefits of this project are detailed in Exhibit 4–2. Since management expects no inflation, costs and benefits are shown in real dollars. Costs and benefits are forecast for five years because management believes that the equipment used in each restaurant will last only five more years. The format in this exhibit is a useful one often employed by financial analysts.

You will note several things about the way the analysis in Exhibit 4–2 is presented. First, the effects this project will have on Consumer's income statement are shown. Included in the changes are any noncash expenses, such as depreciation, that reduce taxable income and thus taxes. Because noncash charges only affect taxes, the format provides for adding them back to net income to calculate cash flow; such a charge does not reduce cash income, only the taxes paid on that income.

The second set of adjustments are capital investments—cash payments for property, plant, and equipment or working capital. Property, plant, and equipment investments are not expensed (and thus do not affect taxes) at the time they are made but over the period allowed by the tax code. The annual expenses are called depreciation. Working-capital investments are expensed neither when they are made nor while the assets are used. The assumption is that these assets can be recovered by the company at its discretion, and thus they remain a part of the firm's capital.

EXHIBIT 4–2 Consumer Breakfast Proposal—Marginal Costs and Benefits (thousands of real dollars)

			Period			
	0	1	2	3	4	5
Income statement changes:						
Sales	$ 0	$15,000	$15,000	$15,000	$15,000	$15,000
Operating expenses	0	(14,250)	(14,250)	(14,250)	(14,250)	(14,250)
Training costs	(1,750)	0	0	0	0	0
Depreciation		0	0	0	0	0
Pre-tax profit	(1,750)	750	750	750	750	750
Less: Taxes (34%)*	595	(255)	(255)	(255)	(255)	(255)
Profit after taxes	(1,155)	495	495	495	495	495
Noncash charges:						
Depreciation	0	0	0	0	0	0
Capital investments:						
Property, plant, and equipment changes	0	0	0	0	0	0
Working capital changes	0	0	0	0	0	0
Net Cash Flow	$(1,155)	$ 495	$ 495	$ 495	$ 495	$ 495

*Note that the positive taxes resulting from the expense of training costs are a tax reduction. This tax reduction is a benefit only if the company has profits in other businesses and tax losses can be used to offset them.

2. Salad-Pasta Bar Proposal

Managers at Consumer, Inc., are also considering adding salad-pasta bars, all-you-can-eat buffets, to their existing lunch and dinner menus. They have already spent $600,000 in developing the salad-pasta bar concept and in limited test-marketing. To introduce the product into all of their restaurants, they estimate that personnel would have to be trained at a cost of $832 per restaurant, and that display cases would have to be bought and installed at $2,800 per bar. The managers expect that the display cases would be scrapped in five years and that the scrap would be offset by disposal costs. Incremental (marginal) operating expenses would include the cost of ingredients, additional refrigeration, and the salary of one additional employee per restaurant to stock the salad-pasta bar. On the basis of test-market results, the marketing staff estimate sales of salad and pasta would be $15 million per year and operating expenses $13,944.

The diverse effects these two proposals would have on Consumer, Inc., illustrate the usefulness of categorizing investments as independent or mutually exclusive. Managers consider the two proposed investments to be mutually exclusive because they do not feel that they could adequately oversee both projects at the same time. The breakfast option would be independent of Consumer's existing business because it would extend the existing product line. The salad-pasta bar, however, would be a partial replacement, since it would affect existing sales of hamburger meals at lunch and dinner. In fact, the marketing staff estimate that half of the salad bar's sales would come from customers who would otherwise have purchased hamburgers and french fries. Thus, while total salad-pasta sales would be $15 million, incremental sales would be only $7.5 million per year.

The salad bar's status as a partial replacement would be responsible not only for lower net cash receipts but also for lower incremental overhead and operating expenses. Unlike the breakfast option, it would add less to current overhead and operating expenses, since it would be offered during existing hours and manned by existing employees. If the analyst did not realize that the salad bar option would be a replacement investment, he or she might erroneously include a portion of the costs of buildings and equipment as part of its incremental costs, or include its total sales of $15 million as a benefit, rather than the $7.5 million incremental sales. The net cash flow for the salad-pasta bars is the net profit plus any noncash charges that were deducted from profit before taxes for the purpose of calculating taxes.

Details of this evaluation of the net benefits of the project appear in Exhibit 4-3. Note that the $600,000 in expenses incurred in developing and test-marketing the salad-pasta bar concept are not included. They are sunk costs: cash already spent and not relevant in making this new decision.

Now that the incremental costs and benefits for the two projects have been estimated, Consumer's management must decide whether to accept one or the other of the plans or reject both projects and seek other oppor-

EXHIBIT 4–3 Consumer Salad-Pasta Bar Proposal—Marginal Costs and Benefits (thousands of real dollars)

			Period			
	0	1	2	3	4	5
Income statement changes:						
Sales		$7,500	$7,500	$7,500	$7,500	$7,500
Operating expenses		(6,972)	(6,972)	(6,972)	(6,972)	(6,972)
Training costs	$ (416)	0	0	0	0	0
Depreciation		(560)	(336)	(202)	(151)	(151)
Pre-tax profit	(416)	(32)	192	326	377	377
Taxes (34%)*	141	11	(65)	(111)	(128)	(128)
Profit after taxes	(275)	(21)	127	215	249	249
Noncash charges:						
Depreciation	0	560	336	202	151	151
Capital investments:						
Property, plant, and equipment changes†	(1,400)	0	0	0	0	0
Working-capital changes	0	0	0	0	0	0
Net Cash Flow	$(1,675)	$ 539	$ 463	$ 417	$ 400	$ 400

*Note that the positive taxes resulting from the expense of training costs are a tax reduction. This tax reduction is a benefit only if the company has profits in other businesses and tax losses can be used to offset them.
†Note that $600,000 spent in developing this concept is not included as a cost because it is a sunk cost.

81

tunities. To make these decisions, the managers need a method of measuring the relative value of the two proposals.

III. CHOOSING AMONG INVESTMENTS

There are a number of different ways to rank the relative attractiveness or value of investments. Each of these methods has advantages and disadvantages.

1. Simple Valuation Methods

Benefit/cost ratio.   The easiest way to compare two investments is to compare their benefit/cost ratios. If the benefits of an investment exceed the costs—if the benefit/cost ratio is greater than 1.0—the project is deemed acceptable using this measure. To choose among several acceptable investments, managers select the project with the highest benefit/cost ratio. For the proposed investment in breakfast service, the benefit/cost ratio is calculated as follows, using the net cash flow figures in Exhibit 4–2.

$$\text{Benefit/cost ratio} = \frac{\text{Net benefits}}{\text{Investment}}$$

$$= \frac{\$495 \times 5}{\$1,155}$$

$$= \$2,475/\$1,155$$

$$= 2.14$$

A comparable analysis of figures in Exhibit 4–3 for the salad-pasta bar yields a ratio of 1.32 ($2,219/$1,675).

Payback Period.   A similar measure, and one that is more widely used, is called *payback period* or just *payback*. Quite simply, payback measures the number of years before the annual net benefits of the project equal its initial cost. For the breakfast proposal, the payback period is calculated as follows:

$$\text{Payback} = \frac{\text{Investment}}{\text{Yearly net benefit}}$$

$$= \$1,155/\$495$$

$$= 2.3 \text{ years}$$

A similar analysis of the salad-pasta bar proposal yields a payback of 3.6 years.

Whether a payback of just over two years is adequate or not is a decision for Consumer's managers. Ordinarily, managers would set a limit on the length of the payback period they would allow and reject those investments that exceed it. To choose among several projects with acceptable payback periods, managers would select the project with the fastest payback period.

Payback can be useful as a quick approximation of a project's relative attractiveness or to indicate whether a firm can recover the project costs in time to make another planned investment. The method ignores all benefits that are derived after the payback date, however; thus it can arbitrarily exclude potentially attractive investments that have longer lives.

Let's look at an example of the problem. Vast Resources, Inc. (VR), has two projects in which it can invest the $1.5 million it has available. VR management uses a payback criterion of three years and will not accept a project that fails to meet this standard. Exhibit 4–4 presents figures for the two projects. Management has chosen to invest in Project A and reject Project B. Do you agree with its choice? Unless VR needs the $1.5 million in the first year, for another investment or to pay an obligation, Project B eventually provides a much larger cash flow.

This example points out obvious problems that can occur when using payback. The same problems can occur using benefit/cost analysis. Neither method takes the timing of cash flows into account. The benefit/cost ratio treats cash received at all points in time as equivalent. We know, however, that investors prefer equivalent amounts of cash received sooner to those received later. The payback method, on the other hand, attempts to take investors' preference for early cash flows into account by ignoring cash flows beyond the payback period. However, although cash flows across time are not equally attractive to the investor, later cash flows are not irrelevant. The benefit/cost ratio and the payback method evaluate investments solely on the size or speed of their returns, and thus neither adequately incorporates the investor's time value of money.

EXHIBIT 4–4 Vast Resources, Inc.—Alternative Investments (in millions)

		Project A	Project B
Cost		$1.5	$1.5
Cash flows:			
Year			
	1	$1.6	0
	2	0	0
	3	0	0
	4	0	0
	5	0	$8.0
Payback		0.94 years	4.19 years

2. Dealing with the Timing of Cash Flow: Discounting Techniques

Investors want to be rewarded for waiting for future returns. They need a method of evaluating investments that will take into account their time value of money and will compensate them for temporary lack of liquidity by giving priority to investments that offer earlier rather than later returns. To give priority to earlier returns, we can use a method called **discounting.** If one applies a discount rate (R) of 5 percent to cash flows five years hence, a single dollar at that time is worth 78 percent of the value of a dollar today. In formula form we can calculate the discount factor thus, where n is the number of years:

$$
\begin{aligned}
\text{Discount factor} &= (1 + R)^n \\
&= (1 + .05)^5 \\
&= 1.28
\end{aligned}
$$

The discounted value, called the **present value,** of the $1.00 cash flow (CF) is:

$$
\begin{aligned}
\text{Present value} &= \frac{CF_n}{(1 + R)^n} \\
&= \frac{\$1.00}{(1.05)^5} \\
&= \frac{\$1.00}{1.28} \\
&= \$0.78
\end{aligned}
$$

At a discount rate of 5 percent, the present value of VR's $8 million in five years is $6.27 million, which is 78.4 percent of $8 million (6.27/8.00 = .784).

Compounding is simply the reverse of the discounting process. If you put $6.27 million in a savings account today at a 5 percent annual compound rate of return, in five years you would have $8 million. This **future value** is calculated as follows:

$$
\begin{aligned}
\text{Future value} &= (1 + R)^n \times (CF) \\
&= (1 + .05)^5 \times \$6,270,000 \\
&= 1.28 \times \$6,270,000 \\
&= \$8,000,000
\end{aligned}
$$

Fortunately one does not have to go through the laborious process of calculating present value factors. Lists of present value factors are available in most finance textbooks. They are not included here because all but the simplest modern calculators perform compounding and discounting functions quite painlessly, rendering the direct use of discount factors an unnecessary step.

EXHIBIT 4–5 Breakfast Proposal—Present Value Payback (in thousands)

Year	Cash Flow	Present Value Cash Flow		Remaining Investment
0	$(1,155)	$\dfrac{\$(1,155)}{(1.05)^0}$ =	$(1,155.00)	$(1,155.00)
1	495	$\dfrac{\$495}{(1.05)^1}$ =	471.43	(683.57)
2	495	$\dfrac{\$495}{(1.05)^2}$ =	448.98	(234.59)
3	495	$\dfrac{\$495}{(1.05)^3}$ =	427.60	193.01

The total present value payback is 2.55 years. The .55 is calculated thus:

$$\frac{\$(234.59)}{\$427.60} = .55 \text{ year.}$$

Present Value Payback. The most simplistic use of the discounting approach is the present value payback. To calculate a present value payback, one first discounts each net cash flow to its equivalent present value. These discounted present values are summed until the total equals the amount of the original investment. Exhibit 4–5 provides the data needed to calculate the discounted payback for the breakfast project. Using 5 percent as the equivalent time value of money, the discounted payback value of the project is 2.6 years. The salad-pasta bar option's discounted payback is 4.2 years.

While including the time value of money, the discounted payback still ignores cash flows beyond the payback period. This is a particularly critical fault when projects with large future returns, such as new products, are being considered. It is neither necessary nor appropriate to discriminate arbitrarily against projects with longer-term returns.

Net present value and **internal rate of return** are two frequently used discounting techniques that take all cash flows into consideration. Either method provides a better measure of value than do the more simplistic ranking methods. We will describe and point out the advantages and disadvantages of each method.

Net Present Value. The net present value—that is, the value as a lump sum today—is the present value of all the current and future benefits less the present value of all current and future costs. The net present value could also be described as the present value of the net worth an investment will contribute to a firm by the end of its useful life. Net present value (NPV) is calculated by means of a discount rate. The discount rate is used to adjust each year's returns according to that year's distance from the date of the initial investment. Net present value is calculated as follows:

$$NPV = \frac{NCF_1}{(1 + R)^1} + \frac{NCF_2}{(1 + R)^2} + \ldots + \frac{NCF_n}{(1 + R)^n} - I$$

where

NCF = The net cash flow per year (cash flow benefits minus cash flow costs)

R = Discount rate

$1, 2, \ldots, n$ = Years from the date of original investment

I = Amount of initial investment

For Consumer, Inc., using 5 percent as a discount rate, the net present value of the breakfast option is calculated as follows:

$$NPV = \frac{\$495,000}{(1 + .05)^1} + \frac{\$495,000}{(1 + .05)^2} + \frac{\$495,000}{(1 + .05)^3} + \frac{\$495,000}{(1 + .05)^4}$$

$$+ \frac{\$495,000}{(1 + .05)^5} - \$1,155,000$$

$$= 988,091$$

The net present value figure is the present value of the net worth the breakfast project will contribute to Consumer by the end of the investment's five-year life. The NPV of the salad-pasta bar project is $260,999 at a 5 percent discount rate. The process is quite simple when a calculator with a net present value function is used.

The NPV approach offers a logical method of evaluating investments. It takes into account the timing of cash flows by placing a higher value on those received immediately and a lower value on those to be received in the future. Once the timing of cash flows has been taken into account, acceptable investments are those with net present values equal to or greater than zero.

Present Value Index.   Some managers prefer to use the profitability or present value index (PVI) rather than net present value. the PVI is simply an adaptation of the benefit/cost ratio:

$$\text{Present value index} = \frac{\text{Present value of net benefits}}{\text{Cost}}$$

Calculating the present value index is simple and straight-forward. Using the breakfast option as an example, and a 5 percent discount rate,

$$\begin{aligned}\text{Present value} \\ \text{index}\end{aligned} = \left[\frac{\$495,000}{(1 + .05)^1} + \frac{\$495,000}{(1 + .05)^2} + \frac{\$495,000}{(1 + .05)^3} + \frac{\$495,000}{(1 + .05)^4} \right.$$

$$\left. + \frac{\$495,000}{(1 + .05)^5} \right] \div \$1,155,000$$

$$= 1.85$$

This means that for each dollar of investment, the breakfast proposal returns a present value of $1.85 of benefits. The present value index for the salad bar project is 1.16. As is the case with any method utilizing a discount rate, the magnitude of the present value index will change if the discount rate is changed.

Internal Rate of Return.   A second discounted cash flow technique is internal rate of return (IRR). This method is used to measure the average rate of return that will be earned over the life of the project. To calculate the IRR, the same formula as that for calculating net present value is used except that we set net present value equal to zero and solve for R.

Solving for R is somewhat more difficult than solving for NPV. To do so we must use a trial-and-error method. We start by choosing an arbitrary discount rate (say 5 percent), calculate the NPV, and see if the NPV is zero. If the NPV is positive, a higher discount rate is next selected and the NPV recalculated. We continue to choose discount rates until we find the discount rate that yields an NPV of zero. With the Consumer, Inc., breakfast project, the IRR is obviously larger than 5 percent, since at that rate the NPV is equal to $988,091. Exhibit 4–6 provides a graph of the results of the trial-

EXHIBIT 4–6   Net Present Value Profile: Salad-Pasta Bar and Breakfast Options

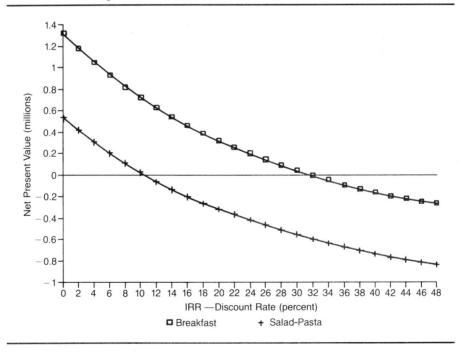

and-error approach. Rates above 5 percent were chosen until the IRR of 32.27 percent was found. The graph is also called a **net present value profile,** since it depicts the project's net present value at various discount rates. Note that at a discount rate of zero, the net present value is the simple sum of the undiscounted cash flows. For the salad-pasta bar project, the IRR is 10.8 percent, and at all discount rates it provides a lower NPV than does the breakfast project. An acceptable IRR for a risk-free project is a return that compensates the investor for his or her time value of money. Here we have used 5 percent. Thus both projects would be acceptable, but the breakfast option is superior.

While the IRR method is purported to be equivalent to the net present value method, it poses special problems for the user. If the investments are of quite different sizes, if the timing of the cash flows is different for each project under consideration, or if negative and positive net cash flows alternate over the life of the project, the internal rate of return can give results that are misleading or difficult to interpret. For instance, in evaluating our sail-assisted tanker project, we noted there would be significant investments at several points over the useful life of the tanker. First, the tanker would be purchased, and later, extensive engine overhauls would be needed. Thus net cash flows would be negative in the first year and at several points in the future. During the intervening years, cash flows would be positive. As a result of alternating positive and negative net cash flows, several different discount rates allow the NPV to equal zero. In other words, the project would have several IRRs.

Exhibit 4–7 shows the net present value profile for the sail-assisted tanker project. There are IRRs of both 8.1 and 21.0 percent. Does this mean that for companies using discount rates below 8.1 and above 21 percent, the

EXHIBIT 4–7   Net Present Value Profile: Sail-Assisted Tanker

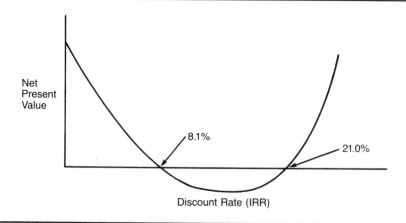

project is acceptable? Yes; and that if the company's rate is between 8.1 and 21 percent, the investment should be rejected. If the analyst had only solved for the IRR and not plotted the net present value profile, the project might have been rejected rather than accepted. Most simple computer models and calculators are designed to solve for one IRR, but the analyst with one IRR may erroneously believe he or she has the complete information necessary to analyze the project. Net present value profiles yield more complete data. For these and other reasons, the net present value technique is the preferred approach.

We have summarized in Exhibit 4–8 the result of using six ranking methods for Consumer's two projects. The benefit/cost ratio and payback period take the size of the cash flows, but not their timing, into account. The net present value and internal rate of return take into account both the size and timing of cash flows. Fortunately for Consumer, Inc., all of our methods indicate that the breakfast option is the more attractive.

3. Ranking Projects

So far we have assumed that if an investment creates value it should be accepted. In doing so, we assumed that the firm had enough capital to invest in all attractive projects. If that were not true, investments would be ranked by their relative value, and the firm would continue to invest in those with the greatest values until its investment resources were exhausted. In most circumstances, that means investing first in those investments with the highest relative values.

For the manager with more projects than cash, projects must be ranked from highest to lowest in value. Our preference is the use of the net present

EXHIBIT 4–8   Summary: Breakfast Option versus Salad-Pasta Bar Option

Method	Breakfast	Salad Bar	Decision Rule
Benefit/cost ratio	2.14	1.32	B/C ≥ 1.0
Payback period	2.3 years	3.6 years	Payback period ≥ Management minimum
Present value payback	2.6	4.2	PV payback ≥ Management minimum
Net present value (in thousands), at discount rate of:			
5%	$988	$261	NPV ≥ 0
10%	$721	$ 32	
Present value index, at discount rate of 5%	1.85	1.16	PVI ≥ 1.0
Internal rate of return	32.3%	10.8%	IRR ≥ Hurdle rate

value method or the present value index to rank projects. These approaches provide a ranking consistent with the assumption that managers are attempting to maximize the value of the firm. Does this mean that the breakfast proposal is the option Consumer management should choose? Maybe, but the breakfast proposal is riskier; customers may not come. The salad-pasta bar will supplement the present hamburger and french fry sales, which is less risky. How should we account for the differences in risk? Since rational investors require larger returns to compensate them for uncertain cash flows, relative value also depends on the risk being taken when making an investment.

4. Dealing with Risk

What do we mean by risk? By risk we mean that our cash flow forecasts might be wrong. Over- or underestimated cash flows result in lower or higher than expected returns. Investors, in addition to preferring large, rapid returns, also prefer certain returns; they do not like to take risks. To induce the typical risk-averse investor to invest in risky projects, larger returns must be anticipated. The higher the risk, the larger the return premium required.

Of all the problems facing the investment analyst, risk is the most troublesome. To date we have not found the ideal method for incorporating risk into the measurement of an investment's value. However, several methods are currently being used by managers. None of these methods is flawless; all are tentative attempts at dealing with a very complex problem.

In most analyses, we assume that the risk of the project is the same as the risk of the firm. That is, cash flows for the project are as predictable (or unpredictable) as cash flows from the firm's current business. Once that assumption is made, we can use, as a discount rate, the firm's average cost of capital.

We can use that cost as a discount rate because the cost of capital is the marginal return required by the firm's providers of capital (creditors and stockholders). These investors require a return for the time value of their investments and for the risk they are taking by allowing the firm the use of their money. Instead of directly estimating the return required for the risk being taken by the firm, we often use the firm's marginal cost of capital as an indication of the fair return as determined by the capital markets. In Chapter 5, we will discuss how this cost is calculated. Meanwhile, we can use the firm's cost of capital as a discount rate if all the firm's investments are of equal risk to that of the firm.

What if the risk of the investment is higher or lower than the corporate average? In this situation, many managers add a premium or deduction to the corporate discount rate to compensate for the difference. The rate that includes the risk differential is called a **hurdle rate**. As the hurdle rate increases—that is, a investors require greater returns as compensation for greater risks—the net present value of an investment diminishes dramatically. Exhibit 4–6 illustrates this decline. When the discount rate is 5 percent, the breakfast and salad-pasta bar options provide net present values of $988,091 and $260,859, respectively. If a hurdle rate of 10 percent is substituted for the discount rate, the net present values diminish to $721,439 and $32,516, as indicated in Exhibit 4–8.

Even discounting the cash flows at a higher rate, the breakfast project still offers greater value to Consumer's shareholders. But these calculations again assume that the risks of the projects are equivalent. On the contrary, opening for breakfast is more risky than adding salad bars. New employees must be hired, a new advertising campaign must be undertaken, new food items will be offered, and a large unrecoverable investment in training is required. Consumer, Inc., managers could be wrong in their forecasts of potential sales and costs of the breakfast option. Salad-pasta bars, on the other hand, add little to the risk of the firm. The initial investment is small and a portion of it recoverable, training costs are low, and few additional employees must be hired. The two projects have different levels of risk. How can these differences in risk be included in the comparison?

So far, neither academics nor businessmen have answered that question very well, although several techniques are currently being used. One approach is to present the problem of risk directly to the managers. Using the cost of capital as a discount rate, managers can determine for themselves whether the net present value compensates for the risk of the project. For instance, the net present value of the breakfast option at a discount rate of 10 percent is greater by $688,993 than that of the salad-pasta bars. Is this amount adequate, in the managers' view, to compensate for the differences in risk between the two investments? It is up to them to decide.

This approach, however, is often too ad hoc for managers who prefer a more structured approach. Another method is to modify the hurdle rate according to the apparent risk of the investment. For example, new products may be considered to have greater risks than the risk of the firm as a whole. Consequently, management will set a higher hurdle rate for new products than the firm's marginal cost of capital. A scheme such as the one shown in Exhibit 4–9 is used by many firms to categorize investments.

EXHIBIT 4–9 Risk Categories

Investment Category	Risk Level	Hurdle Rate
Cost reduction	Less than firm's average risk	Lower than firm's marginal average cost of capital
Plant expansion	Average risk	Marginal average cost of capital
New products	Higher than average risk	Higher rate than marginal average cost of capital

Managers who use this scheme believe that investments in cost reductions are less risky than their firm's average risk, and that new products are more risky. Using this scheme, Consumer's management might discount the salad-pasta bar's cash flows at the cost of capital, 10 percent. But since breakfast is a new product, it may be considered riskier, and its cash flows may be discounted at an even higher rate.

While this scheme is often used, it leads to predictable results—new products are less attractive, whereas cost-reduction projects are usually acceptable. These conclusions may or may not be appropriate for the specific firm or investment. Furthermore, it is difficult to determine the appropriate changes to make to the hurdle rate.

Managers with a number of divisions or lines of business have attempted to adapt their corporate hurdle rate for the specific risks of the division or product line. Since the cost of capital for a division is not available, a number of methods are used to estimate the appropriate discount rate. Most often the rate is calculated by using the average of the costs of capital for a number of publicly traded proxy firms—firms with similar characteristics. These proxy methods are imprecise but hold more promise than using a single rate for businesses with very different levels of risk in their various investments.

Some suggest that manipulating cash flows is more appropriate than varying the discount rate for risk. The most simplistic method of revising the cash flows for risk is conservative forecasting, which typically involves overestimating costs and underestimating revenues. Rather than being conservative, it is wrong. Such estimates permit an inaccurate picture of the real potential (upside and down) of the project. While such "conservatism" is broadly practiced, the good analyst will seek the most accurate forecasts and analyze risk using a different method.

Another useful method of adjusting cash flows can be employed. The investor, or the manager on the investor's behalf, examines the forecasted net cash flow for each year of the project's life. The manager then determines the **certainty equivalent** for each of those cash flows and discounts them at the time value of money. A certainty equivalent is an estimate of an absolutely risk-free amount that the investor would take for the uncertain cash flow that is actually forecast. For instance, for the breakfast project, the managers forecast a cash flow of $495,000 in the first year. However, they were very uncertain about the success of the project. Sales or costs could exceed or be considerably below expectations. The actual net cash flow might be as low as $86,000 or as high as $1,029,000. Instead of masking the risk, management would assess the certainty equivalent. In this case, it might be $495,000—the certain amount that would induce management, on behalf of the shareholders, to give up the chance of higher returns and avoid lower ones as well. The certainty equivalent—the risk-free sum—is then discounted at the risk-free rate, the time value of money.

The certainty equivalent includes the risk preference of the individual manager determining the sum. Thus, while the idea is theoretically appealing, the problems with certainty equivalents are obvious: who will make the judgment on the shareholders' behalf?

Finally, there are two methods for incorporating risk directly into investment valuation. Both are based on the analyst's forecasting several probable outcomes (costs and benefits), multiple scenarios, for an investment. The analyst then incorporates this information into the investment analysis.

In the simple use of multiple-scenario analysis, an analyst forecasts just three alternative outcomes—optimistic, pessimistic, and most likely— for each of the project's costs and benefits. The result of this analysis is three forecasts and three sets of measures of value for each investment. For instance, the management of Consumer, Inc., might decide that the breakfast proposal has a possibility of much greater success as well as real potential for failure. Its success or failure will depend on whether the customer will perceive a fast-food restaurant as a place for breakfast. The forecasts made for the breakfast project (shown in Exhibit 4–2) were the most likely estimates—but management was quite uncertain about what would occur if they opened their restaurants for breakfast. If sales from their new breakfast menu exceeded their most likely estimate of $15 million, they would expect the operating cost percentage to be slightly lower, since some costs (for instance, maintenance) will not increase with sales. Likewise, if sales were lower than expected, operating costs would not decrease as fast as sales and the net profit woulç be lower. Exhibit 4–10 provides the annual cash flows for optimistic, most likely, and pessimistic scenarios for the breakfast proposal. The net present value for each scenario is listed at the bottom of the exhibit. The investment cost of $1.155 million would remain the same regardless of the success of the project. Quite obviously, if the breakfast project

EXHIBIT 4–10 Consumer Breakfast Proposal—Annual Cash Flow
(in thousands of real dollars)

	Pessimistic	Most Likely	Optimistic
Incremental sales	$ 3,300	$ 15,000	$ 26,000
Operating expenses*	(3,170)	(14,250)	(24,440)
Depreciation	0	0	0
Pre-tax profit	130	750	1,560
Taxes (34%)	(44)	(255)	(530)
Profit after tax	86	495	1,029
Noncash charges	0	0	0
Net cash flow	$ 86	$ 495	$ 1,029
Net present value (at 5%)	$ (783)	$ 988	$ 3,300

*Operating expenses are projected by management to decline as sales increase—to be 96, 95, and 94% of sales, respectively.

is not successful, the value to Consumer is negative—costs exceed benefits. Using a higher discount rate would make the net present value even lower. However, if customers find the new breakfast menu appealing, the project could be quite a boon to Consumer and its shareholders—the net present value would be very attractive. To decide whether to proceed with the breakfast proposal, management must decide on the likelihood of the pessimistic scenario occurring and whether the most likely and optimistic scenarios could create enough value to offset this danger.

Most managers who use this three-scenario analysis implicitly assume that each scenario is equally likely, and they use the information in the analysis to decide whether the company could afford the project if the pessimistic scenario were the one that occurred. Note that in making these forecasts, the analyst must take care that all three sets of forecasts are probable, not just possible. If the analyst were to take the worst (or best) outcome possible for every cost and benefit, the result would be a forecast that was possible but not very probable. Possible but not probable forecasts give managers very little information on which to base decisions.

Managers do not need to believe that each of the scenarios is equally likely to happen. Using the breakfast proposal as an example, the management of Consumer might think it most likely that, based on the experience of other fast-food restaurants in introducing a breakfast menu, the breakfast proposal would have sales of $15 million as predicted in Exhibit 4–2. While $15 million is a good estimate of the expected sales, there is a reasonable chance that the innovative menu Consumer management is planning will be very successful. The analyst could estimate the likelihood, or probability, that each of the three scenarios shown in Exhibit 4–10 will occur. In fact, the analyst could estimate the probabilities of more than three likely outcomes occurring. Instead of only three scenarios, the analyst might estimate five or more. In Exhibit 4–11, the analyst has estimated five alternative outcomes for the breakfast proposal and the likelihood that each will occur.

To put the forecasts into perspective, the analyst weights the net present values for each of the scenarios by the probability it will occur to obtain

EXHIBIT 4–11   Probabilistic Analysis—Breakfast Proposal (in thousands of real dollars)

Probability	Net Present Value	Weighted Value
15%	$ (783)	$ (117)
20	(102)	(20)
30	988	296
20	2,100	420
15	3,300	495
Expected value (weighted average)		$1,074

what is called an **expected value**—the probability-weighted net present value. Exhibit 4–11 provides the result of such an analysis. While the net present value of $1,074,000 is not one that the analyst explicitly forecast, it represents a sort of average for the project. The analyst also could compute a standard deviation to obtain a measure of risk.

In a more complex investment analysis, where there are numerous costs and benefits for which an analyst could assess a probability distribution, computer-assisted analysis, especially simulation, provides a good means for analyzing complex data and estimating the expected value and standard deviation for a project.

One word of caution in the use of multiple-scenario expected value analysis: the veracity of this method depends on the company engaging in a number of projects at the same time, or over time, for the net present value to represent the average net present value the firm will receive from its projects. If only one project is undertaken, only one outcome can occur—no other projects exist to average the results. Thus probabilistic analysis can yield rich information for a knowledgeable user but hold dangers for the naive.

Simulation analysis, described in Appendix A, is used by an increasing number of companies. Managers find that the discipline of deciding what might occur for each of the various costs and benefits keeps their assumptions reasonable and makes the analysis useful. However, this technique (simulation) is time-consuming and requires a computer. The increasing use of microcomputers has made multiple-scenario, not simulation, analysis, more accessible and useful for managers. As computer simulation models become readily available for use on the microcomputer, simulation may also become a widely used method of risk assessment.

None of these available risk-adjustment methods is completely satisfactory. New methods for incorporating risk into capital-investment decision making are being developed. Some firms assign different hurdle rates to divisions or strategic business units that are exposed to different levels of risk. Other firms attempt to quantify risk differences for each individual investment. Still other firms use statistical techniques, such as probabilistic simulation analysis, to estimate directly the riskiness of investments. To date, risk is the most difficult problem in assessing value.

IV. OTHER CONSIDERATIONS IN CREATING VALUE

Not all investments are as complex or as risky as these two examples. Some are simple replacements of old, antiquated, or technologically inferior equipment. Analysis of one of these replacement investments will allow us to examine the impact of such things as different methods of depreciation and the effect of taxes. Consumer, Inc., management is considering just such a replacement investment—microwave ovens.

Currently each of Consumer's restaurants uses conventional electric ovens to heat some sandwiches and desserts. Such ovens are large, take an average of 10 minutes to heat the food, and, since they warm up slowly, must be kept hot whether they are being used or not.

Microwave ovens have been proposed to replace these ovens. They are small, cook much more rapidly, and, since the method of heating and cooking is totally different, need only be turned on when actually in use. Thus the primary savings would be in the expense for electricity.

Management has made the following estimates of the costs and benefits associated with each new oven.

1. Microwave ovens can be purchased, fully installed, for $630.

2. The old ovens can be sold to a used-equipment dealer for their book value of $25 each.

3. While annual usage and costs of electricity vary from restaurant to restaurant, the average cost per year per oven has been $300. The new ovens would use about one third the electricity, for a cost of $100 per oven per year.

4. The new ovens are expected to be fully useful for five years. After that time, the ovens will be obsolete or in need of substantial repair. Management believes the ovens would have no salvage value at the end of the fifth year. Management would depreciate the new ovens over five years, according to provisions of the 1986 tax code.

This is a very straightforward problem. As you can see in Exhibit 4–12, reduced costs are treated the same as increased income. Using double-declining balance five-year depreciation, the IRR is 14.7 percent and the NPV (at a 10 percent discount rate) is $68.99 per oven, seemingly a reasonable investment opportunity.[1]

However, there are changes within management's discretion that can increase the value of the investment. As an example, under certain tax codes, management could have elected to use straight-line or another rapid method of depreciation. The 1981 tax code used one accelerated method, the 1986 code another. Let's examine the effect of using other depreciation methods on the value of the microwave oven investment.

The yearly depreciation changes that would result from using other methods of depreciation are shown in Exhibit 4–13. The effect on the net cash flow of using other methods is shown in Exhibit 4–14. The double-declining balance method used under the 1986 code yields the largest increase in the project's value.

At first glance, this may seem like numerical black magic, but it is, in fact, a real change in the value of the project to the firm. While the same

---

[1] An analysis for ovens for all 500 restaurants would yield the same IRR, 14.6% but an NPV of $34,495 (500 × $68.99).

EXHIBIT 4–12 Investment Analysis per Oven (Microwave Oven Investment)

			Period			
	0	*1*	*2*	*3*	*4*	*5*
Income statement changes:						
Revenues		0	0	0	0	0
Electricity:						
Old oven		$(300)	$(300)	$(300)	$(300)	$(300)
New oven		(100)	(100)	(100)	(100)	(100)
Net electricity		200	200	200	200	200
Depreciation:						
Old depreciation		0	0	0	0	0
New depreciation		(252)	(151)	(91)	(68)	(68)
Net depreciation		(252)	(151)	(91)	(68)	(68)
Pre-tax profit		(52)	49	109	132	132
Taxes (@ 34%)		18	(17)	(37)	(45)	(45)
Profit after taxes		(34)	32	72	87	87
Noncash charges:						
Net depreciation		252	151	91	68	68
Asset changes:						
Property, plant, equipment:						
Microwave oven	$(630)					
Old oven salvage value	25					
New oven salvage value						
Working capital	0					
Net cash flow	$(605)	$ 218	$ 183	$ 163	$ 155	$ 155

Net present value at 10% = $69

Internal rate of return = 14.7%

total depreciation is taken, the amount taken in each year is different, and thus the timing of the taxes paid by the firm is different. Since the discounting process deems earlier cash flows as more valuable and accelerated depreciation methods provide larger, earlier cash flows, the method of depreciation chosen by management can create value. As shown in Exhibit 4–14, under ACRS rules the net present value would have been $55.80 per oven, for a total of $27,900. The net present value under the 1986 tax code is $34,495 for all 500 ovens.

Changes in the tax laws illustrate the impact external factors can have on the operations and decisions of the company. With the tax shield having a significant impact on the attractiveness of a project, the analyst should always be informed of not only current tax regulations but pending legislation as well. Keeping abreast of the economic, social, and political environment is essential for the analyst to properly analyze managerial decisions.

EXHIBIT 4–13   Yearly Depreciation Charge—Different Depreciation Methods
(microwave oven investment)

Year	Straight-Line*	Double-Declining Balance†	Sum-of-Years' Digits‡	ACRS§
1	$126	$252	$210	$ 95
2	126	151	168	139
3	126	91	126	132
4	126	68	84	132
5	126	68	42	132
Total	$630	$630	$630	$630

*The depreciation rate is calculated by dividing 100% by number of years. In this case, the depreciation rate is 100/5 = 20% per year. To determine yearly depreciation, multiply the purchase price, minus the salvage value, by the depreciation rate.
†Double the straight-line depreciation rate is multiplied by the full *undepreciated* value of the asset. In the final year, the remaining depreciation, less the salvage value, is taken.
‡To calculate the sum-of-the years' digits factor:
a. Sum the numbers of the years, in this case 5 + 4 + 3 + 2 + 1 = 15.
b. For each year divide the number of remaining years by the summed years. In this case, the depreciation factor for the first year is 5/15 or .33.
c. Multiply the depreciable value by this factor.
§Five-year ACRS rates are 15% the first year, 22% the second year, and 21% the remaining three years.

We have looked at three investments Consumer, Inc., could make—the breakfast service, the salad-pasta bar, and installing microwave ovens. Each had a different net present value. While the breakfast option appears to be the best choice, we have failed to take note of one more thing: Consumer's investments will require different amounts of capital. Thus, if we simply compare the net present values of the three alternatives, we have not considered the amount of invested capital. As an example, all 500 microwave ovens require a net investment of only $302,500, while the breakfast proposal requires $1.155 million. We have not determined what use Consumer management could make of the available difference, $852,500, if the microwave ovens alone were bought. If we simply compare the net present values, or any other measure of relative return, we could make a bad decision; we would be comparing unequal corporate strategies.

Must managers have an intended use for the extra capital in order to compare the projects? No. They can examine the value the added investments will create for the firm. Exhibit 4–15 analyzes the value the breakfast option would create for Consumer, Inc., shareholders. If we deduct the microwave option's cash flows from those of the breakfast option, we can determine the return we gain from the added investment of the added $852,500. The added net present value is $687,590. The incremental investment does create value.

EXHIBIT 4–14 Changes in Net Cash Flow, IRR, and NPV for Microwave Oven—Different Depreciation Methods*

Method	0	1	2	3	4	5
			Year			
Double-declining balance:						
Net costs and benefits after tax, excluding depreciation	$(605)	$132	$132	$132	$132	$132
Depreciation tax shield	0	86	51	31	23	23
Net cash flow	$(605)	$218	$183	$163	$155	$155
IRR = 14.6%						
NPV (@ 10%) = $67.69						
Accelerated cost recovery system:						
Net costs and benefits after tax, excluding depreciation	$(605)	$132	$132	$132	$132	$132
Depreciation tax shield	0	32	47	45	45	45
Net cash flow	$(605)	$164	$179	$177	$177	$177
IRR = 13.5%						
NPV (@ 10%) = $55.80						
Straight-line:						
Net costs and benefits after tax, excluding depreciation	$(605)	$132	$132	$132	$132	$132
Depreciation tax shield	0	43	43	43	43	43
Net cash flow	$(605)	$175	$175	$175	$175	$175
IRR = 13.7%						
NPV (@ 10%) = $58.39						
Sum-of-years' digits:						
Net costs and benefits after tax, excluding depreciation	$(605)	$132	$132	$132	$132	$132
Depreciation tax shield	0	71	57	43	29	14
Net cash flow	$(605)	$203	$189	$175	$161	$144
IRR = 14.5%						
NPV (@ 10%) = $66.60						

*Based on the microwave oven analysis in Exhibit 4–12, the 1986 tax code rate of 34%, and no investment tax credit.

EXHIBIT 4–15   Consumer, Inc., Net Cash Flows—Two Alternatives (in thousands)

	(1) *Breakfast Option*	*(2)* *500 Microwave Ovens*	*(1) – (2)* *Difference*
Net investment	$ 1,155.0	$ 302.5	
Annual net cash flows, year:			
0	$(1,155.0)	$(302.5)	$(852.5)
1	495.0	108.8	386.2
2	495.0	91.7	403.3
3	495.0	81.4	413.6
4	495.0	77.1	417.9
5	495.0	77.1	417.9
NPV (at 10%)	$ 721.44	$ 34.50	$ 687.59
IRR	32.3%	14.6%	37.7%

Because we do not have alternating negative and positive cash flows, we are reasonably safe in using the internal rate of return to examine value creation in this case. The IRR for the differential cash flows is 37.7 percent. Except in the most inflationary environments, this return should be quite acceptable.

There is one last problem analysts and managers must consider every time they analyze the value of an investment—inflation. You will notice that all the cash flows that Consumer management forecast were in real terms, they did not include inflation. Inflation can have a neutral, positive, or negative effect on the value of a project depending on whether managers can pass on their costs in the form of prompt price increases. If cost increases can be passed on immediately and fully, the relative value of the project will remain the same. If there is a lag between the time the company's costs increase and the time when it can raise prices, however, inflation can have a very negative effect on the value of a project.

Inflation can have yet other effects. Revenues themselves may rise or fall depending on the rate of inflation. For instance, if more people eat breakfast at fast-food restaurants than at traditional restaurants when inflation and prices rise, Consumer, Inc., may find that its revenues rise in both real terms (more customers are eating breakfast) and nominal terms (prices rise to account for the increased costs of producing the same number of breakfasts). The effects of these increases should be well understood by the manager. Exhibit 4–16 provides a forecast for the salad-pasta bar proposal that Consumer, Inc., management is considering. In this example, there is no increase in revenues greater than that driven by the 10 percent expected inflation: the unit sales remain the same.

EXHIBIT 4–16 Consumer Salad-Pasta Bar Proposal—Marginal Costs and Benefits with Annual Inflation of 10% (thousands of dollars)

			Period			
	0	*1*	*2*	*3*	*4*	*5*
Income statement changes:						
Sales		$8,250	$9,075	$9,983	$10,981	$12,079
Operating expenses		(7,673)	(8,440)	(9,284)	(10,212)	(11,233)
Training costs	$ (416)	0	0	0	0	0
Depreciation		(560)	(336)	(202)	(151)	(151)
Pre-tax profit	(416)	18	299	497	617	695
Taxes (34%)	141	(6)	(102)	(169)	(210)	(236)
Profit after taxes	(275)	12	198	328	408	458
Noncash charges:						
Depreciation	0	560	336	202	151	151
Capital investments:						
Property, plant, and equipment changes	(1,400)	0	0	0	0	0
Working-capital changes	0	0	0	0	0	0
Net cash flow	$(1,675)	$ 572	$ 534	$ 530	$ 559	$ 609

101

You will note in comparing Exhibit 4–16 to Exhibit 4–3 that inflation does not affect depreciation. As the rate of inflation increases, the taxes that are deferred by the depreciation tax shield decrease, making the investment less valuable. This is one of the insidious costs of inflation, a cost that occurs in countries where the depreciation schedules for capitalized property are calculated on the basis of historical cost, as is done in the United States. In other countries, particularly those with high inflation, companies are allowed to increase the book value of fixed assets, and hence the depreciation, with increases in inflation. Because of this practice, profits actually increase at a rate comparable to inflation.

Exhibit 4–16 is a simple example of the effect inflation can have on the value of an investment. Of course, individual costs and revenues could increase at rates slower or faster than inflation. However, a simple increase in inflation, to 10 percent, increases the net present value of this project, at a discount rate of 10 percent, from $32,446 to $444,465. Why, if inflation appears to be so beneficial to the shareholders' value, do we avoid it so fearfully? It is not that inflation is beneficial; it is that we have not fully included it in our Exhibit 4–16 analysis. In our earlier analysis, we used a discount rate of 10 percent to cover time and risk, but not inflation. To cover the expected losses from inflation, we would have to discount the Exhibit 4–16 cash flows at a total rate of 20 percent. At that discount rate, the net present value is a loss of $6,464. Inflation can really have an impact on value.

We will investigate how investors determine their required returns, and thus how companies decide on the appropriate hurdle rate, in the next chapter. In the meantime, however, remember that investors certainly expect returns to cover their time value of money, *in nominal terms*. Therefore, leaving all other risks aside, investors expect a real return.

V. SUMMARY

Good investments are critical to the future of the firm. The analyst's job is to gather and analyze the relevant information and present it in such a way that the future is adequately foreseen. Analysts have three major problems in assessing potential investments. First, the appropriate cash costs and benefits must be determined. That process, as we have suggested, can be difficult, particularly when evaluating replacement investments. The analyst's second problem is to evaluate the relative attractiveness of the investment's net marginal benefits. We suggest that the net present value method is the most appropriate technique to use in measuring this value. Third, the problem of incorporating risk into the evaluation of any investment is a particularly vexing one. If all of the investments are of a risk similar to that of the firm, an appropriate method is to use the firm's marginal cost of capital for a hurdle rate. If the investment is more or less risky than the firm, the analyst may leave it to the managers to decide subjectively whether the return is adequate to compensate for the risk or if they should use one of the hurdle-rate adjustment techniques. However, until risk analysis is refined, we are left with methods that do not fully satisfy our needs.

SELECTED REFERENCES

For comprehensive reviews of the capital budgeting process, see:
Bierman, Harold, Jr., and Seymour Smidt. *The Capital Budgeting Decision.* 5th ed. New York: MacMillan, 1980.

Levy, Haim, and Marshall Sarnot. *Capital Investment and Financial Decisions.* Englewood Cliffs, N.J.: Prentice-Hall International, 1978.

For corporate strategy and capital budgeting, see:
Shapiro, Alan, "Corporate Strategy and the Capital Budgeting Decision," *Midland Corporate Finance Journal,* Spring 1985, pp. 22–36.

For an analysis of the capital-budgeting and planning process in one firm, see:
Bower, Joseph. *Managing the Resource Allocation Process: A Study of Corporate Planning and Investments.* Homewood, Ill.: Richard D. Irwin, 1970.

For descriptions of various approaches to risk analysis, see:
Bower, Richard S., and J. M. Jenks. "Divisional Screening Rates." *Financial Management,* Autumn 1975, pp. 42–49.

Hertz, David B. "Risk Analysis in Capital Investment." *Harvard Business Review,* September-October 1979, pp. 169–81.

Hull, J. C. *The Evaluation of Risk in Business Investment.* Elmsford, N.Y.: Pergammon Press, 1980.

Sick, Gordon A. "A Certainty-Equivalent Approach to Capital Budgeting." *Financial Management,* Winter 1986, pp. 23–32.

Weston, J. Fred. "Investment Decisions Using the Capital Asset Pricing Model." *Financial Management,* Spring 1973, pp. 25–33.

For information on the effects of inflation on capital budgeting analysis, see:
Rappaport, Alfred, and Robert A. Taggart, Jr., "Evaluation of Capital Expenditure Proposals Under Inflation." *Financial Management,* Spring 1982, pp. 5–13.

For approaches to determining the cost of capital for divisions, see:
Harrington, Diana R. "Stock Prices, Beta, and Strategic Planning." *Harvard Business Review,* May/June 1985, pp. 157–164.

Gup, Benton E., and Samuel W. Norwood III. "Divisional Cost of Capital: A Practical Approach." *Financial Management,* Spring 1982, pp. 20–24.

STUDY QUESTIONS

1. In December 1988, the Marvel Corporation was considering the development of a new assembly line. The necessary machinery was estimated to cost $800,000. The 1986 tax code would allow the equipment to be depreciated in 20 years, its useful life, using the double-declining balance method of depreciation with a switch to straight-line depreciation when

advantageous. Marvel management estimated that the costs associated with owning and running the machinery (gas, minor repairs, etc.) would be constant over time and total $200,000 over its 20-year estimated life. Thirty people would be required to work the assembly line. These would be new employees, each earning an average of $15,000 a year in salary and benefits. Sales from the new assembly line were estimated to total $1.25 million a year, with raw materials representing 37 percent of that amount. No other costs specific to the project were anticipated. The Marvel Corporation had a 34 percent tax rate and a required payback period of four years on all new projects. Should they develop the assembly line? What is the project's benefit/cost ratio?

2. The SUN Company was considering an investment which would cost $200,000 initially. The new equipment was estimated to have a useful life of five years but would require an additional investment of $60,000 in year two for specialized equipment. The initial investment would be depreciated under the 1986 tax code for 5 years. The second investment would meet the guidelines for the three-year class. Sales specific to the project were forecasted at $120,000 in year one, increasing 15 percent a year to $209,881 in year five. Necessary raw materials, labor, etc., were estimated at 39 percent of sales. Compute the project's net present value using a 10 percent discount rate and a 34 percent tax rate.

   What is the major factor creating the project's net present value?

3. The Kertin Company was trying to decide between the two capital projects described below. Evaluate each of the projects on the basis of their payback period, benefit/cost ratio, and net present value. Which project would you recommend Kertin Company undertake? Why?

   Project 1: Expand existing production by acquiring new machinery costing $800,000 and having a productive life of 10 years:
   a. Incremental sales = $500,000/year.
   b. Cost of goods sold = $49 percent of sales.
   c. Advertising = Constant $50,000 a year.
   d. Depreciation computed according to the 1986 tax code for 10 years.

   Project 2: Expand product line by undertaking a project estimated to cost $600,000 for production facilities, depreciable for 10 years, and $200,000 for production training for employees. Kertin management had already funded $100,000 worth of market research which had documented the product's sales potential. Kertin hoped to recoup this outlay through further sales.
   a. Sales in year 1 estimated to be $350,000, increasing 10 percent a year in years 2–4, 15 percent a year in years 5–7; and 10 percent a year in years 8–10.
   b. Cost of goods sold projected at 50 percent of sales.
   c. Advertising to be 25 percent of sales for first three years and to level off at $100,000 thereafter.

   Kertin had a 34 percent tax rate and used a 10 percent discount rate to evaluate all projects.

CHAPTER 5

The Cost of Capital

In Chapter 4, we followed the financial analyst through the evaluation of investment opportunities for Consumer, Inc. We used two projects to investigate incremental cash flow analysis and to demonstrate several methods for evaluating the value of those investments to a company's owners. We showed that the net present value technique is both intuitively acceptable and unambiguous. While there can be confusion about whether an investment is appropriate when other ways of valuing and ranking investments are used, there is no doubt about whether value will be created by the investment when the net present value (NPV) is used as the criterion. Investments with a positive net present value are expected to create value. Those with a zero NPV neither create nor destroy value. Those with a negative NPV should be rejected, and available funds used for value-creating investments or returned to the shareholders. The shareholders could do better by investing those funds in other securities in the capital markets than by allowing Consumer, Inc. to fund unacceptable investments.

To evaluate investments using the net present value method, we needed two estimates: (1) the cash flows expected over the life of the project and (2) a rate at which to discount those cash flows. In the last chapter, we first used a discount rate designed to compensate investors only for the timing of cash flows. We later augmented this rate to compensate investors for risk (including inflation). The discount rate that included components for time and risk, called a hurdle rate, was set at an amount equal to Consumer's cost of capital. We used the cost of capital as the hurdle rate because, although we can estimate the cash flows expected from an investment, it is very difficult to determine whether the return is enough to compensate for the risk of the investment. This fair return for risk, or market price of risk, is so difficult to determine that we turn for help to the experts—those who determine the fair return for different levels of risk all the time—the capital markets. The most direct information the capital markets give us about the market price of risk for any company is the return required by those investing in the company: the company's shareholders *and* lenders. The cost of capital is the return required by investors for the risk the company is taking. The use of the firm's cost of capital as the hurdle rate is acceptable so long as the investments being considered are as risky as the firm itself.

What determines lenders' and shareholders' required returns? First, since lenders or shareholders are inconvenienced by no longer having funds available to spend at will, they require a rate of return that compensates for not being able to use their money whenever they choose. The **illiquidity premium,** or **time value of money,** is what the investor expects to make while his or her money is unavailable. If the investor expects inflation to erode the value of the money, we can be certain that the illiquidity premium includes in it a return to compensate for the inflation expected. When the return required includes a premium for inflation, we call it a **nominal return.** A return that is net of inflation is called a **real return.**

There is a second part of an investor's required return: a premium that compensates for risk, the possibility that the funds will never be regained (the loan may not be repaid, or the stock's price may fall). The cost of any type of capital is the investor's compensation for these two factors, illiquidity and risk. The riskier the investment, the higher must be its expected return. That is why common stocks have higher expected returns than debt or preferred stock, both of which have claims on the firm's earnings and assets that supersede the claims of common shareholders.

To understand the cost of capital better and to see how investors determine what return they expect on their investments, a brief discussion of the capital markets will be helpful. It is in these markets that the users of funds (corporations) and the providers of funds (investors) meet.

I. CAPITAL MARKETS

The market for long-term funds for corporations is called the **capital market.** The capital market differs from the money market discussed in Chapter 2 by the nature of the funds that are invested. Money-market funds are short-term investments with maturities of under one year. Capital-market funds are long-term investments, exceeding one year. In addition to providing funds with a stated maturity—debt—the capital markets provide equity funds that have no stated maturity.

Capital markets exist on two levels, the **primary market** and the **secondary market.** Primary-market transactions occur when companies issue securities, debt or equity, to investors. Typically these securities are sold through investment bankers, who, through their relationships with brokers, act as agents for the companies selling the instruments. The proceeds from the sales of financial instruments, minus the investment bankers' commissions, are paid to the issuing companies. The primary market is a major source of capital for companies.

After the securities have been sold initially, the purchaser of the securities, equity or debt, may then trade them in the secondary market. Financial instruments may be sold individually or bundled together and then traded between individuals or institutions who may have no relationship with the original issuing company. While the company does not gain direct benefit from this trading, it is not indifferent to activities in the secondary market. Prices of its securities may change as a result of changing prospects for the company, its industry, and the economy. The prices for securities that are reported in such publications as *The Wall Street Journal, Barron's,* and most local daily newspapers reflect trading in the secondary market.

In recent years, several new instruments such as options and futures have been introduced in the financial markets. These instruments, which are designed to provide a means of protecting investors against price movements in the capital markets, are all secondary-market instruments. They are not a source of capital for corporations.

Trading in capital-market instruments can take place in organized market exchanges or "over the counter" (OTC). Organized exchanges such as the New York Stock Exchange (NYSE) and the American Stock Exchange (AMEX) allow trading only in listed securities. To achieve listed status, companies must meet specific qualifications of the exchange, including such things as the size of the company, the total market value of the publicly traded shares, and the amount of trading in the company's securities. Trading on these exchanges can only be done by members of the exchange who own one of a limited number of seats. Members of the exchange are typically brokerage companies who buy and sell securities for their customers.

Unlike the exchanges, which have a specific location where trading takes place, the OTC market consists of numerous traders located throughout the country. These traders "make a market"—buy, sell, and keep an inventory—in one or several securities. Brokerage firms are market makers. A computerized network called NASDAQ, sponsored by the National Association of Securities Dealers, ties these various market makers together. Many more securities are traded over-the-counter than on the exchanges. Because listed companies tend to be larger, the average trading volume for the securities listed on the exchanges is much greater.

In addition to the public markets, capital can be raised through **private placements.** Public issues are regulated by the Securities and Exchange Commission (SEC), which requires the issuing company to disclose specific information about the company's business activities, the financial instrument being issued, and the use of the proceeds. Such disclosure provides the public with information that facilitates subsequent trading in the secondary market. Private placements are direct placements of the securities with investors such as large insurance companies. They are not registered with the SEC and therefore cannot be traded in the secondary market. However, because the issuer can negotiate directly with the investor, private placements allow more complicated and specialized financial arrangements between borrower and lender, company and shareholder, than are available in the public capital markets.

Private institutional investors such as mutual funds, insurance companies, and pension funds are the largest investors in the capital markets.

Although precise data are difficult to obtain, estimates suggest that well over half of publicly traded securities are owned by these institutions. Individual shareholders account for the remainder.

While the two primary types of securities used by companies to raise long-term capital are debt and equity, some instruments combine the two types through "convertible" provisions. Convertible instruments typically allow the investor to convert a debt instrument or preferred stock into equity, usually common stock, at a specified conversion price and usually for a particular period of time.

1. Debt Markets

Long-term debt instruments are frequently called **bonds.** A bond is a contractual debt obligation to repay a stated amount (called the **principal** or **par value,** typically $1,000) on a specified date (termed the **maturity**) and to make periodic interest, or **coupon,** payments. Specific features of the bonds issued are described in a contract called an **indenture agreement.** The stated interest or coupon payments are determined by a specified interest rate or coupon rate at the time the bond is issued. If the contractually obligated payments are not made, the bond is in default and the bondholders may have to call on the assets of the company as compensation.

For most bonds, the coupon rate is fixed for the life of the bond. Because of large fluctuations in interest rates in recent years, some bonds have been issued with variable, or floating, interest rates. For variable-rate bonds, the interest rate is restated at specified intervals based on a particular market index of interest rates—for example, LIBOR (the London Interbank Offering Rate); or the prime rate, the rate charged the best customers of a bank.

For fixed-coupon bonds, changes in interest rates subsequent to the date of issue affect the bond price in the secondary market. If general market interest rates go up (or down), the price of the bond will go down (or up) in order to continue to provide a fair rate of return in the subsequent interest rate environment. These adjustments occur so that the bond's **yield to maturity** (interest plus principal repayments) will approximate the current market rate of interest for bonds of similar maturity and quality. Thus the price that an investor is willing to pay for a bond is a function of the par value of the bond, the coupon rate, the maturity, and prevailing interest rates. The formula for determining the proper secondary price shown below is similar to the present value calculations discussed in Chapter 4:

$$P = \frac{CP_1}{(1 + R)^1} + \frac{CP_2}{(1 + R)^2} + \ldots + \frac{CP_m}{(1 + R)^m} + \frac{PAR}{(1 + R)^m} \qquad (1)$$

where

P = Market price of the bond
CP = Periodic coupon payment (interest payment)
R = Current market interest rate

PAR = Par value of the bond
m = Maturity period of the bond

If, for instance, a company like Consumer, our example firm in Chapter 4, had issued $2 million in bonds at 12 percent and the rate of interest on bonds of a similar maturity and quality rose from 12 to 15.7 percent, the market price of Consumer's bonds with two years remaining until maturity would drop from $2 million to under $1.9 million in order to provide a 15.7 percent yield to new purchasers:

$$P = \frac{\$240,000}{(1 + .157)^1} + \frac{\$240,000}{(1 + .157)^2} + \frac{\$2,000,000}{(1 + .157)^2}$$

$$P = \$1,880,762$$

Conversely, if market rates dropped to, say 10 percent, the bond price would rise to over $2 million:

$$P = \frac{\$240,000}{(1 + .10)^1} + \frac{\$240,000}{(1 + .10)^2} + \frac{\$2,000,000}{(1 + .10)^2}$$

$$P = \$2,069,421$$

Present values (prices) of bonds with longer maturities are more affected by interest rate changes than are values of bonds with short maturities.

If the market price of a bond is known but the effective interest rate (the yield to maturity) is not, it is possible, using the same formula, to calculate the yield to maturity. The method for determining the yield to maturity is like that used in Chapter 4 for calculating the internal rate of return. A calculator is all you need.

For conventional bonds, the amount the company borrows is the same as the principal or par value of the bond, net of issue costs, of course. This statement is not true for **zero-coupon bonds**. These bonds do not require any periodic coupon payments. Instead, the par value of the bond is much larger than the amount originally borrowed (the cost of the bond to the investor): essentially, interest is accrued during the bond's life and paid at the time the initial principal is repaid as a part of the final payment. Determining the return on these bonds is a simplification of the yield-to-maturity calculation, because there are no coupon payments. The following simplified formula would be used, where i is the yield to maturity:

$$\text{Price} = \frac{\text{PAR}}{(1 + i)^m} \qquad (2)$$

Using this formula, if a firm issues a zero-coupon bond today at a price of $275 per bond returning $1,000 in 10 years, the effective yield, or yield to maturity, is 13.8 percent.

Not all bonds retire the entire principal amount at the specified maturity date of the bond. Many bonds require periodic principal reductions called **sinking funds.** The purpose of these sinking funds is to reduce the risk that the borrower will not be able to repay the par amount. While the amount going into the sinking fund may be placed in a trust account to be held until the maturity date, this practice is not typical today. It is more likely that when the sinking-fund payments are due, the company will retire a portion of the issued bonds, even though they have not reached maturity. The way in which bonds are chosen to be purchased or retired before maturity is specified at the time the bonds are first issued by the company and noted in the indenture agreement. For publicly traded bonds, it is more common for the company simply to purchase some of the existing bonds in the market, reducing the total amount of bonds outstanding.

In addition to reducing the amount of bonds outstanding through sinking-fund requirements, companies may choose to retire the bonds before the specified maturity. This process is termed **refunding** or **calling** the bonds. Companies are especially interested in refunding if interest rates fall. They can call the existing bonds and then refinance with lower-cost debt. To protect against this possibility, many bonds have **call protection:** most bonds cannot be called for a specified period of time or may be called only if a stated premium is paid to the bondholders. Call provisions are also specified in the indenture agreement.

As a further protection for bondholders, the bond contract or indenture may limit the company in other ways. Frequently the company will be required to maintain certain levels of assets or to limit its total amount of debt. Often these restrictions or **covenants** are specified in the form of ratios—the kind we discussed in Chapter 1. If any of the bond covenants are violated, the bond is deemed to be in technical default and is immediately due for payment. It is up to the bondholder whether the company will be forced to pay or whether the covenant will be waived or rewritten.

The general risk to the borrower is reflected in the **bond rating.** Bond ratings are important because bonds with higher potential for default (lower ratings) must pay a higher coupon interest rate to compensate investors for the risk. Several organizations publish bond ratings; Moody's and Standard & Poor's (S&P) are the two most widely known. Based on these independent organizations' assessments of the general credit risk of the borrower, bonds are assigned a rating, with Aaa (Moody's) or AAA (S&P) indicating the most creditworthy bonds—those with the lowest risk of default. The ratings decrease through Aa/AA, and so on, to high-risk bonds rated Caa/CCC or below. High-risk bonds are called **high-yield bonds** or **junk bonds.**

A company may have several kinds of debt at the same time. The debt may have been issued by different lenders, at different times, and under different market conditions. The indenture agreement will stipulate the differences: the amount of debt, the coupon rate of interest, payment terms, specific assets on which the lenders may call in event of default, the priority in which the lenders' claims will be settled, and criteria the company must meet in order to have the debt without covenant revision. Debt that holds claim to specific assets in event of default is usually called **mortgage debt.**

Debt that, by contract, allows other debt precedence in event of default is called **subordinated debt.** Different issues of debt are listed separately on a company's balance sheet. The balance sheet and the accompanying notes will describe the major differences in each debt instrument. The bond guides by S&P and Moody's provide more detail for the potential investor or company analyst.

2. Equity Markets

There are two types of equity, **common stock** and **preferred stock.** Both of these equity instruments differ from debt in that there is no contractual obligation to provide any return to the investor. Dividends may be paid to equity investors, but only after all obligations have been paid to bondholders.

Preferred stockholders do have a preferential position over common stockholders, hence the name "preferred" stock. The dividend that is to be paid on preferred stock is a stated amount. This dividend must be paid before any dividend can be paid to the common shareholders. If the company has insufficient funds to pay the dividend, however, the dividend may be omitted without causing a default. Usually, any previously omitted preferred dividends must be paid before dividends can be paid to common shareholders. Preferred stock with this provision is termed **cumulative preferred.** However, because the dividend is stated, like an interest payment, preferred stock is similar to debt. Since the company has no obligation to pay the dividends, the preferred shareholder's return is uncertain. Thus it is also similar to equity.

After the required preferred dividend has been paid, the common shareholders may receive any dividend that management deems appropriate and the board of directors approves. Dividend income is the smaller part of the potential return. Most investors buy common stock with the expectation that the company will grow and prosper and the price of the stock will increase. The change in the market price of the stock is termed **capital appreciation** if the change is positive. In addition to owning the residual income of the company, common shareholders elect the board of directors.

Whereas changes in the prices of bonds are primarily related to interest rate changes, the determinants of changes in stock prices are not quite so easy to isolate. Factors that affect the general economy, such as interest rates and the rate of economic growth, affect stock prices. In addition, the market price may be affected by the industry outlook as well as by the prospects for the specific company. Whereas bond prices tend to move in unison with interest rate movements, at any given time some stock prices will be rising and some will be falling as company and industry prospects change.

The combination of dividend income and capital appreciation determines the return earned by equity investors. Since future return is uncertain at the time equity is purchased, investors use several methods to forecast their total return.

A continuing controversy surrounds the question of whether analysts can forecast market price movements. The argument rests on whether the capital markets are efficient. In an **efficient market,** all available information known to market participants is reflected in current market prices. Many managers and investors believe, however, that the market may not always be efficient and that an astute analyst can find information that has not been adequately evaluated by the market and reflected in the price. This situation might allow particular stocks or bonds to be overvalued or undervalued at a given time. While academic evidence shows that the capital markets are relatively efficient, several recent studies have suggested that there may be some inefficiencies that astute investors can exploit.

Regardless of whether inefficiencies exist in the capital markets, the manager's job is to manage his or her company in a way that increases the shareholders' value—to increase the market value of the company. In order to increase share price, the manager invests in projects or assets that yield a return larger than the projects' costs, including the cost of capital—a fair or required return for the risk being taken. To maximize the value of the company, the manager will want to maximize positive cash flows and minimize the required return.

To maximize cash flows, the manager will seek those investments for which the company has special product or market power, such as a patent, and can ward off the competition. To minimize the return required, managers will want to obtain capital at the lowest possible cost, using the two basic sources of capital, debt and equity. The proportion of debt the firm uses as part of its total capital is called **leverage.** Managers want to leverage the firm in such a way as to minimize the weighted-average cost of capital.[1]

All the manager has to sell to investors, lenders and shareholders, is the company. Whether capital providers make their investments in the form of debt, with the security of its contract and superior claims, or in the form of equity, with its residual benefits, really depends only on the investors' desires. The investors in an all-equity company will require the same return as would be required *on average* by the lenders and shareholders of a company that has some leverage: lenders require a smaller return than shareholders because they are more secure. The company's risk does not change, only the portion of the risk taken on by the various providers of capital. Thus the return required of the company depends on the risk being taken in the company's businesses, not on what the investors choose to call their investments. The cost of capital for a company is thus the same regardless

---

[1] While there are conflicting theories about the impact of leverage on the cost of capital, here we assume that moderate amounts of debt are desirable and will lower the average cost of capital. Only with high debt levels do shareholders begin to require added return for the risk of increased leverage.

of its capital structure, and managers can create value only through the investments the firm makes, not the way the company is financed.

The way a company finances itself, its **capital structure,** cannot create value unless a particular capital structure increases the company's cash flow or reduces its risk. The idea of reducing risk merely by changing capital structure assumes that there are investors who do not really understand the risk of their position and thus will allow the company to have money at a rate lower than is reasonable for the real risk. In efficient capital markets, this situation would seem to be unlikely—or at best, rare.

Lenders do appear to charge lower rates than do providers of equity capital, but they also take less risk than do shareholders because their claims supersede those of either common or preferred shareholders in case of bankruptcy. That is why lenders are willing to charge a somewhat lower rate than the implicit rate required for equity.[2] However, because lenders' claims take precedence over shareholders' claims, shareholders are put in a riskier position and thus should charge more. The lower cost of debt should therefore be balanced in the firm's overall capital cost by the higher cost of equity; the weighted-average cost of capital should not change unless either lenders or shareholders misprice their risk (charge too low a rate).

Although finding mispriced debt or equity is unlikely, it is still possible for leverage to increase a company's cash flows. The shareholders' required return is the company's cost of the equity; however, the lenders' required return is not the company's cost of debt. The U.S. Internal Revenue Service's tax code, and the tax codes of many other countries, allow the company to take the interest paid on debt as a tax-deductible expense, which effectively increases the company's net cash flow and decreases its cost of debt.

Exhibit 5–1 shows the differences in shareholders' profits and cash flows that would occur if Extra Company leveraged itself simply by replacing some of its equity with debt. As you can see, shareholders would gain $.14 if Extra replaced 30 percent of its equity with debt—that is, without making a single new investment. (Note that without the tax deduction for interest, earnings per share would not change as debt is added.) So, how much debt should a company use?

Exhibit 5–2 shows that while the capital providers' average required return is the same regardless of leverage, the cost of the company's capital declines as leverage increases, because of taxes. Thus, unless something like taxes interferes with the pricing of debt or equity, a company should leverage as much as possible.

Since companies do not have extremely high degrees of leverage, something else is probably affecting the cost of debt or equity, or both. Some believe that managers prefer to have little debt because lenders have con-

---

[2] In fact, lenders may establish their own priorities. For instance, the claims on the company by holders of debentures (a form of debt) take precedence over the claims of holders of subordinated debentures.

EXHIBIT 5–1   Extra Company Value with Varying Capital Structure
(in thousands except per share data)

	Without Debt	*With 30% Debt*
Total capital	$100	$100
Debt	$ 0	$ 30
Interest rate	NA	10%
Number of shares	10	7
Book value per share	$ 10	$ 10
Revenues	$100	$100
Costs	(80)	(80)
Depreciation	(5)	(5)
Interest	0	(3)
Profit before tax	15	12
Taxes (34%)	(5)	(4)
Profit after tax	10	8
Depreciation	5	5
New property, plant, and equipment	(5)	(5)
Added working capital	0	0
Cash flow	$ 10	$ 8
Profit per share	$1.00	$1.14
Cash flow per share	$1.00	$1.14

NA = not applicable.

tracts and thus can have more impact on the company. Others believe that, at some level of debt, lenders' and shareholders' concerns about bankruptcy increase their required returns. As shown in Exhibit 5–3, it is at this point that capital providers increase the return they require, and the average cost of capital increases from what it otherwise would have been. The point at which the cost of capital begins to rise is called the **optimal capital structure.** It is also the point at which the value of the company is at its highest. Just how management goes about choosing the amount of leverage it will use will be discussed in Chapter 7. For determining the cost of capital, we will assume an appropriate capital structure has been chosen.

To calculate the weighted-average cost of capital, analysts need three basic pieces of information:[3]

1. The marginal after-tax cost of debt.

2. The marginal cost of equity.

3. The proportions of debt and equity expected to be used to finance the company.

---

[3] In making investment decisions, we are investing new or marginal funds into projects. These new funds may come from the shareholders, in the form of retained profits or new issues of common stock, or from newly placed debt.

EXHIBIT 5-2 Tax Impact on Capital Costs

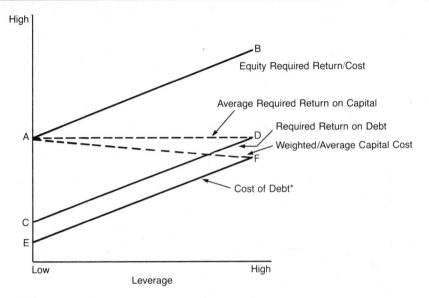

*Debt cost = Debt required return × (1 − Tax rate)

EXHIBIT 5-3 Required Return and Capital Cost with and without Bankruptcy Considerations

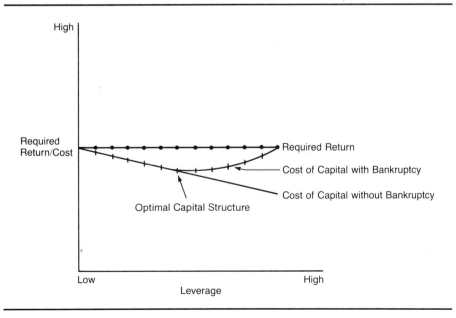

This chapter will discuss the means of calculating each of these three factors. Note that because we are concerned about evaluating investments that can be but have not yet been made, we use in these evaluations the *expected* cash costs and benefits, the expected or **marginal costs** of debt and equity and capital structure. We are evaluating not the past but the value of future actions. Every step requires the analyst's judgment as well as mathematical skill.

II. DETERMINING THE COST OF DEBT

Most firms use debt to finance a portion of their assets. As shown in Exhibit 5–4, over the past 18 years the proportion of debt used by U.S. firms has risen dramatically.

Exhibit 5–5 shows the market rates of interest during the last 15 years on publicly traded debt of varying qualities. Note that the interest rate on the best quality corporate debt is higher than that on government debt of the same maturity.

Just as the reliability of the borrower affects the interest rate, so does the length of time the borrower wishes to use the principal. Exhibit 5–6 shows the market rate of interest on debt of the same quality but different maturities at several points in time. The normal line is upward-sloping like that shown for June 1, 1980. An upward slope is normal because lenders

EXHIBIT 5–4   Annual Growth of Capital Structure and Its Composition
(all nonfinancial business corporations)

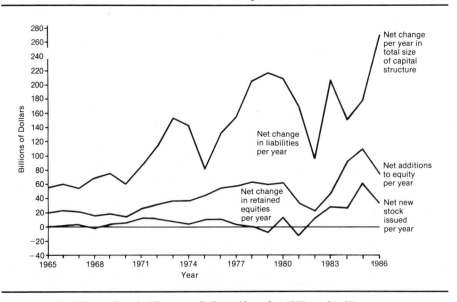

SOURCE: Federal Reserve Board of Governors Bulletin, November 1987, pp. 34–35.

EXHIBIT 5–5   Interest Rates for Debt of Different Qualities

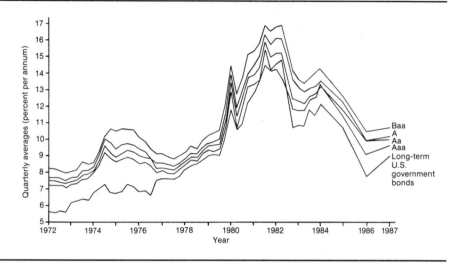

SOURCES: *Moody's Bond Record,* August 1981–87, for corporate yields; Board of Governors, Federal Reserve System, *Federal Reserve Bulletin,* 1976–87, for U.S. government bond yields.

who provide capital for longer times require, quite logically, more return. At some points in time, this upward-sloping curve, the **yield curve,** does not exist. This has been particularly true in periods of high inflation. For instance, during the 1970s, the relationship between the market rate of interest and debt of different maturities was sometimes perverse. Exhibit 5–6 shows two typical and two inverse (the March 1, 1981, and December 1, 1981) yield curves.

In addition to interest payments, a number of special features may be required by the lender. For example, specific assets may be pledged to support the loan; the lender may require seniority over others' claims in the case of bankruptcy; or the loan may be convertible into common or preferred stock under certain conditions. Each feature offers the lender different levels of protection from risk and thus carries a somewhat different cost, which is reflected in the interest rate.

The pre-tax cost of debt is the ratio of the interest rate to the principal amount of the debt. Since interest payments are tax deductible, we calculate all capital costs on an after-tax basis. To determine the after-tax cost of debt, this ratio is multiplied by one minus the corporate tax rate. In other words,

$$R_d = \frac{CP}{PAR} (1 - t) \tag{3}$$

where

$$R_d = \text{After-tax cost of debt}$$
$$CP = \text{Coupon, interest, payment}$$
$$PAR = \text{Principal received by the company}$$
$$t = \text{Corporate tax rate}$$

EXHIBIT 5–6   Interest Rates for Debt of Different Maturities

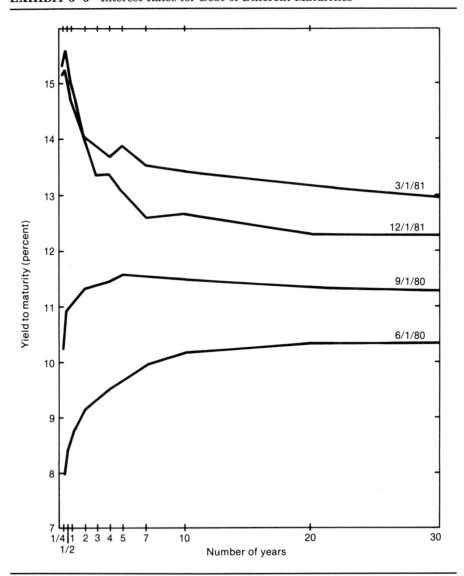

SOURCE: Salomon Bros., *An Analytical Record of Yields and Yield Spreads,* May 1981.

For example, if Consumer, Inc., wanted to borrow $3.5 million, the lender expected interest of $345,000 per year, and Consumer had a corporate tax rate of 34 percent, the after-tax cost of this debt would be calculated as follows:

$$R_d = \frac{\$345,000}{\$3,500,000} (1 - .34)$$

$$= .0986 (1 - .34)$$

$$= .065 \text{ or } 6.5\%$$

For purposes of investment analyses, the after-tax cost of debt should not be based on the debt the firm has already borrowed. That debt has already been used by the firm to finance assets currently in use. The interest payments Consumer, Inc., is currently making are not relevant to future investment decisions. Only costs of the new, marginal, funds are relevant.

Calculating the marginal cost of debt is simple enough if the firm is currently negotiating a loan. How does the analyst estimate the marginal cost of debt if the firm is not negotiating with lenders for debt funds?

There are several ways in which the analyst can obtain the needed estimates. First, by looking at rates charged other firms of the same risk or quality, the analyst can determine the current rate of interest for comparable firms. For a company like Consumer, Inc., the analyst might look at the yield on publicly traded debt issued by such fast-food firms as Wendy's or McDonald's.

A second approach is to examine the cost of a company's publicly traded debt, its bonds. Bonds traded in the public markets are often sold at a price that is different from the price at which they were originally sold by the issuing firm. The current yield to maturity, described earlier in this chapter, can then be used to obtain an estimate of the cost of issuing new debt.

The analyst may decide that the company will be issuing several different kinds of debt. Some debt may be placed with banks or insurance companies, and other debt may be sold to the public. Each kind of debt will have different features—maturity, coupon, and security—and thus different interest rates. The marginal debt cost is an average of the costs of several kinds of debt used by the company. Most analysts exclude short-term (current) debt from calculation of the marginal cost of debt, primarily because it will be repaid within one year. Recently, however, analysts have reconsidered the exclusion of short-term debt. Short-term financing has become an important source of funds for many firms, either because borrowers wait for long-term rates to drop or because lenders prefer frequent rate revisions. The best rule for an analyst to follow in dealing with short-term debt is to exclude it if it is being used to supply temporary needs (such as seasonal inventory) but to include it and its cost if the short-term funds represent permanent financing for the firm's assets.

III. DETERMINING THE COST OF EQUITY

Shareholders, like other lenders, expect to earn a return on the funds they provide—a return that compensates them for both the time that the funds are made available to the firm and the risk that the firm will not provide the expected return. Returns for common stock, however, come from quite a different source than returns from debt. Returns on common stock come from the dividends the common shareholder receives over the term of his or her investment in the firm and from any gains realized by the investor on the sale of the stock, resulting from increases in its market price.

How do analysts estimate the returns shareholders will require? If the firm were owned by a single shareholder or a small group of shareholders, the analyst could simply ask them, "What return do you expect this firm to earn on your behalf?" If the shareholder replied, "Fifteen percent would satisfy me; I would not want to buy a larger share of the firm, nor would I want to sell the ownership position I already have," the analyst would know that the shareholder's required return—the cost of equity—was 15 percent. However, firms whose stock is bought and sold on the stock exchange do not have such limited ownership. As a result, we must find a way to estimate the return required by a large number of dispersed shareholders.

There are two categories of methods for estimating the cost of equity. The first category places a value on shareholders' returns. Since part of the value of a shareholder's stock in the firm is created by reinvested earnings (retained earnings), analysts often estimate the cost of equity by evaluating the earnings of the firm. The second group of approaches could be called capital-market estimations. Because investors require higher returns for riskier securities, capital-market methods categorize all securities by risk and then estimate the cost of equity according to the stock's risk.

1. Cash Flow Valuation: The Dividend Discount Method

To determine the fair value of a share of common stock, its price (MP_0), we must first forecast the cash flows the investor will receive now and in the future. One simple way analysts estimate the investor's future cash flows is to look to the company's expected annual earnings per share (EPS_1) and discount them at the investor's required return (R_e):

$$MP_0 = \frac{EPS_1}{R_e} \tag{4}$$

By simply rearranging this formula, using the current market price and earnings per share, we can determine the investor's required return:

$$R_e = \frac{EPS_1}{MP_0} \tag{5}$$

or

$$R_e = \frac{1}{MP_0 / EPS_1} \tag{6}$$

$$= \frac{1}{Price/earnings\ ratio}$$

We will use this approach to estimate the cost of equity for Consumer, Inc.

Consumer's current stock price is $15 per share, and the earnings estimated for the next 12 months are $1.80 per share. Consumer's cost of equity is calculated as follows:

$$R_e = \frac{\$1.80}{\$15.00}$$

$$= .12\ or\ 12\%$$

We do not adjust the equity cost for taxes because common stock dividends are not tax deductible by the company and are therefore already an after-tax cost. Using formula (6), we find the cost of equity would be the same: $1/(\$15.00/\$1.80) = 1/8.3 = .12$ or 12 percent.

By itself, however, equation (5) is actually only a rough measure of the cost of equity. To use this equation, we must assume that Consumer, Inc. pays 100 percent of its earnings to shareholders—or that if it does reinvest any funds, they do not create any value for the shareholders. In other words, the equation assumes that the net present value of all Consumer's investments is zero. Suppose for a moment that these assumptions are valid in this case: Consumer, Inc., will pay out all of its earnings. In this circumstance, we can rephrase equations (4) and (5) by substituting the next year's dividends (D_1) for the next year's earnings per share. In other words,

$$MP_0 = \frac{EPS_1}{R_e} = \frac{D_1}{R_e} \tag{7}$$

or

$$R_e = \frac{EPS_1}{MP_0} = \frac{D_1}{MP_0} \tag{8}$$

Only for the most mature companies in stable, highly competitive industries, however, are these formulas anything more than an approximation of what an investor expects. For companies in declining industries, investors may believe that today's earnings and dividends are higher than they will be in the future. For new companies in growing markets, present earnings and dividends often are less than investors expect to gain in the future. When a portion of the company's earnings will be reinvested in the firm and these investments will create value—that is, the firm will grow in value over time—formulas (4) through (8) are much too simplistic.

To include the expectation of growth in value, we could use the following formula:

$$MP_0 = \frac{D_1}{(1 + R_e)} + \frac{D_1(1 + g)}{(1 + R_e)^2} + \frac{D_2(1 + g)}{(1 + R_e)^3} + \ldots + \frac{D_{n-1}(1 + g)}{(1 + R_e)^n} \quad (9)$$

The growth rate, g, is the rate at which dividends are expected to grow each year. To estimate shareholders' required return, we must forecast the dividends the company will pay from now on. This process is tedious; but it can be cut short for a firm that is growing at a constant rate, which is often the case with mature firms. We can take this expected growth into account quite easily be rewriting equation (9) in the following way:

$$MP_0 = \frac{D_1}{R_e - g} \quad (10)$$

or

$$R_e = \frac{D_1}{P_0} + g \quad (11)$$

Equations (10) and (11) are versions of what is known as the **dividend discount** or **dividend growth model,** a widely used and accepted method for valuing a firm's shares.

Let's apply the dividend discount model to Consumer, Inc. The expected dividend for the next year (D_1) is $0.40, the market price is $15 per share, and the firm is paying out 30 percent of its earnings in dividends:

$$R_e = \frac{\$0.40}{\$15.00} + g$$

$$R_e = 2.7\% + g$$

The problem for the analyst now is to determine g—that is, to determine the growth that shareholders expect from the 70 percent of earnings Consumer is retaining and investing in the business.

There are several ways to estimate expected growth. One is to use the firm's average historic rate of growth. Another, superior, method is to forecast the expected growth. Forecasting expected growth in dividends requires that the analyst know the company and its prospects quite well. Forecasts for market growth, market share, and product prices, and for marketing, production, and administrative costs must also be made. Analysts looking for a shortcut often turn to the sustainable rate of growth, described in Chapter 1, to make their first growth estimate:

$$g = (1 - DPO) \times (ROE) \quad (12)$$

where

ROE = Expected return on equity
DPO = Percentage of earnings expected to be paid out as dividends

While there are other ways to estimate future growth, this method forces the analyst to evaluate the effects of new investments in the firm. If Consumer, Inc., continued to pay out 30 percent of its earnings as dividends and expected its return on equity to maintain the historic 20 percent rate, we could calculate Consumer's sustainable growth and an estimate of the shareholders' expected growth by using equation (12) as follows:

$$g = (1 - .30) \times (.20)$$
$$= .14 \text{ or } 14\%$$

With this growth rate, Consumer's cost of equity would be calculated thus:

$$R_e = \frac{\$0.40}{\$15.00} + .14$$

$$= .167 \text{ or } 16.7\%$$

Remember that the sustainable rate of growth will be the actual growth rate *only* if the company maintains its current ratios of return on equity (the current return on sales, asset efficiency, and leverage) and dividend payout. For a company that is likely to grow at a rate that is more or less than its sustainable growth rate, the analyst must make specific forecasts for the future.

There are a number of problems with the simple dividend discount model shown in equation (11). It cannot be used in the following circumstances:

1. The firm pays no dividends.
2. The expected growth rate is higher than the discount rate.
3. The expected growth rate is not constant.

Many firms do not pay dividends and do not have constant growth rates. For such firms, other methods of calculating the cost of equity are available. Many of these methods draw upon rearranged and expanded versions of the dividend discount model, as shown below.

Our simple, constant growth model, equation (10), is:

$$MP_0 = \frac{D_1}{R_e - g}$$

Variations are:

$$MP_0 = \frac{D_1}{(1 + R_e)^1} + \frac{D_2}{(1 + R_e)^2} + \ldots + \frac{D_n}{(1 + R_e)^n} \qquad (13)$$

$$MP_0 = \frac{D_1}{(1 + R_e)^1} + \frac{D_2}{(1 + R_e)^2} + \ldots + \frac{D_n}{(R_e - g)} \qquad (14)$$

$$MP_0 = \frac{D_1}{(1 + R_e)^1} + \frac{D_2}{(1 + R_e)^2} + \ldots + \frac{MP_n}{(1 + R_e)^n} \qquad (15)$$

These models are all versions of equation (9) and can be very useful in different circumstances. Equation (13), for instance, allows the analyst to forecast the dividend the firm is expected to pay each year in the future.[4] For firms that are not growing at a constant rate, this version of the model allows the analyst to avoid the use of a constant rate of growth—a rate needed when equation (10) is used. It is, however, quite difficult to forecast dividends into the distant future.

Equation (14) affords the analyst the best features of equations (9) and (10). To use equation (14), the analyst explicitly forecasts dividends for a short time into the future, perhaps until the firm has matured and can be expected to grow at a more normal and constant rate. The analyst then uses the constant growth formula (10) to account for all dividends beyond that point. This method is often used by investment analysts to value the common stocks they follow. Typically, their year-by-year forecast of dividends is for 5 to 10 years.

Finally, equation (15) can be used by assuming the stock is held for a period of time and then sold. The analyst forecasts year-by-year dividends for several years and the anticipated price for which the stock will be sold in the future. That price, of course, will reflect the value the new buyer places on dividends he or she will receive once the transfer is made. However, many analysts find it easier to forecast a price for which the stock can be sold at a later date than to forecast constant growth rates or dividends year-by-year over a long period.

The many versions of equation (9) were presented not to confuse the reader but to give the financial analyst, confronted with different companies in different situations and with various kinds of data, a variety of useful tools. One method will not work in every circumstance.

2. Capital-Market Estimations: Risk-Premium Methods

The dividend discount model, as we have seen, uses dividend forecasts and the current stock price to calculate the cost of equity for the firm. At times, however, estimating earnings or dividends may be difficult. An analyst can estimate the cost of equity according to the security's risk by comparing it with other investments in the marketplace. The marketplace is the great arbitrager of risk and return. This approach, called **capital-market estimation,** assumes that investors require additional return to

---

[4] We could use yet another version of the dividend discount method. Instead of using dividends, we would use free cash flow—cash not retained and reinvested in the business: Free cash flow = Revenues − Costs − Investment + Noncash charges (e.g., depreciation). Simply replace the estimated dividends with free cash flow. This is especially useful in evaluating firms that pay out dividends in excess of revenues—dividends that are not really funds available to shareholders but a return of capital. This formula assumes, of course, that investors like both current dividends and growth equally and discount them at the same rate.

compensate them for added risk. This extra return is known as the **risk premium.** The concept can be expressed mathematically thus:

$$R_e = R_f + R_p \qquad (16)$$

where

R_e = The total return investors require

R_f = The return received on a hypothetical risk-free security

R_p = The risk premium

Several different ways of using this simple concept to estimate the cost of equity have been developed. We will discuss two methods: the stock-bond yield-spread method, and the capital asset pricing model.

The stock-bond yield-spread method.   This simple model estimates the cost of equity by means of two key variables: (1) the firm's marginal pre-tax cost of debt and (2) the historical difference between the firm's costs of debt and equity. Expressed mathematically,

$$R_e = R_d + (\dot{R}_e - \dot{R}_d) \qquad (17)$$

where

R_e = The required return on equity

R_d = The required return (pre-tax) on debt (pre-tax; for instance, the yield to maturity on the firm's bonds)

$\cdot$ = Indicates historic data

Let us use this formula to calculate Consumer's cost of equity. If the historic equity/debt cost difference (the spread) has been 6 percent and the company's marginal pre-tax cost of debt is 9.9 percent, we can calculate Consumer's cost of equity in this way:

$$
\begin{aligned}
R_e &= R_d + (\dot{R}_e - \dot{R}_d) \\
&= 9.9\% + 6.0\% \\
&= 15.9\%
\end{aligned}
$$

This percentage is 0.8 percent below the 16.7 percent cost of equity we calculated with the dividend discount model. The two methods usually do not yield the same results. If they do not, the difference in results may be because the difference between the yields of stocks and bonds is not always constant. Exhibit 5–7 shows annual returns on Standard & Poor's 500 Index and a high-grade corporate bond index. This exhibit shows that the differences between stock and bond returns are not as constant as the stock-bond yield-spread method implies. This approach provides a quick estimate, but should not be used unless its results are to be verified by another method.

EXHIBIT 5–7   Total Realized Returns on Common Stocks and Corporate Bonds

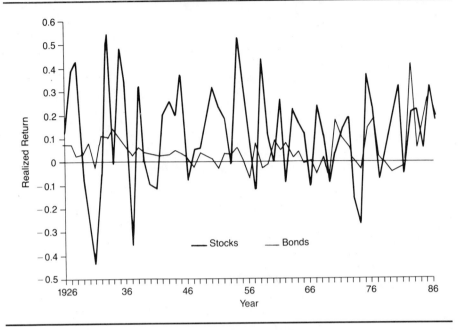

SOURCE: Ibbotson Assoc., *Stocks, Bonds, Bills, and Inflation* 1988 Yearbook.

The capital asset pricing model.   The simple risk-premium model described by equation (16) could be rewritten to include a term denoting the difference between the average risk of all securities in the market and the risk of one firm's security. We would write the new equation thus:

$$R_{ej} = R_f + x_j(R_m - R_f) \qquad (18)$$

where

$$_j = \text{A term to denote a particular company}$$
$$x = \text{A measure of the risk for a stock}$$
$$R_m = \text{The return required on an asset of average risk}$$
$$R_f = \text{The return required on a hypothetical risk-free security}$$

This formula could also be called the **relative risk-premium model** because it contains a factor, x_j, to indicate the relative risk of the particular security. Notice that in this formula, only x_j changes; all other factors remain constant from company to company.

The capital asset pricing model is a very intriguing adaptation of this basic relative risk-premium approach. The model suggests that there is a relationship between risk and return; in fact, the higher the risk, the higher the expected return. Exhibit 5–8 depicts this relationship. Since investors

EXHIBIT 5–7   (*concluded*) Spread between Common Stock and Bond Returns

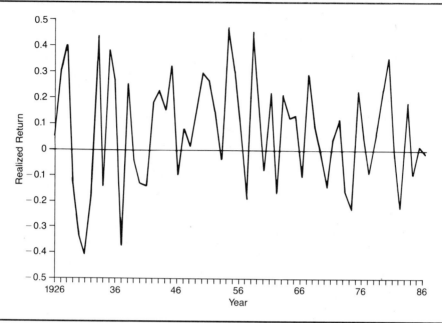

require a return for illiquidity, the line starts at R_f, the return required from a riskless security. The solid line represents the return required at each level of risk. This risk/return concept seems quite realistic: investors do expect greater rewards for taking greater risks, and the expected return for the common stock of any company is relative to its risk. However, in order to use this method, we must define and measure risk.

The capital asset pricing model (CAPM) is an attempt to make the relative risk-premium model usable. In the CAPM, risk is defined as the covariance of a stock's returns with those of an asset of average risk. This definition is a bit different from the usual definition of risk as total variability. Covariance rests on a simple idea: it is not the total variability of the returns of each security that is important to the investor. Instead, what is important is how each security's variability contributes to the total variability of an investor's portfolio. We could, for instance, place a security with cyclical returns (such as an automobile company's common stock) with a security whose returns are countercyclical (such as an automobile replacement-parts manufacturer's common stock). As shown in Exhibit 5–9, when the auto manufacturer is doing well, the replacement-parts manufacturer is experiencing a slump. The reverse is also true: Replacement parts sell when people defer new-car purchases. As you can see, returns from the portfolio containing both stocks would be quite stable: that is, they

EXHIBIT 5–8   Risk/Return Trade-Off

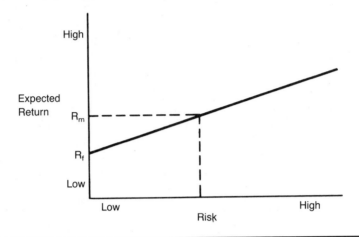

would not be very risky according to the CAPM's definition of risk even though the returns from each are quite risky. Note our optimism: we show the returns for both the companies growing, not diminishing, over time.

The only differences between the relative risk-premium formula (18) and the CAPM is that the CAPM defines risk as the covariability of stock returns. According to the CAPM,

$$R_{ej} = R_f + \beta_j (R_m - R_f) \tag{19}$$

where

β_j = Beta, a measure of the covariance between the returns (dividends plus capital gains) of the market average and those of the company's stock. All other factors as defined for equation (18).

To estimate Consumer's cost of equity based on the CAPM approach, we must estimate the risk-free rate of return, the expected return on the average asset, and the covariability of the returns on Consumer's stock with those on the average asset.[5] To use the CAPM, we need forecasts for R_f, R_m, and β. To demonstrate how the analyst might use the model, we will use 10.2 percent as the current yield on a 10-year U.S. Treasury for R_f; and 14.5 percent, a forecast of the return for the Standard & Poor's 500 Index as estimated by a group of financial analysts, for R_m and for the covariability, or risk, of Consumer's returns, β_j, we will use 1.5, an estimate based on the

---

[5] Considerable controversy surrounds the theory and use of the CAPM. The reader should become familiar with the problems before becoming a frequent user. Since these problems are lengthy and complex, they are beyond the scope of this book. See, for instance, Harrington (1987) for a description of the uses of and problems with the CAPM.

EXHIBIT 5–9   Two-Asset Portfolio Risk

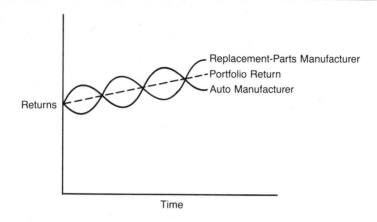

historical relationship of Consumer's returns with those of the Standard & Poor's 500 Index.[6] Using these estimates, we can calculate Consumer's cost of equity thus:

$$R_{ej} = R_f + \beta_j (R_m - R_f)$$
$$= 10.2 + 1.5 (14.5 - 10.2)$$
$$= 16.7\%$$

While in this case the CAPM provides a result that is quite close to those of other methods, that is not always true. The analyst is wise to use several approaches to corroborate any cost-of-equity estimate.

Each of these models requires considerable judgment on the part of the analyst. If the results are approximately the same, the analyst can have more confidence in the estimate. However, if each method results in a very different cost of equity, the analyst must think carefully about the source of the variations. The analyst's choice of data could be inconsistent from

---

[6] The typical method of estimating a beta is to use a version of the simple linear regression and the monthly total rates of return for the stock and for an index like the S&P 500:

$$R_j - R_f = \alpha_j + \beta_j(R_m - R_f) + \epsilon_j$$

where

α = The intercept of the linear regression
β = The slope of the line
ϵ = The errors that occur because of a nonperfect
        fit of the line to the data
j = The designated stock or portfolio

As any financial analyst knows, however, using history as a predictor for the future is dangerous. The danger is no less here than elsewhere.

model to model; the forecasts could be optimistic or pessimistic; or the share-holder's concept of future returns could be quite different from that of the analyst. After careful execution of each model, the analyst must corroborate the forecasts, remembering that the purpose of all forecasts and calculations is to capture the shareholder's expectations of future returns, not the analyst's or management's hopes and beliefs.

3. Other Concerns in Determining Equity Costs

New equity issues.   When a firm issues new equity, it incurs additional expenses that we have not yet discussed. The firm issuing new equity must register the issue with the Securities and Exchange Commission, and the firm must rely on the advice of lawyers, accountants, and underwriters to do so. In addition to registering the stock, the underwriter usually buys the issue from the firm, thus guaranteeing its sale. The underwriter then resells the stock to the public—for a fee.[7] The average cost of these services can range from 4 to 15 percent of the equity issue, depending on the size of the company, the amount of stock to be issued, and the underwriter's confidence that the firm's stock will sell quickly.

Using the dividend discount method, equation (11), we can calculate the cost of newly issued equity by using the following equation. For Consumer, Inc., a small regional company, a new issue would be more expensive than the average stock issue. Let us assume that new issue costs, N, would be 8 percent for Consumer. We can then calculate the cost of newly issued equity as follows:

$$R_{ej} = \frac{D_1}{MP_0(1 - N)} + g \qquad (20)$$

$$= \frac{\$0.40}{\$15.00(1 - .08)} + 14.0\%$$

$$= \frac{\$0.40}{\$13.80} + 14.0\%$$

$$= 2.9\% + 14.0\%$$

$$= 16.9\%$$

To maintain the value of Consumer, Inc., the newly issued equity funds would have to be invested at a slightly higher return than would retained earnings, because newly issued common stock has the additional cost of issuance to be covered.

---

[7] For a smaller fee, the underwriter may make a "best effort" to sell the stocks or bonds. In a "best-effort" sale, the underwriter does not guarantee the sale of the securities.

Cost of retained earnings.   Each year a firm can generate net income after taxes and dividends (retained earnings). Managers may use these funds to increase the firm's assets or to reduce its debt, or the funds may be held temporarily in cash or marketable securities. Some managers consider retained earnings to be "free" funds, but that is certainly not true from the stockholders' point of view. If managers had returned the funds to the stockholders, they could have invested the funds themselves. Thus retained earnings have a cost—the cost of the opportunity shareholders lose when funds are retained by the firm.

In exchange for this **opportunity cost**, stockholders expect retained earnings to create value for them. So the cost of retaining earnings is the cost of equity.

Preferred stock.   Preferred stock presents additional problems because preferred stock is a cross between debt and equity. Like debt, preferred stock offers a fixed payment—fixed dividends. In bankruptcy, preferred shareholders take precedence over common shareholders. However, if preferred dividends are not paid, the firm cannot be forced into bankruptcy, as it may be if it fails to pay the interest on debt. For investors, owning preferred equity is somewhat less risky than holding common stock and more risky than being a lender. Preferred stock is also unlike debt in that the firm does not repay the principal amount.

Keeping these things in mind, we can calculate the cost of preferred stock as follows:

$$R_p = \frac{PD}{PP_0} \tag{21}$$

where

$$PD = \text{Preferred dividend}$$
$$PP_0 = \text{Preferred stock price}$$
$$R_p = \text{The cost or return required on preferred stock}$$

Consumer, Inc., had issued a very small amount of preferred stock when it was founded. It was subsequently repurchased by the firm. At the time of repurchase, the dividend was $1.30 per share per year and the market price was $9.25 per share. The cost of preferred at the time it was retired was:

$$R_p = \frac{\$1.30}{\$9.25}$$
$$= .141 \text{ or } 14.1\%$$

Once again, there is no tax adjustment because preferred dividends are not a tax-deductible expense. However, because Consumer no longer has preferred stock, and management does not expect to issue more in the future, the marginal cost of preferred stock is not relevant in estimating Consumer's marginal cost of capital.

IV. CALCULATING THE WEIGHTED-AVERAGE COST OF CAPITAL

Our intention in this chapter is to calculate the weighted-average cost of new or marginal capital. A weighted average can be calculated by multiplying the costs of debt and equity by their respective portions to be raised by the firm. In other words,

$$R_{wacc} = R_d \frac{D}{V} + R_e \frac{E}{V} \qquad (22)$$

where

R_{wacc} = Weighted-average cost of capital
D = Amount of debt expected in the firm's capital structure
E = Amount of equity expected in the firm's capital structure
V = D + E, the value of the firm's capital
R_d = Marginal after-tax cost of debt
R_e = Marginal cost of equity

Thus far we have estimated R_d (7.2%) and R_e (approximately 16.7%) for Consumer, Inc., but we have not yet estimated the proportions of debt and equity used by the firm.

While calculating the amounts of debt and equity used to finance the firm might appear to be quite simple, it is, like most of the analyst's jobs, not completely straightforward. The capital structure we want to use in calculating the weighted-average cost of capital is what investors believe will be the way funds are raised by the company in the future. It is the company's marginal or "target" capital structure—that structure wherein sufficient capital is raised to finance all value-creating investments. For some firms, the target capital structure is one in which the cost of capital is at its minimum. For other firms, the marginal capital structure reflects managers' decision to keep the leverage within a certain range.

For simplicity, let's assume for a moment that Consumer, Inc.'s current book-value capital structure is the same as its market-value and target capital structures. The **book-value** capital structure is the percentage of debt and equity currently financing the assets of the firm. It can be calculated directly from the balance sheet. The **market-value** capital structure is calculated by taking the current market values of the company's debt and equity and recalculating the same percentages. In Consumer's book-value capital structure, 65 percent of the capital is equity and 35 percent is debt. We will also assume that the managers expect to have $250,000 in new retained earnings for the year. Since 65 percent of the capital structure is equity, the maximum funds available for investment are $384,000 ($250,000/

EXHIBIT 5–10   Weighted-Average Cost of Capital (up to $384,000)

(1) Component	(2) Proportion	(3) Cost	(4) (2) × (3)
Debt (taxes = 34%)	35%	6.5%	2.3%
Equity:			
Retained earnings	65	16.7	10.9
New common equity	0	16.9	0
Weighted-average cost of capital			13.2%

EXHIBIT 5–11   Weighted-Average Cost of New Capital ($1 million budget)

(1) Component	(2) Proportion	(3) Cost	(4) (2) × (3)
Debt (taxes = 34%)	35%	6.5%	2.3%
Equity:			
Retained earnings ($250,000)	25	16.7	4.2
New common equity	40	16.9	6.8
Weighted-average cost of capital			13.3%

.65) unless new equity is issued. If the Consumer management plans capital expenditures of no more than $384,615, then the cost of capital will be 13.2 percent, as shown in Exhibit 5–10.

If Consumer needs more than $384,000 to finance its capital budget and keep the capital structure at the targeted proportion of 65 percent equity, it will have to resort to newly issued stock to finance an increasing portion of the needs. Thus, if the budget is $1 million, because of the costs of issuing new equity, the cost of capital will be slightly higher, 13.3 percent, as shown in Exhibit 5–11. Similar changes would have to be made whenever Consumer, Inc., fully exploited any source of debt or equity and resorted to the next available, but more expensive, source.

We made this example especially easy by assuming that the book value (the balance sheet value), the market value (the balance sheet value recalculated using the market values of securities), and management's target capital structure were all the same. If they were not, we might use the current market value to provide a clue to investors' expectations, or we might turn to statements made by management about its future intentions.[8]

---

[8] While many firms use their book-value structure as the target, as analysts we are concerned with the market value of the marginal capital raised. If the target is the same as the book-value capital structure, the market value of the capital raised will be in the same proportions as the book value, regardless of the market value of the capital already in use by the firm.

It is not appropriate to use either book value or market value if they differ from the target for the funds being raised.

Once again, we have a deceptively simple calculation. A firm in need of capital usually does not simultaneously issue debt and equity securities just to fit its target capital structure. Rather, the firm would issue first one and then the other, depending on prices and availability in the capital markets. Over time, however, the firm would issue sufficient debt and equity to meet its targeted capital structure. Thus, while the actual capital raised in a single period might be all equity and its cost higher than average, we would still use the weighted-average cost of capital as the return required for any project that is of the same risk as the firm. For investments where the risk is not equal to that of the firm, adjustments such as those described in Chapter 4 would be necessary.

V. SUMMARY

In estimating the weighted-average cost of marginal capital, the analyst's judgment is required again and again. The cost of equity is particularly elusive: we are trying to estimate what investors expect from owning a share of our firm. While we have several approaches that will help the analyst make the estimate, each must be used thoughtfully. Furthermore, as conditions in the world and domestic economies change, the capital markets react, and investors' expectations change—sometimes quite rapidly. When these changes occur, the firm itself may change—new projects may be announced, and old projects succeed or fail. Once again investors' expectations will change, and so will their required return on equity. The analyst must not only estimate an elusive figure but do so at the same time that figure is changing. Skill and judgment take the financial analyst's job beyond the mechanical and the routine, making it a continual challenge.

SELECTED REFERENCES

For general information about the stock and bond markets, see:
Fogler, H. Russell, Frank Fabozzi, and Diana Harrington. *Analyzing the Stock Market.* 2d ed. Chicago: Probus Publishing, 1988.

Reilly, Frank, *Investments.* 2d ed. Hinsdale, Ill.: Dryden Press, 1987.

Sharpe, William F. *Investments.* 3d ed. Englewood Cliffs, N.J.: Prentice-Hall, 1985.

For further explanations of the process and problems in calculating the costs of debt and equity, see:
Brealey, Richard, and Stewart Myers. *Principles of Corporate Finance.* 2d ed. New York: McGraw-Hill, 1984, chap. 9.

Solomon, Ezra, and John J. Pringle. *An Introduction to Financial Management.* 2d ed. Santa Monica, Cal.: Goodyear Publishing, 1980.

Weston, J. F., and E. F. Brigham. *Essentials of Managerial Finance.* 8th ed. Hinsdale, Ill.: Dryden Press, 1988, chap. 17.

For those with a further interest in the capital asset pricing model and discounted cash flow methods of equity valuation, see:

Brealey, Richard, and Stewart Myers. *Principles of Corporate Finance.* 3d ed. New York: McGraw-Hill, 1988, chaps. 4 and 8.

Harrington, Diana R. *Modern Portfolio Theory, The Capital Asset Pricing Model and Arbitrage Pricing Theory: A Users Guide.* 2d ed. Englewood Cliffs, N.J.: Prentice-Hall, 1987.

Ross, Stephen, and R. W. Westerfield. *Corporate Finance,* St. Louis, Mo.: Times Mirror/Mosby, 1988, chaps. 7–9.

For historic data from the stock and bond markets and information about comparable firms, see:

Dun & Bradstreet, *Key Business Ratios.*

Ibbotson Associates. *Stocks, Bonds, Bills and Inflation,* 1988 Yearbook.

Robert Morris Associates, *Annual Statement Studies.*

Arnold Bernhard & Co., Inc., *Value Line Investment Survey.*

For information about the effects of different financing instruments on the cost of capital, see:

Smith, Clifford W. "Raising Capital: Theory and Evidence." *Midland Corporate Finance Journal,* Spring 1986, pp. 6–22.

STUDY QUESTIONS

1. Bakelite Company was a commercial bakery, specializing in biscuit making, located in rural Ohio. Recent substantial declines in grain prices had resulted in significant raw material savings. Since prices did not need to be cut—Bakelite was already at the low-priced end of the market—cash reserves had built up well beyond historical levels. This wealth of cash spurred management, with the support of the board, to consider some capital investments they had long deferred. The various division heads were asked to propose capital investments to Carl Borg, vice president for finance. Mr. Borg was given the job of evaluating the projects and making recommendations to the board. Because it had been years since Bakelite made any really significant investments, Mr. Borg was concerned about choosing the right ones. To get some advice about making these decisions, he called an old college friend, Jane Wilson, now a finance professor at a nearby university. Professor Wilson said that since Mr. Borg already had cash flow forecasts from the divisions, the only thing left was to discount the flows at the relevant cost of capital.

   Mr. Borg was well aware that the company's bonds had been rated B when they were issued two years earlier. The coupon rate was 17.3 percent. At present the bonds were all held by two insurance companies, so they did not trade. The current yield on newly issued B-rated bonds was 14.5 percent.

   Bakelite was too small a company to be followed by investment services like Value Line. It paid a $3 dividend, and its current market price in the over-the-counter market was $25. However, a regional investment banker had just published a brief report on the company. It included a beta of 1.32, and the analyst's estimates for Bakelite's nominal long-term growth was 4.9 percent, a figure with which management agreed. At present U.S. Treasury seven-year bonds were yielding 8.9 percent and 90-day Treasury bills 6.5 percent. Historically, the stock market had yielded about 8.5 percent above Treasury bills and 6 percent above longer-term bonds. Bakelite's balance sheet is shown below.

Bakelite Corporation

Assets		Liabilities and Equity	
Cash	$0.2	Accounts payable	$0.8
Marketable securities	2.3	Taxes payable	0.3
Accounts receivable	1.1	Total current liabilities	1.1
Total current assets	3.6	Long-term debt	1.3
Net property, plant,		Common stock	0.5
and equipment	1.2	Retained earnings	1.9
Total assets	$4.8	Total equity	2.4
		Total liabilities and	
		equity	$4.8

Mr. Borg believed that the capital structure Bakelite currently had represented the mix that the company would continue to use. Its taxes were 49 percent. What is Bakelite's weighted-average cost of capital?

2. The Select Company was in the process of developing a discount rate to evaluate capital projects that had been proposed for the following year. The company, with net income of $504,000 in 1987, had been growing steadily, with both sales and earnings increasing at about 10 percent per year. The firm's return on equity had also been fairly constant at about 12 percent per year. Absent any change in the company's strategy, these trends were expected to continue into the future. At the end of 1987, the Select Company had an A bond rating. Debt on the balance sheet had been issued at an average rate of 10 percent. Long-term A-rated bonds were currently being sold at 10.4 percent. Select's stock was selling for $6.90; 300,000 shares were outstanding; and the company consistently paid out 24 percent of earnings in dividends. Because of its steady growth and performance, Select's returns were estimated to have a beta of 0.98.

   Based on the following data, compute the company's marginal weighted-average cost of capital using:

   a. The dividend discount model, where $g = (1 - \text{Payout})(\text{ROE})$.

   b. The capital asset pricing model (six-month Treasury bills were selling for approximately 8.5%, U.S. Treasury 7-year bonds for 10.1%, and the expected market return was 16%).

Select Company

	1986	1987	1988 (projected)
Profit after tax (34% tax rate)	$ 458,182	$ 504,000	$ 554,400
Earnings per share	$1.52	$1.68	$1.85
End-of-year market price/share	$7.40	$8.60	$6.90
Current assets	$2,255,665	$2,383,661	$2,729,354
Net long-term assets	4,793,289	5,305,569	5,799,876
Total assets	$7,048,954	$7,689,230	$8,529,230
Current liabilities	$1,174,826	$1,227,692	$1,421,538
Long-term debt	2,055,945	2,261,538	2,487,692
Common stock ($5 par value)	1,500,000	1,500,000	1,500,000
Retained earnings	2,318,185	2,700,000	3,120,000
Total long-term debt and equity	$5,874,128	$6,461,538	$7,107,692
Total liabilities and equity	$7,048,954	$7,689,230	$8,529,230

CHAPTER 6

Valuation 2: Acquisitions and Divestitures*

Analyzing a corporate strategy—whether the investment is in property, plant, or equipment; a line of business; or a whole company—uses valuation tools. The only real differences between capital budgeting and corporate valuation lie in the scope and availability of the data needed to create estimated cash flows and discount rates. Because acquisitions and divestitures are large, are strategically important, and often require special analytical approaches, we consider their analysis a separate topic in valuation.

Merger activity in the United States by domestic and nondomestic firms has burgeoned, particularly during the late 1960s and early 1980s, as shown in Exhibit 6–1. Managers engaged in this activity have given a number of reasons for making acquisitions:

1. To lower financing costs.
2. To diversify and thus reduce risk.
3. To increase the earnings per share of the acquiring firm.
4. To use excess funds.
5. To provide needed funds.
6. To purchase an undervalued company.
7. To take advantage of economies of scale or size.

These are seven quite different reasons for an acquisition or merger. However, all these reasons can be reduced to one: to create value for the firm's shareholders. This creation of value comes only as the result of synergy between the merging firms.

Creating value is a familiar goal, one that was discussed in relation to capital-investment decisions in Chapter 4. The goal is the same here. Although an acquisition is usually larger than the typical capital investment,

---

* In the past, the words *merger* and *acquisition* were used to denote different forms of corporate combinations. Now *merger* is used to designate the physical combining of companies after acquisition is complete.

EXHIBIT 6–1   Net Merger-Acquisition Announcements

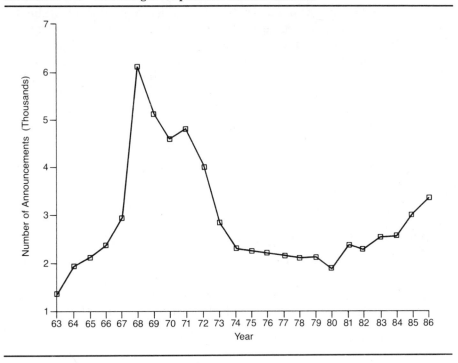

SOURCE: *Mergerstat Review 1986*. Chicago, Ill.: W. T. Grimm, 1987, p. 2.

the acquired firm, division, or line of business must still generate an adequate return for the acquiring shareholders. If an acquisition is just like any other corporate investment, why then do we devote another chapter to its discussion?

There are four reasons. First, since acquisitions usually require large investments, firms frequently have separate staffs of acquisition analysts. Second, these analysts often borrow the analytical tools of stock analysts to use instead of or as a supplement to traditional valuation (capital-investment) techniques and criteria. The stock analyst's approach is used because many acquisitions are made by purchasing the stock of the acquired firm with cash or securities of the acquiring firm. Because stock is used or exchanged in the transaction, stock analysis techniques appear appropriate. Third, acquisitions are a separate topic because the real benefits of an acquisition can be difficult to identify and awkward to evaluate, since the costs and benefits are unusually influenced by tax and accounting issues. Fourth, the acquisition decision is an excellent example of the way a manager can create value for the company.

Despite the difficulties, an acquisition is essentially a complex capital investment. Thus the capital-investment framework presented in Chapter

4 and the cost of capital analysis presented in Chapter 5 can be adapted and used to determine whether a potential acquisition will create value for the acquiring firm's shareholders. In this chapter, we will recommend and describe present value analysis of cash flows as a method of valuing and pricing acquisitions. We will then discuss some of the other valuation techniques currently used by acquisition analysts that focus particularly on earnings. Note that acquisition is our primary focus. A divestiture is the same transaction seen through the seller's eyes, and the analysis is the same.

Now, armed with our knowledge about basic valuation techniques (Chapter 4) and cost of capital determination (Chapter 5), we are ready to value lines of business, divisions, or whole companies.

I. PRESENT VALUE ANALYSIS OF CASH FLOWS

The analyst must follow two steps in valuing an acquisition:

1. Identify the present value of the equity of the company to be acquired (NPV_A).
2. Identify the present values of the synergies that may result as the acquired firm's business is joined with that of the acquirer (NPV_{AS}).

The marginal value of the acquisition depends on both the value of the company to be acquired and the synergies:

$$\text{Acquisition value} = NPV_A + NPV_{AS} \qquad (1)$$

Let's follow an example to demonstrate the analysis of an acquisition using these two steps and the problems an analyst will face.

1. Calculating the Marginal Value of an Acquisition without Synergy

Consider two mature firms, both growing just enough to offset the effects of inflation; in real terms, neither is growing. One firm, Kitchen Craft Industries (KC), manufactures kitchen cabinets and is interested in acquiring the other firm, Zeus, Inc., a printer, binder, and distributor of religious pamphlets and books. For the present, let's suppose that Zeus's current net cash flow is a good estimate of its annual cash flows over the foreseeable future. Zeus is slightly less risky than KC, and although its net cash flows are lower, its cost of equity is also lower. To calculate the marginal value of the acquisition, we first need to measure the net present value of Zeus to its shareholders.

Zeus's sales in 1988 are expected to be $9.147 million, operating expenses 92 percent of sales, and depreciation $50,000. Taxes will be 34 percent of income before taxes, net income will be $450,000, and the company has no interest expense because it has no long-term debt. Exhibit 6–2 shows management's forecasted 1988 income statement and cash flow. Income and

EXHIBIT 6–2   Zeus 1988 Income Statement and Cash Flow (in thousands)

Sales	$9,147
Operating expenses	(8,415)
Depreciation	(50)
Interest	0
Income before taxes	682
Taxes (34%)	(232)
Income after taxes	450
Depreciation	50
Increase in property, plant, and equipment	(50)
Increase in working capital	0
Payment on debt principal	0
Residual net cash flow*	$ 450

*Cash flow to equity shareholders.

costs from 1988 onward are not expected to grow. Because net cash flow will remain the same every year in perpetuity, we can calculate the net present value of a whole company thus:

$$NPV_A = \frac{NCF_A}{R_{eA}} \qquad (2)$$

where

R_{eA} = The cost of equity for company A[1]

NCF_A = The yearly residual net cash flow for company A

NPV_A = The net present value of equity cash flows for company A

As we saw in the chapter on cost of equity, Chapter 5, this method of calculating net present value is appropriate only for a firm that is not growing.[1]

Because management expects no growth, and with a marginal cost of equity of 13.8 percent, the value of Zeus is:

$$NPV_Z = \frac{NCF_Z}{R_{eZ}}$$

$$= \frac{\$450,000}{.138}$$

$$= \$3,260,870$$

---

[1]We can also value the equity by discounting the net cash flows to all capital providers (NCF_{WACCA}) by the weighted-average cost of capital (WACCA) and deducting the debt principal:

$$NPV_A = \frac{NCF_{WACCA}}{WACC_A}$$

The cash flows to all capital providers do not have interest or principal payments deducted.

At a value of $3.3 million, should KC acquire Zeus? It depends on the price.

If KC pays a fair price for Zeus, there is no benefit or loss to the shareholders of either firm. A fair price for Zeus is one that neither creates nor destroys value—one that exactly equals the present value of the benefits from Zeus, $3.3 million. These benefits are exactly offset by the $3.3 million cost. If, by skillful negotiation, KC management can acquire Zeus for less than $3.3 million, KC's shareholders will gain value, while investors holding Zeus stock will lose value. A simple formula can be used to show the important relationship between price and value:

$$NRC_A = Q_A - NPV_A \tag{3}$$

where

NRC_A = The net real cost to acquire the target
Q_A = The purchase price
NPV_A = The present value of the target
firm with no synergistic benefits

If KC pays $3.3 million for Zeus, the value created for KC's shareholders will be:

$$NRC_Z = \$3.3 - \$3.3$$
$$= \$0$$

If KC pays more than $3.3 million, its shareholders lose value. For instance, if the price were $3.8 million, the loss would be $500,000, as shown below.

$$NRC_Z = \$3.8 - \$3.3$$
$$= \$0.5 \text{ million}$$

And if KC negotiated skillfully and paid $2.8 million for the $3.3 million in benefits, $500,000 in value would be transferred to KC's shareholders. Thus, in the simplest case, managers face two problems. First, they must place a value on what they are acquiring, and second, a price must be determined. The two are not the same.

2. Calculating the Marginal Benefit of an Acquisition with Synergy

Our calculations thus far have assumed that the acquisition offers no new benefits, no synergies. What if the combined companies are expected to have cash flows in excess of those the two firms would have had without each other? The increased cash flows might come from a variety of synergies. For example, Zeus might be operating at full capacity with a large backlog of orders for its products. Kitchen Craft might have an empty manufacturing facility that could be used, with little change, to produce religious tracts for

Zeus's customers. KC's unused capacity combined with Zeus's need for capacity would increase cash flows without incurring fully offsetting costs: more pamphlets could be printed and sold without adding to the combined firm's plant capacity. Thus the combination of Zeus and KC would provide a value that is greater than the value of the two companies operating alone.

There are two ways Kitchen Craft's analysts might go about estimating the value of such synergies. First, the analysts could forecast the synergies' cash flows and discount them. They would estimate the increase in the sale of Zeus's religious tracts, the marginal costs incurred in using KC's plant, and any other new costs associated with producing, selling, and delivering the religious tracts. The cash flows from the increase in sales would be discounted by a rate reflecting their risk and added to the NPV of Zeus alone. The total is the value of the synergies and Zeus.

For analysts who find directly estimating the values of synergies difficult, there is another way to make the forecast. As shown in Exhibit 6–3, analysis can determine the values of Zeus (NPV_Z) and KC (NPV_{KC}), each operating alone, and the value of the combined company (NPV_{KCZ}). The difference between the values of the independent firms and the combined company value is the value of the synergies (ΔNPV_{KCZ}):

$$\Delta NPV_{KCZ} = NPV_{KCZ} - (NPV_{KC} + NPV_Z) \tag{4}$$
$$= \$9.3 - (\$5.0 + \$3.3)$$
$$= \$9.3 - \$8.3$$
$$= \$1.0 \text{ million}$$

As a result of combining the two firms, an additional $1 million in present value benefits (synergies) is gained. Value is created through the merger. Of course, the price paid by KC for Zeus plus the synergies will determine which firm's stockholders benefit from the acquisition and profit from the synergies.

Let us calculate the value to KC's stockholders if KC were to pay $3.3 million for the acquisition. Remember, this acquisition creates new benefits as a result of synergies. Thus formula (3) cannot be used without adjustments. The value to the acquirer's stockholders (V_B) equals the marginal value of the acquisition minus the net real cost (the price paid to acquire):

$$V_B = \Delta NPV_{AB} - NRC_A \tag{5}$$

EXHIBIT 6–3 Net Present Value of Combined Firms: Synergistic Benefits

	Kitchen Craft	Zeus	KC–Zeus
Residual net cash flow per year	$600,000	$450,000	$1,190,000
Cost of equity	12.0%	13.8%	12.8%
Net present value	$5.0 million	$3.3 million	$9.3 million

Using formulas (1) and (3), we can rewrite this equation so that we can determine the value KC's shareholders will receive:

$$
\begin{aligned}
V_{KC} &= \Delta NPV_{KCZ} - NRC_Z \\
&= [NPV_{KCZ} - (NPV_{KC} + NPV_Z)] - (Q_Z - NPV_Z) \qquad (6) \\
&= [\$9.3 - (\$5.0 + \$3.3)] - (\$3.3 - \$3.3) \\
&= \$1.0 \text{ million}
\end{aligned}
$$

Since the change in value as a result of the acquisition is $1 million and the change in value for KC's shareholders is also $1 million, Kitchen Craft stockholders receive $1 million of new value created by the acquisition.

If V_{KC} were less than $1 million, the gain from the acquisition (and the increase in value) would be shared by the shareholders of both firms. For instance, if KC paid $3.6 million, the value gained by KC's stockholders, calculated using formula (6), would be:

$$
\begin{aligned}
V_{KC} &= [\$9.3 - (\$5.0 + \$3.3)] - (\$3.6 - \$3.3) \\
&= \$1.0 - \$0.3 \\
&= \$0.7
\end{aligned}
$$

And Zeus's shareholders would receive the remainder:

$$
\begin{aligned}
V_Z &= NPV_{KCZ} - V_{KC} \\
&= \$1.0 - \$0.7 \\
&= \$0.3
\end{aligned}
$$

Only at a price of $3.8 million would the two groups of stockholders share equally in the increased value.

These formulas are simply a means of examining the price and value of benefits. However, we made the analysis deceptively straightforward by assuming that the benefits and the resulting present values had already been determined. The practicing analyst must estimate these benefits. Projecting the costs and benefits of the synergies of the combined companies is subject to even greater forecasting error than is forecasting the cash flows for the original entities. For example, we said that Zeus might benefit by using KC's excess capacity. However, the benefits of using that space could depend on such factors as the availability of local labor, the suitability of the space, and unpredictable conversion costs. The benefits may be quite different from those originally forecast. Most acquisitions provide far greater forecasting ambiguity.

Risk and the impact of an acquisition on risk are also difficult to estimate. In the KC–Zeus example, we made the analyst's life simple by assuming that the business risk of the new firm was simply the average of the two firms' risks prior to acquisition. This simplifying assumption rarely holds true in practice. For example, joining a cyclical to a countercyclical firm will greatly reduce the risk of the combined firm, all other factors being equal. Joining two firms with the same cyclicality would have the opposite effect.

Rarely, also, will an analyst find either or both of two firms without real growth. To value growing firms, the analyst must forecast the net annual cash flow for a number of years. Since companies must invest in assets to grow, the analyst must include estimates of the increase in assets in the forecasts. As an example, if Zeus were to introduce a new product that would spur real growth of 5 percent, for the next five years, it would need increases in net working capital (current assets minus current liabilities) and in property, plant, and equipment. Exhibit 6–4 provides the forecast for Zeus.

After five years, Zeus is expected to stop growing. At that point, we can estimate the value of Zeus using the perpetuity method. Each of the cash flows, including the terminal value, is discounted at Zeus's cost of capital (13.8 percent) for a present value of $3.6 million. This value is greater than the one we found for Zeus without real growth.

One other factor can affect valuation. That is inflation. Inflation affects both the cash flows and the discount rate. Let's assume for a moment that the 13.8 percent required return on equity includes 5 percent to compensate for expected inflation. In *real* terms, net of inflation's effects, the investors expect to get a return of 8.8 percent. Therefore, unless Zeus's managers expect sales to decline in real terms, they must take into account the impact of inflation on revenues and costs, as well as the cost of capital. If management expected to be able to keep up with inflation—just keep up—their forecasts would be as shown in Exhibit 6–5. Notice that this forecast is somewhat different from that shown in Exhibit 6–4. First, depreciation changes only to account for increases in property, plant, or equipment purchases. It does not rise with inflation, because the U.S. tax code bases depreciation expense on the initial purchase price of the item to be depreciated, not on any current market value. There are some tax codes, notably those in highly inflationary environments, that do base depreciation on prices revalued for inflation.

The second major difference is that management expects growth to keep up with long-term inflation. Thus, the terminal value, using the perpetuity method, is:

$$\text{Perpetuity value} = \frac{\text{Annual cash flow}}{\text{Cost of capital} - \text{Growth}}$$

$$= \frac{\$459}{.138 - .05} \tag{7}$$

$$= \$5,216$$

This value is in great contrast to the terminal value of $4,159 when there is no expected growth, even from inflation; but it is slightly lower than $5,216, the terminal value with perpetual real growth of 5 percent. The difference between the two is the depreciation penalty under inflation.

EXHIBIT 6–4 Zeus, Inc., Income and Cash Flow—5% Real Growth for Five Years (in thousands)

	1988	1989	1990	1991	1992	1993
Sales	$ 9,147	$ 9,605	$ 10,085	$ 10,589	$ 11,118	$ 11,674
Operating expenses	(8,415)	(8,836)	(9,278)	(9,742)	(10,229)	(10,740)
Depreciation	(50)	(53)	(55)	(58)	(61)	(64)
Interest	0	0	0	0	0	0
Income before taxes	682	716	752	789	828	870
Taxes (34%)	(232)	(243)	(256)	(268)	(282)	(296)
Income after taxes	450	472	496	521	546	574
Depreciation	50	53	55	58	61	64
Change in property, plant, and equipment	(50)	(53)	(55)	(58)	(61)	(64)
Change in working capital	0	(91)	(96)	(101)	(106)	(111)
Change in debt principal	0	0	0	0	0	0
Free cash flow	450	381	400	420	440	463
Terminal value†	0	0	0	0	0	4,159
Total cash flow	$ 450	$ 381	$ 400	$ 420	$ 440	$ 4,622

Net present value* = $3,570

*At a discount rate of 13.8%.

†Without growth, working capital increases will cease. Thus terminal value is the perpetuity value of $574,000 at a discount rate of 13.8% and no real growth from 1993 onwards $\left(\dfrac{CF}{R_e - g} = \dfrac{\$463 + \$111}{13.8 - 0.0} \right)$; with 5% perpetual growth, the terminal value would be $5,261 (i.e., $463,000/ 13.8 − 5.0).

EXHIBIT 6–5 Zeus, Inc., Income and Cash Flow—5% Inflation (in thousands)

	1988	1989	1990	1991	1992	1993
Sales	$ 9,147	$ 9,604	$ 10,085	$ 10,589	$ 11,118	$ 11,674
Operating expenses	(8,415)	(8,836)	(9,278)	(9,742)	(10,229)	(10,740)
Depreciation	(50)	(50)	(51)	(51)	(52)	(52)
Income before taxes	682	718	756	796	837	882
Taxes (34%)	(232)	(244)	(257)	(271)	(285)	(300)
Income after taxes	450	474	499	525	552	582
Depreciation	50	50	51	51	52	52
Increase in property, plant, and equipment	(50)	(53)	(55)	(58)	(61)	(64)
Increase in working capital	0	(91)	(96)	(101)	(106)	(111)
Free cash flow	450	380	399	417	437	459
Terminal value†	0	0	0	0	0	5,216
Total cash flow	$ 450	$ 380	$ 399	$ 417	$ 437	$ 5,675
Net present value* = $ 4,050						

*At a discount rate of 13.8%.

†With 5% inflation beyond 1993, working capital increases will continue, and the terminal value is the perpetuity value of $459,000 at a discount rate of 13.8% and with growth equal only to 5% inflation.

147

The important thing this analysis points out is that forecasts of the discount rate and the cash flows must both rest on the same scenario for the future. If management really thinks cash flows will decline in real terms—that the cash flows will not grow to offset the erosive effects of inflation—the value of the company will decline as inflation rises.

II. EARNINGS VALUATION METHOD

To avoid elaborate projections of cash flows, benefits, and risks, some analysts use the relationship of a firm's projected earnings to its present earnings to calculate a crude approximation of an acquisition's value or of a cash flow terminal value. To use this approach, the analyst first estimates the earnings of the firm to be acquired (or uses historical earnings as an estimate of future earnings) and estimates the relationship between those earnings and the stock price, the price/earnings ratio (P/E). From this ratio, the analyst estimates the price per share for the business to be acquired as follows:

$$\text{Price per share} = \text{EPS} \times \text{P/E} \tag{8}$$

where

EPS = Earnings per share
P/E = The firm's estimated price/earnings ratio after acquisition

Or the price for the whole company would be:

$$\text{Price} = \text{Earnings} \times \text{P/E} \tag{9}$$

where earnings are equal to annual net income.

Suppose that Zeus's earnings over the past 12 months have been $450,000 and that 100,000 shares of stock are outstanding. Earnings per share are $4.50 ($450,000/100,000). Zeus is not publicly traded, however, and thus it has no market price or price/earnings ratio to use as a starting point. To overcome this lack, analysts often use the average P/E for a group of similar but publicly traded firms as a proxy for this unobtainable P/E. To use this proxy method, the analyst must assume that firms in the same industry or with similar earnings records are equally risky and that the market will pay a standard multiple of earnings for stocks of equivalent risk. However, these assumptions are not always valid. The price/earnings multiples of comparable stocks in comparable industries can be very different. As an example, Exhibit 6–6 shows varying price/earnings ratios for an industry similar to Zeus's, the publishing industry.

If the analyst estimates a price/earnings ratio for Zeus equal to the 1986 industry average of 20.8 for Zeus, the estimated price per Zeus share would be:

$$\begin{aligned}
\text{Price per share} &= \text{EPS} \times \text{P/E} \\
&= \$4.50 \times 20.8 \\
&= \$93.60
\end{aligned}$$

EXHIBIT 6–6 Selected Publishers (average annual price/earnings ratios)

Company	1984	1985	1986
Advanced Systems	25.5	10.2	13.0
Banta	6.2	11.2	14.9
Browne & Co.	14.9	12.4	10.5
Commerce Clearing House	13.5	16.1	22.1
R. R. Donnelley & Sons	11.6	14.3	16.9
Grolier, Inc.	10.8	11.8	15.0
Houghton Mifflin	10.6	13.9	20.3
McGraw-Hill	14.4	15.7	18.5
Meredith Corp.	10.7	12.6	15.7
Average	13.7	16.3	20.8

SOURCE: Value Line, *Investment Survey*, Sept. 11, 1987.

At a price per share of $93.60, the total price for the company would be $9.36 million ($93.60 × 100,000 shares). This price is more than the net present value calculated for Zeus by the cash flow projection method using a 5 percent real or nominal growth rate.

The price/earnings method requires a P/E estimate, which can be difficult to make. The method is easiest to use with a company that is not growing and is unlikely to create synergies with its merger partner. Such a target is rare. Most interesting acquisitions (and divestitures, for that matter) are growing and will provide opportunities for synergies. The fact that we found Zeus's value using the cash flow and the earnings methods to be quite different is typical.

Several other factors can make us question the validity of the price/earnings ratio method for valuation. First, in using this approach, we assume that recent earnings represent the real earning power of the firm. In the past several years, the reported earnings of U.S. corporations have become less and less representative of the firms' *economic* earnings. The effects of inflation, and the accounting treatment of those effects, combined with changes in accounting methods for such items as unrealized foreign exchange losses and gains, have made the reported earnings of U.S. corporations resemble only vaguely the firms' real earning power.

Second, this method also assumes that the price/earnings ratio is a reliable indicator of value. While the current P/E of a publicly traded firm reflects its shareholders' present estimates of its future as an independent company, it is just the relationship between the market price of the company's stock and its earnings. It does not reflect the potential synergies that might result from a merger. To estimate the value of synergies using the earnings valuation approach, the analyst must forecast the new earnings after the merger and the P/E ratio if the merger were known to investors.

The current P/E reflects prospects without a merger, and a P/E reflecting the potential for a merger is difficult to estimate. If the acquisition is expected to create value, the analyst is justified in using a higher estimate. The problem is that there is no simple method for making this estimate.

There are still other assumptions behind the earnings valuation method: that the earnings stream will remain constant over time; that short-term earnings and market prices are good indicators of value. The net present value method, on the other hand, assumes that any acquisition with a positive marginal value will increase the value of the firm and that the increased value will eventually be reflected in the market price of the firm's stock. The logic behind the net present value method is clear and powerful.

While we would dismiss the price/earnings multiple method as the sole approach to valuing an acquisition, it can be put to good use by the analyst. It can be used to put the present value analysis into a capital-market perspective. We can compare the P/E that is *implied* by a present value analysis to a P/E estimated using the earnings analysis. For Zeus we had the following information:

Cash flow per year	$450,000
Earnings per year	$450,000
Discount rate	13.8%
Net present value with 5% inflation	$4.1 million
Number of shares	100,000

The implied price/earnings ratio is equal to the present value per share divided by the earnings per share:

$$\text{Implied P/E} = \frac{\text{PV/Share}}{\text{Earnings/Share}} \qquad (10)$$

$$= \frac{\$4,049,991/100,000}{\$450,000/100,000}$$

$$= \frac{\$40.50}{\$4.50}$$

$$= 9.0$$

Since the implied P/E is lower than the average ratio for most companies in the group in Exhibit 6–5, the difference in price/earnings ratios indicates that our present value estimate is lower than the value the market is likely to set on the common stock. There are several possible reasons for the discrepancy: (1) our predicted cash flows (growth) may be less than those the market is forecasting, (2) our predicted risk (incorporated in the cost of capital estimate) could be higher than the market's prediction, (3) we could have made an error in our inflation forecasts, or (4) the P/E of Zeus could be lower than the industry.

III. OTHER VALUATION TECHNIQUES

Several other valuation techniques are used by acquisition analysts. These methods should be used only as supplements to the present value analysis, not as substitutes for it.

1. Book Value

This valuation technique is quite simple and lacks any but the most simplistic reasons for its use. Book value (net assets minus liabilities), calculated by using the balance sheet figures, is a poor estimate of economic value for several reasons:

1. Book value depends on the accounting practices of a firm. It is usually only a vague approximation of the real economic value of a firm.
2. Book value ignores intangible assets. Intangibles—copyrights, trademarks, patents, franchise licenses, and contracts—protect a company's right to market its goods and services and thus have value. If the book value of the assets is less than the present value of the cash flows of the firm, intangible assets can account for the discrepancy.
3. Book value ignores the price appreciation of real assets. Since assets are valued on the balance sheet at their depreciated costs, some assets (for instance, land, precious metals, and mineral reserves) may be valued far below even their liquidation value.

Particularly with privately or closely held firms, owners may believe that book value is the least they should receive when selling the company. When this is true, book value provides a floor below which a successful price offer is unlikely to go.

2. Liquidation Value

Liquidation value is the cash value the acquirer would receive if the assets of the acquired firm were sold. This method of valuation is useful if the acquirer intends to sell the assets of the acquired firm. It may also be used to aid in determining the fair book value of under- or overvalued assets. Analysts sometimes use liquidation value as a floor price for an acquisition. If liquidation value exceeds the present value, the company will be worth more if its assets are sold.

3. Replacement Cost

Replacement cost is a measure of the cost of replacing the assets of the potential acquisition. While some analysts use it to set a ceiling price on the acquisition, replacement cost estimates can be difficult to make.

4. Market Value

Often a good starting point in estimating an acquisition's price is the market value of the firm's stock. If the stock is publicly traded, its market value is simply the market price per share times the number of shares. The reason market value is only a starting point should be clear from the present value analysis we performed for Zeus and Kitchen Craft. If the acquisition is expected to increase value for the shareholders of one or both firms, this increase in value is unlikely to be reflected in the public price of the common stock of either firm. (Of course, the expectation of increased value may be reflected in the price once the merger becomes public knowledge.) Thus, if there are synergies and value will be created, the current market prices underestimate the present value of the merging firms. Still, the market price of the stock is a benchmark from which the analyst can begin.

Under a certain set of circumstances, all these values should be the same. Liquidation value should reflect what a buyer is willing to pay for the earning power of the firm's assets. Thus a liquidation value, if it can be obtained, should be close to the value estimated using the present value analysis. Likewise book value, if it truly reflects the economic value (the earning power of the assets), will be similar. Only because of estimation errors and accounting conventions, coupled with inflation's impact, are the values different.

IV. SUMMARY

There is only one purpose in making an acquisition—to create value for the shareholder. Value can be created through increased returns or reduced risk, changes that the shareholders could not make by themselves. In general, this increase in value comes from increased capacity being matched with a need for that resource—a matching that cannot occur unless the two firms merge. The analyst's task is to estimate the effect of a merger on a firm's return and risk characteristics. Since earnings are, at best, only a vague indication of real value, the analyst should project cash flows with and without the benefits of the merger. Other valuation techniques, such as earnings analysis, should be used merely to corroborate the present value analysis.

SELECTED REFERENCES

For methods of analyzing a merger, see:
Brealey, Richard, and Stewart Myers. *Principles of Corporate Finance*, 3d ed. New York: McGraw Hill, 1988, chap. 33.

Myers, Stewart C. "A Framework for Evaluating Mergers." In *Modern Developments in Financial Management*. New York: Frederick A. Praeger, 1976.

————. "The Evaluation of an Acquisition Target." *Midland Corporate Finance Journal*, Winter 1983, pp. 39–46.

Rappaport, Alfred. *Creating Shareholder Value*. New York: Free Press, 1986.

————. "What We Know and Don't Know About Mergers." *Midland Corporate Finance Journal*, Winter 1983, pp. 63–67.

Ross, Steven, and Randolph Westerfeld. *Corporate Finance*. St. Louis, Mo.: Times Mirror/Mosby, 1988, chap. 26.

Salter, Malcolm S., and Wolf A. Weinhold. *Diversification Through Acquisition*. New York: Free Press, 1979, part II.

Shrives, Ronald E., and Mary M. Pashley. "Evidence on Association Between Mergers and Capital Structure." *Financial Management*, Autumn 1984, pp. 39–48.

Weston, J. F., and Eugene Brigham. *Essentials of Managerial Finance*. 8th ed. Hinsdale, Ill.: Dryden Press, 1987, chap. 23.

For two studies on the relative values of mergers, see:
Mueller, D. C. "The Effects of Conglomerate Mergers: A Survey of the Empirical Evidence." *Journal of Banking and Finance*, December 1977, pp. 315–48.

Rumult, Richard. *Strategy, Structure and Economic Performance*. Boston: Division of Research, Harvard Business School, 1974.

For a description of current merger activity, see:
"A New Strain of Merger Mania." *Business Week*. March 21, 1988, pp. 122–26.

STUDY QUESTIONS

1. The Single-Firm Company, a growth-oriented enterprise, was considering making an acquisition in the spring of 1986. It had two prospects, which it designated as X Company and Y Company for confidentiality reasons. Based only on these data, which company would you recommend that Single-Firm Company pursue?

	Company X		Company Y	
	Shares of Common Stock	*Cash Flow per Share*	*Shares of Common Stock*	*Cash Flow per Share*
1981	400,000	$1.75	300,000	$1.67
1982	400,000	$1.89	305,000	$1.84
1983	400,000	$2.04	500,000	$1.25
1984	400,000	$2.20	505,000	$1.39
1985	400,000	$2.38	507,000	$1.55

2. Compute the maximum price the management (for the shareholders) of the Kupp Corporation should be willing to pay to acquire the Klick Company, and the minimum price Klick's management should accept. Both companies operate in the same industry, and although neither is experiencing any rapid growth, both provide a steady stream of earnings. Kupp's management is encouraging the acquisition because of the excess plant capacity available at Klick, which it hopes to use. The Klick Company has 50,000 shares of common stock outstanding, which are selling at about $6 per share. Other data are shown in the following table.

	Kupp Corporation	Klick Company	Combined Entity
Profit after tax	$48,000	$30,000	$ 92,000
Residual net cash flow/year	$60,000	$40,000	$120,000
Cost of equity capital	12.5%	11.25%	12%

KLICK COMPANY
Balance Sheet

Assets		Liabilities and Owners' Equity	
Current assets	$273,000	Current liabilities	$137,000
Net PP&E	215,000	Long-term liabilities	111,000
Other	55,000	Owners' equity	295,000
		Total liabilities and	
Total assets	$543,000	owners' equity	$543,000

3. Smyth Instrument Company wishes to acquire Robinson Research Lab through a merger. Smyth Instrument expects to gain operating efficiency from the merger through distribution economies, advertising, manufacturing, and purchasing.

   The weighted-average costs of capital for Smyth and Robinson are 12.2 percent and 10.5 percent, respectively. Neither company has any long-term debt outstanding. The effective cost of capital after the merger is estimated to be 11 percent. The projected growth rate for both of the firms is 4 percent per year. The current net cash flow per year is $6.45 million for Smyth and $2.2 million for Robinson. Based on an analysis of the synergies for the combined company, the combined net cash flow would have been $9.45 million if the two had been combined for the past year.

   Calculate the price Smyth Instrument should offer to acquire Robinson Research and the price above which Robinson should accept the merger offer.

4. The Action Corporation made cardboard boxes for a wide range of clients. The industry was experiencing a severe slowdown in terms of sales. Several substitute products were threatening to win over Action's major clients. In spite of the fact that entry into the industry was relatively cheap, fixed assets accounted for a large percentage of the total expenses. Volume was thus important, and there was pressure on margins.

   In late 1987, Action was approached by a large packaging company that wanted to add a cardboard box manufacturer to its portfolio of companies. Mr. Santiago, CFO at Action, was concerned about the price he should expect for this acquisition and was wondering how best to maximize the return to Action's stockholders.

   Action was rated by Moody's as a moderate risk, and bonds of similar-risk companies were yielding around 10.1 percent. Mr. Santiago felt that his stockholders would demand at least a 12 percent return on their investment. Sales in 1987 were $250 million and were expected to grow at 3 percent annually; cost of sales was 75 percent of sales; and selling general, and administrative expenses were 10 percent of sales. Taxes would be 34 percent. Depreciation was fixed at $7 million, and PP&E and working capital investments would total $7 million per year. In the past, Action had paid dividends of 10 percent of net income, and the return on the investment had been about 3.4 percent. The company currently had obtained 15 percent of its capital from lenders. The coupon on the debt was 15 percent. What price should Mr. Santiago sell for to provide the shareholders a fair return?

CHAPTER 7

Obtaining Outside Capital

In Chapter 5 we learned how to estimate the fair return that should be expected for an investment. We found that all investors require a return for:

1. *Illiquidity:* the time that money is invested.
2. *Inflation:* losses caused by changes in the purchasing power of money.
3. *Risk:* the chance that the returns from an investment may be higher or lower than was expected.

The following formula can be used to determine this required, or expected, return:

$$\text{Required return} = \text{Risk-free rate} + \text{Inflation} + \text{Risk premium}$$

The rate from a U.S. Treasury security is an estimate of the return required for both the time value of money and inflation. As for risk, we know that investors expect more return for increased risk. But how do we determine how much more, and how do we measure risk?

Estimating the fair return for risk is so difficult that in Chapter 5 we turned to capital-market experts and asked them what they believed was a fair return for risk—their market price of risk. To determine this fair return for a company, we estimated the returns required by its capital providers for their particular stakes. The weighted average of the capital costs that resulted from this analysis was our best estimate of investors' required return for the risks being taken by that particular company at that particular time—that is, the company's investors' fair return for risk, and the company's cost of capital. For a company that has 30 percent of its capital in the form of long-term debt and marginal costs of debt and equity of 10 and 15 percent, respectively, the cost of capital is 12.5 percent, as shown in Exhibit 7–1.

You will recall from Chapter 5 that the cost of debt is lower than the cost of equity because lenders have explicit rights, usually in the form of a contract with the borrower. Equity shareholders have no contract, but they do have residual rights. Thus, regardless of the condition of the company, shareholders have a less secure, more risky position, and as a result, should and do require a higher return.

EXHIBIT 7–1   Weighted-Average Cost of Capital

	After-Tax Cost	Proportion
Long-term debt:	$(1 - .34)\ 10.0\%$	30%
Equity	15.0%	70%
Weighted-average cost of capital = 12.5%		

You will also recall from Chapter 5 that, to determine the proportions of debt and equity for the cost of capital calculation, we said that we should use the proportions investors expect. Since getting into investors' minds is impossible, we used whatever information we could—management words or actions, or information about past practices, or industry norms—to make a judgment about management's target capital structure and thus about what was expected. But how does management decide what its target should be?

In this chapter we will examine how a company's management makes that decision. We will learn whether adding debt to the capital structure of the company can create value for the shareholders, and if so, how to go about deciding the appropriate amount of debt to use. To do this we will use most of the tools of analysis we have learned about so far: ratio analysis, forecasting, and valuation.

Let's keep in mind what owners want the managers of their company to do. All other things being equal, shareholders want the highest return, as soon as possible, while taking the least risk. In other words, shareholders want managers to create value. To create value, the manager must make decisions that will increase the present value of the company by either reducing risk, increasing return (cash flow), or both. Keeping these objectives in mind, let's see if some method of financing the corporation—some particular mixture of debt and equity—can actually make the company worth more. If a financing strategy does not affect the value of the company, then the way a company finances itself is irrelevant.

I. THE VALUE OF LEVERAGE

To decide whether a particular capital structure can enhance shareholders' value, let's look at Greenway Corporation. Greenway currently has no debt, operates in a world where interest on debt is *not tax-deductible,* and has the cash flows and value shown in Exhibit 7–2.

Column 1 of Exhibit 7–2 shows that the company's market value, the shareholders' value, is $66.67 million. Column 2 shows that, if leverage is increased to 10 percent (the firm obtains 10 percent of its capital from lenders and repurchases shares), the cost of capital drops to 14.5 percent and the value of the total company is $68.96 million, or $6.92 per share. Note that

EXHIBIT 7–2

GREENWAY CORPORATION
Income Statement
(dollars in millions except per share data)

	All-Equity Financed	10% Debt/Capital (Equity Cost 15.0%)	10% Debt/Capital (Equity Cost 15.6%)
Profit before taxes	$15	$15	$15
Taxes	(5)	(5)	(5)
Profit after taxes	10	10	10
Depreciation	5	5	5
New equipment	(5)	(5)	(5)
Added working capital	0	0	0
Cash flow to all capital providers . . .	$10	$10	$10
Number of shares outstanding	10	9	9
Book value of firm	$66.67	$66.67	$66.67
Book value of equity	$66.67	$60.00	$60.00
Book value of debt	$ 0	$ 6.67	$ 6.67
Return on book equity	15.0%	15.0%	15.0%
Cost of equity	15.0%	15.0%	15.6%
Cost of debt	10.0%	10.0%	10.0%
Weighted-average cost of capital	15.0%	14.5%	15.0%
Total market value*	$66.67	$68.96	$66.67
Equity market value/share†	$ 6.67	$ 6.92	$ 6.67

*Total market value calculated using the nongrowth perpetuity method of valuation:

Annual cash flow to all capital providers/Weighted-average cost of capital, e.g.,

$$= \frac{\$10.00}{15.0\%}$$

$$= \$66.67.$$

†(Total market value − Value of debt)/Number of shares.

leverage does not change the company's capital nor, because this is a taxless world, its earnings and cash flow. The only thing that changes is the cost of capital.

Leverage increased, and so did the shareholders' value, by $0.25 per share; but notice that the cost of equity did not change as leverage increased—*even though the shareholders' position became a little less secure.* If you were a shareholder, would you require the same return from Greenway leveraged as unleveraged? Not if you recognized that although the risk (i.e., the variability) of the company's earnings and cash flow *before* financing costs did not change as leverage increased, the net income after interest charges did, and the shareholders' position did become more risky.

Exhibit 7–3 demonstrates what happens to the shareholders' return (ROE), with and without leverage, when Greenway's revenues rise or fall from those originally forecast. It is clear that ROE changes as the company's income rises or falls, and that increased leverage makes the range of possible outcomes wider. Increase leverage more and the range of ROEs will widen further. Shareholders recognize this fact, so as the risk increases, so does

EXHIBIT 7–3

GREENWAY CORPORATION
Forecasted Earnings and Cash Flows—Three Outcomes
(dollars in millions)

	Bad Times	Most Likely	Good Times
Profit before taxes	$ 5.0	$15.0	$25.0
Taxes	(1.7)	(5.0)	(8.5)
Profit after taxes	3.3	10.0	16.5
Depreciation	5.0	5.0	5.0
New plant and equipment	(5.0)	(5.0)	(5.0)
Added working capital	0	0	0
Without Leverage			
Net income and cash flow to:			
All capital providers	$ 3.3	$10.0	$16.5
Shareholders	$ 3.3	$10.0	$16.5
Book value of equity	$66.67	$66.67	$66.67
Return on equity	4.95%	15.00%	24.75%
10% Debt/Total Capital*			
Net income and cash flow to:			
All capital providers	$ 3.3	$10.0	$16.5
Shareholders	$ 2.6	$ 9.3	$15.8
Book value of equity	$60.00	$60.00	$60.00
Return on equity	3.83%	15.50%	26.33%

*Interest rate on debt = 10%.

their required return. In fact, with 10 percent leverage, Greenway's share-holders require a return of about 15.6 percent on their equity. As column 3 of Exhibit 7–2 shows, with a required return on equity of 15.6 percent and on debt of 10 percent before taxes, Greenway's cost of capital is 15 percent and shareholders' value is $6.67 per share.

The total return required by Greenway's investors does not change when leverage changes, even though the returns required by lenders *and* share-holders rise as their risk increases. Exhibit 7–4 shows this result graphi-cally. As risks rise, so do investors' required returns, but not the weighted-average cost of capital: because the risk of the company does not change, neither does the required return for the risk being taken. At low levels of debt, lenders charge less than do equity providers because they are protected by contracts. However, the cost of capital stays the same, because the less expensive debt offsets increases in the cost of equity. Thus the value of Greenway is $66.67 million, $6.67 per share, regardless of leverage.

Leverage does not affect shareholders' value in a *taxless* world. In a world where interest is tax-deductible, however, although the required re-turn on equity is the company's cost of equity, the required return on debt is not the company's cost of debt. Because the U.S. tax code (and the tax codes of many other countries) allows interest but not dividends to be a tax-deductible expense, debt is more attractive to borrowers than it would oth-

EXHIBIT 7–4   Greenway Corporation: Costs of Capital in a Tax-Free World

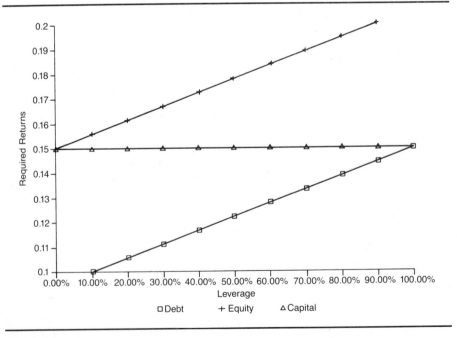

erwise be. Exhibit 7–5 shows the impact of this feature of the tax code on Greenway's cost of capital and its shareholders' value. Exhibit 7–6 shows the effect of taxes on the cost of capital graphically.

Although debt and equity costs rise as lenders finance an increasing proportion of a company, the value of the company is maximized with as much debt as it can get. The increase in value comes from an increase in return that is not offset by an increase in company risk. Why then don't companies finance themselves with more debt? And why has there been so much discussion about the amount of debt held by U.S. corporations and about the risk of leveraged buyouts? Either leverage doesn't increase risk or it does. Which is it?

On a personal level, we certainly feel that we are in a riskier position as we take on more debt, because lenders have a contract requiring that certain conditions be met—for instance, that interest be paid and principal repaid. Companies with large amounts of debt have large interest and principal payments. Thus the more debt the company has, the more likely that it will be financially embarrassed (unable to pay the interest) or financially distressed (unable to pay interest and principal).

Financial distress can result in bankruptcy: the contract with the lender is broken, and the lender, because it has a contract, can still require debt payment. In the case of modest amounts of debt, most lenders do not worry about the possibility of a company going bankrupt. As the amount of debt rises, however, bankruptcy becomes more probable, and lenders begin to incorporate the expected costs of possible bankruptcy into their required

EXHIBIT 7–5

GREENWAY CORPORATION
Tax Effect of Capital-Structure Changes with 10 Percent Debt/Total Capital
(dollars in millions except per share value)

	Interest Not Deductible	Interest Deductible
Profit before interest and tax	$15.0	$15.0
Interest	0.0	(0.7)
Earnings before tax	15.0	14.3
Taxes (34%)	(5.0)	(4.9)
Profit after taxes	$10.0	$ 9.4
Weighted-average capital cost	15.0%	14.7%
Corporate value	$66.67	$67.34*
Equity value	$60.00	$60.60
Value per share	$ 6.00	$ 6.00

*Calculated by dividing the before-interest, after-tax profit by the weighted-average cost of capital. If after-interest, after-tax earnings were divided by the weighted-average cost, interest expense would be double-counted—once in the cash flow and once in the cost of capital.

EXHIBIT 7–6   Greenway Corporation: Costs of Capital in a Taxable World with
and without Bankruptcy

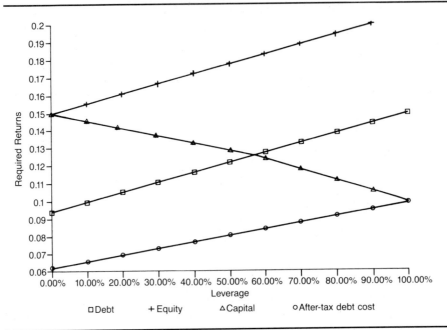

return. Thus at the point that lenders begin to be concerned about bankruptcy, they add an extra charge to the cost of debt. Exhibit 7–6 shows what
happens to a company's cost of capital when lenders and shareholders are
not concerned about bankruptcy. With bankruptcy, the costs of debt and
equity jump and the cost of capital would start its rise.

What makes the cost of debt rise? The explicit contract between lender
and borrower and the need for fixed payments appear to make bankruptcy
more likely for a highly leveraged, distressed company. The same company,
equally distressed but financed only by shareholders who have no explicit
contract, will not be in as difficult a position. Obviously shareholders are
not happy when a company is financially distressed, but they have no contract, only expectations. Shareholders whose expectations are not met will
sell their shares, and the price of the shares will decline. They may also use
their voting rights to change the board of directors.

We have suggested that the lender's return increases when the probability of bankruptcy becomes real enough for its costs to be priced. This is
one theory that may explain a jump in the cost of capital as leverage increases. Other theories, such as agency costs, have been used to explain the
phenomenon. Whatever the reasons, however, there does appear to be a
point at which the weighted-average cost of capital begins to rise, and the

value of the company thus starts to decline. The point where this jump in the cost of debt occurs is called the **optimal capital structure.** It is optimal because beyond this point, as the cost of capital rises and the value of the company declines, so does shareholders' value.

How do we determine the optimal capital structure—the point at which bankruptcy becomes an important, and priceable, consideration? In assessing what the optimal debt level should be, managers must recognize that the use of any debt brings some risks as well as advantages. Because debt entails contractual obligations to make cash payments for interest and principal, the company incurs the risk that there will be insufficient cash available. Obviously, the greater the leverage, the higher this financial risk will be. Thus while high leverage might lower the cost of capital for the company, it also places the company at risk of bankruptcy or insolvency.

The manager must consider all the risks and returns in determining the appropriate mix of debt and equity. In some ways, this task is a marketing problem, in that the manager is faced with several different products (the company's financial securities) and several different markets (potential investors in the company). The financial manager must match securities with investors in a way that creates the greatest value for the company. He or she does so by analyzing the potential effects of various financing alternatives on the total market value of the company.

II. RICHS ANALYSIS

A convenient framework for analyzing the many different factors that affect the capital-structure decision is provided by the RICHS process. The acronym represents five major factors the manager should consider:

> **R** – Risk
> **I** – Income
> **C** – Control
> **H** – Hedging
> **S** – Speculating

These factors are not listed in order of priority or importance; for each firm, and in different economic environments, the relative importance of the factors will differ. However, the manager should ensure that all have been analyzed.

The RICHS analytical process is more art than science. It is not a strictly mechanical process in which computational abilities can be substituted for analytical skill and judgment; the manager must interpret the results of the analysis. For this reason, the RICHS analytical process can best be explained through a specific example. We will use the Greenway Corporation's decision about whether to finance a $6 million expansion in production capacity through a public equity offering or through a privately placed debt issue.

Greenway is the leading producer and marketer of sand-trap graders for golf courses. The company was a market leader in both manufacture and sale of the graders until the rising value of the dollar made it economically attractive to sell Greenway's production plants and produce the needed parts in a joint venture with a Japanese firm. Earnings before interest and taxes have been under $4.0 million per year. Up to 1989, parts for the graders were manufactured in Japan and assembled and sold in the United States by Greenway. Exhibits 7–7 and 7–8 show historical and forecasted income statements and balance sheets Greenway managers made for the company in 1989. (The forecasts do not include a new plant the company is considering purchasing). Recently the value of the dollar has declined relative to the Japanese yen and it has become economically attractive to manufacture as well as assemble the grader parts in the United States. Greenway has thus decided to buy a parts manufacturing plant, and one that is readily adaptable is available. Exhibits 7–9 and 7–10 show the management forecasts for Greenway with the new plant investment. The increased earnings before interest and taxes (EBIT) are expected to come from a reduction in transportation and manufacturing costs.

To make the investment, Greenway will need a total of $6 million: $4.5 million to pay for plant and equipment and $1.5 million for new working capital (to be invested largely in inventory). Greenway will need the money in January 1989, and the new plant will start full operation shortly thereafter. Greenway currently has 20 percent of its $36 million of long-term capital in the form of debt issued in 1984. The coupon, or interest rate, on that debt is 9.74 percent. It is 30-year debt with no principal repayments due until the tenth year, 1994.

Greenway can get the $6 million it needs from either debt or equity—the sale of common stock.

Common Stock.   Greenway has 926,376 shares outstanding. The market price of the shares is $27.17 per share. To obtain the needed capital, Greenway's investment banker has said that the company can issue up to 230,769 new shares at $26 per share. Greenway has paid its shareholders, and expects to continue to pay, $2.40 per share. This dividend represents a payout ratio of almost 100 percent. The high payout ratio reflects the wishes of Mr. Jim Greenway, the company founder, and the rest of his family. They hold the single largest block of stock in the company, about 30 percent of the outstanding shares. The rest of the shares are widely held in the locale in which the company operates.

Bonds.   Greenway already has some debt. Any new debt would be subordinated to the old debt—that is, it would not have as strong a contract. The investment banker believes that Greenway would have to offer a coupon of 12 percent to attract buyers. These would be 20-year bonds, with interest payable yearly and principal to amortize the debt fully due starting in 1994.

EXHIBIT 7–7

GREENWAY CORPORATION
Historical and Forecasted Income Statements without New Plant
(in millions)

	1985	1986	1987	1988	Forecast 1989	1990	1991	1992	1993
Sales	$28.80	$30.24	$31.44	$32.72	$36.00	$38.48	$41.12	$44.00	$47.12
Manufacturing expenses	(23.76)	(24.95)	(25.94)	(26.99)	(29.70)	(31.75)	(33.92)	(36.30)	(38.87)
Depreciation	(1.44)	(1.51)	(1.57)	(1.64)	(1.80)	(1.92)	(2.06)	(2.20)	(2.36)
Earnings before interest and taxes	3.60	3.78	3.93	4.09	4.50	4.81	5.14	5.50	5.89
Interest	(0.07)	(0.07)	(0.70)	(0.70)	(0.70)	(0.70)	(0.70)	(0.70)	(0.70)
Earnings before taxes	3.53	3.71	3.86	3.39	3.80	4.11	4.44	4.80	5.19
Taxes*	(1.69)	(1.78)	(1.31)	(1.15)	(1.29)	(1.40)	(1.51)	(1.63)	(1.76)
Net earnings	1.84	1.93	2.55	2.24	2.51	2.71	2.93	3.17	3.43
Cash flow:									
Depreciation	1.44	1.51	1.57	1.64	1.80	1.92	2.06	2.20	2.36
Change in property, plant, and equipment	(1.00)	(1.00)	(1.00)	(1.00)	(1.00)	(1.00)	(1.00)	(1.00)	(1.00)
Working-capital changes	(0.45)	(0.51)	(0.57)	(0.64)	(0.80)	(0.92)	(1.06)	(1.20)	(1.36)
Debt	0	0	0	0	0	0	0	0	0
Net cash flow†	$ 1.83	$ 1.93	$ 2.55	$ 2.24	$ 2.51	$ 2.71	$ 2.93	$ 3.17	$ 3.43

*Tax rate in 1985 and 1986 of 48%; 34% thereafter.
†Not accounting for dividend payments of $2.2 million per year.

EXHIBIT 7–8

GREENWAY CORPORATION
Historical and Forecasted Balance Sheets Without New Plant
(in millions)

	1988	1989	1990	1991	1992	1993
		Forecast				
Total current assets	$27.72	$28.92	$30.30	$31.89	$33.69	$35.73
Net property, plant, and equipment	15.00	14.20	13.28	12.22	11.02	9.66
Total assets	$42.72	$43.12	$43.58	$44.11	$44.71	$45.39
Total current liabilities	$ 7.24	$ 7.35	$ 7.32	$ 7.14	$ 6.79	$ 6.27
Long-term debt	7.20	7.20	7.20	7.20	7.20	7.20
Equity	28.28	28.57	29.06	29.77	30.72	31.92
Total liabilities and equity	$42.72	$43.12	$43.58	$44.11	$44.71	$45.39

EXHIBIT 7–9

GREENWAY CORPORATION
Historical and Forecasted Income Statements with New Plant
(in millions)

	1988	1989	1990	1991	1992	1993
		Forecast				
Sales	$32.72	$42.40	$44.64	$46.96	$49.36	$51.92
Expenses	(26.99)	(34.98)	(36.83)	(38.74)	(40.72)	(42.83)
Depreciation	(1.64)	(2.12)	(2.23)	(2.35)	(2.47)	(2.60)
Earnings before interest and taxes	4.09	5.30	5.58	5.87	6.17	6.49
Interest	(0.70)	(0.70)	(0.70)	(0.70)	(0.70)	(0.70)
Earnings before taxes	3.39	4.60	4.88	5.17	5.47	5.79
Taxes*	(1.15)	(1.56)	(1.66)	(1.76)	(1.86)	(1.97)
Net earnings	2.24	3.04	3.22	3.41	3.61	3.82
Cash flow:						
Depreciation	1.64	2.12	2.23	2.35	2.47	2.60
Change in property, plant and equipment	(1.00)	(1.00)	(1.00)	(1.00)	(1.00)	(1.00)
Working-capital changes	(0.64)	(1.12)	(1.23)	(1.35)	(1.47)	(1.60)
Debt	0	0	0	0	0	0
Net cash flow†	$ 2.24	$ 3.04	$ 3.22	$ 3.41	$ 3.61	$ 3.82

*Tax rate 34%.
†Not accounting for dividend payments of $2.2 million per year.

EXHIBIT 7-10

GREENWAY CORPORATION
Historical and Forecasted Balance Sheets with New Plant
(in millions)

	1988	Forecast 1989	1990	1991	1992	1993
Total current assets	$27.72	$30.90	$32.75	$34.77	$36.97	$39.37
Net property, plant, and equipment	15.00	18.38	17.15	15.80	14.33	12.73
Total assets	$42.72	$49.28	$49.90	$50.57	$51.31	$52.11
Total current liabilities	$ 7.24	$ 6.98	$ 6.60	$ 6.08	$ 5.43	$ 4.62
Long-term debt	7.20	7.20	7.20	7.20	7.20	7.20
Equity	28.28	29.10	30.10	31.29	32.68	34.28
Subtotal	42.72	43.28	43.90	44.57	45.31	46.11
Financing needed	0.00	6.00	6.00	6.00	6.00	6.00
Total liabilities and equity	$42.72	$49.28	$49.90	$50.57	$51.31	$52.11

To decide which is better, management will want to determine which financing method will increase the value of the company more. First, let's look at the impact on the first factor in RICHS, risk.

1. Risk to Lenders

Affordability. To ensure that the company can remain solvent, management should determine how much cash is available to service debt obligations. This cash availability then provides a limit on the amount the company should borrow. A company that takes on financial obligations in excess of its ability to service them is courting disaster.

During good times, with a steady, predictable cash flow, companies are not likely to encounter financial embarrassment or distress. It is during the "down" times, when cash flow is reduced, that problems are encountered. Thus, the cash flow determinant of debt serviceability should be based on scenarios of cash shortage.

The factors that might lead to a cash shortage will be different for each firm. For some companies, an unusual demand for its products and the resulting need for cash to finance growth might be the downside scenario. For other companies, an economic recession with a decline in sales might cause cash problems. Whatever the case, the company should examine the cash flows under the maximum likely cash shortfall to determine its ability to meet debt payments and remain solvent.

There may be actions a company can take to free up cash during these difficult periods. For example, during a recession a company might postpone capital investments. If the problem is caused by too rapid growth, the company might decide to reduce its credit terms and decrease accounts receivable. After evaluating the impact of all these alternatives, the company can determine how much cash will be available to pay debt obligations. The amount of debt this cash can service should establish a company's debt limit or **debt capacity**.

Companies may decide to borrow less than their capacity. The actual leverage the company decides to obtain is termed the **debt policy**. Whereas debt capacity is determined by the ability of the company to service the debt, the debt policy is determined by market reaction. The objective of debt policy is to maximize the market value of the company by minimizing the cost of capital.

Current Situation.   To measure Greenway's ability to meet its cash obligations, we can use the coverage ratios discussed in Chapter 1. These ratios focus on the relationship between the company's fixed obligations, primarily debt service, and the resources available to meet them. Obviously, the higher the ratio, the more margin for error. As shown in Exhibit 7–7, projected earnings before interest and taxes in 1989 will cover interest, with room to spare, and will do so through 1993:

$$\text{Earnings/Interest coverage} = \frac{\text{EBIT}}{\text{Interest}}$$

$$= \frac{\$4.5}{\$0.7}$$

$$= 6.43 \text{ or } 643\%.$$

Even companies without earnings before interest and taxes can afford some debt, since interest is paid with cash. Because Greenway invests an amount equal to its depreciation in working-capital increases (WCI in the following formulas) and property, plant, and equipment (PP&E), its ratio of cash flow to interest coverage is the same as its ratio of earnings to interest coverage. If Greenway did not reinvest an amount equal to depreciation, the ratio would rise to 9.0 or 900 percent:

$$\text{Cash flow/Interest coverage} = \frac{\text{EBIT} + \text{Depreciation} - (\text{PP\&E} + \text{WCI})}{\text{Interest}}$$

$$= \frac{\$4.5 + \$1.8 - (\$1.0 + \$0.8)}{\$0.7}$$

$$= 6.43 \text{ or } 643\%$$

Interest expense may not be the only contractual payment Greenway must make. The ratio may be adapted to include, for instance, any principal payments the company must make.

$$\text{Cash flow/Debt-service coverage} = \frac{\text{EBIT} + \text{Depreciation} - (\text{PP\&E} + \text{WCI})}{\text{Interest} + [\text{Principal}/(1 - \text{Tax rate})]}$$

Because Greenway does not have principal payments until 1994, this ratio would be the same as that for cash flow–interest coverage. Notice that since principal payments are made from after-tax funds, the payment must be adjusted to a before-tax basis. Greenway's effective tax rate is 34 percent, so each $1 of principal requires $1.52 [$1.00/(1 − .34)] of earnings before taxes.

Interest is not the only payment Greenway management wants to make. Dividends, because of the Greenway family's policies, are a high priority. Therefore, management may want to add dividends to the payments to be covered. This move would reduce the coverage ratio in 1989 to 111 percent, still providing for an 11 percent decline in cash flow before Greenway management would have to consider changing the dividend policy.

Exhibit 7–11 shows what will happen to the ratios of earnings to interest coverage if Greenway chooses either debt or equity. Because the projected cost savings are not certain, it also shows what will happen to the ratio if EBIT is only $4.5 million. If the company finances its need with debt, the ratio is lower by half, but interest expense can still be covered easily. When management includes dividends, however, the contractual payment coverage ratios are less than 100 percent if new earnings do not materialize. Even if earnings do materialize, the coverage ratios leave little room for error the first year the new plant is owned and operated.

EXHIBIT 7–11   Greenway 1989 Interest Coverage Ratios: Alternative Financing Schemes (dollars in thousands)

	Old EBIT		New EBIT	
	Debt	Equity	Debt	Equity
EBIT	$4,500	$4,500	$5,300	$5,300
Old interest	$ 700	$ 700	$ 700	$ 700
New interest	$ 720	. . .	$ 720	. . .
Total interest	$1,420	$ 700	$1,420	$ 700
EBIT/Interest	316.9%	642.9%	373.2%	757.1%
Dividends	$2,223	$2,777	$2,223	$2,777
EBIT/Contractual payments	93.9%	91.7%	110.7%	108.0%

If new earnings materialize, the company can cover its debt obligations and dividend payments. In later years, because management expects EBIT to grow, coverage ratios will improve. We can conclude that lenders will feel assured that their interest payments will be met—or will they? In 1989, EBIT covers interest more than three times. Is this enough of a cushion to comfort lenders? That depends on how volatile Greenway's earnings might be. Lenders to companies with very volatile earnings will want a larger cushion than lenders to companies whose earnings are quite stable.

Risk.   The most common source of risk and unstable earnings is the impact of business cycles. Cyclical expansions and contractions strain a firm's ability to service product demand, maintain proper inventories, and control its resources adequately. These strains are most vividly seen in their effects on earnings and cash flow. As economic conditions deteriorate, companies will be pressed to find adequate cash flow to meet their obligations.

In addition to the problems caused by business cycles, companies face other types of risks. In some industries, strikes occur with almost the same regularity as business cycles. These disruptions cause problems not only for the companies being struck but also for their suppliers and customers. There are other unforeseeable problems, such as periodic market gluts and shortages of basic raw materials, that can affect particular industries or companies. In each of these situations, a company's ability to marshal its cash resources is critical to its ability to service debt.

Greenway's earnings and revenues have been very stable in the past. Management has been able to secure equipment orders far in advance of delivery and has not been badly hurt by previous recessions. Thus the coverage ratios should hearten lenders, if not shareholders. However, regardless of the alternative financing method chosen, Greenway will be somewhat more risky in 1989 than it was, or than it would be without the new plant. Therefore, of the two methods, common stock financing provides better coverage in 1989.

It is important to note that these calculations provide only an approximation of the cash available to service obligations during an adverse cycle. Greenway may be able to generate additional cash internally through astute management of inventories, accounts payable, accounts receivable, and capital expenditures. Thus cash could increase during periods of declining sales and decline during periods of increasing sales. This strategy is, in fact, what most companies have discovered. The critical factor in the management of a company is to identify the economic situation and respond quickly to minimize any adverse impact it may have on the cash position of the company.

Lenders are not only concerned with interest payments; they want to be certain the principal they have lent can be repaid. Since a lender's business is to make money by lending money, the lender does not want the money returned (that means the loss of interest income or the need to find another customer); they do want to be sure the money could be repaid. When firms are financially embarrassed, they cannot pay the interest on their debt; when they are distressed, they cannot repay the principal. To determine whether they could lose their principal, lenders often use ratios that measure the relative proportion of the company's capital they have provided. The ratio of debt to total capital is a good measure of the exposure of a lender's principal to loss.

Greenway currently has 20.3 percent of its capital in the form of debt. Exhibit 7–12 shows what will happen when Greenway adds $6 million in either debt or equity. Greenway's ratio of debt to total capital increases to 31.8 percent if it uses debt but drops to 17.4 percent if equity is raised. Increased leverage does increase the lender's risk; but does it raise it beyond a level that is acceptable?

To determine what the impact on leverage might be and whether it is acceptable, analysts often examine what others in the same industry are doing. Exhibit 7–13 provides information on others in Greenway's industry. Producers of lawn and garden equipment obtain about one third of their capital from lenders—more debt than Greenway will have if it raises $6 million in debt. In addition, Greenway's net EBIT/interest ratio would be above others in that industry. Based on these comparisons, if Greenway raises debt it would be following a conservative financing plan. Greenway does not really fall into the lawn and garden equipment industry, however. A better comparison is with producers of golf course equipment. In this case, Greenway would be following a more aggressive strategy.

Management must ask itself, "Why do golf course equipment producers have less debt and higher coverage ratios?" The likely answer is that they are more affected by economic cycles than sellers of lawn and garden equipment. Lenders have thus decided that they require more protection and will lend less to producers of golf equipment.

EXHIBIT 7–12   Greenway Corporation Debt to Total Capital: Alternative Financing Methods (dollars in thousands)

	Debt Financing	Equity Financing
Total capital:		
Old	$35,480	$35,480
New	6,000	6,000
Total	$41,480	$41,480
Debt outstanding:		
Old	$ 7,200	$ 7,200
New	6,000	0
Total debt	$13,200	$ 7,200
Debt to total long-term capital:		
Old	20.3%	20.3%
New	31.8%	17.4%

EXHIBIT 7–13   Industry Comparisons

	Interest Coverage	Debt to Total Capital
Lawn and garden equipment producers:		
RideRite Enterprises	310.3%	33.1%
Topflight Irrigators	253.7	34.3
General Cropharvester, Inc.	304.5	46.0
Greenway Corporation	642.0	31.8
Golf course equipment producers:		
Fairway Products, Inc.	1,430.3	11.2
Greenskeepers Corporation	2,103.1	18.1
Sam Speed, Inc.	1,836.1	15.3
Greenway Corporation	642.0%	31.8%

While Greenway may well be stronger and more able to handle higher levels of debt than others in its industry, following a different financing plan is likely to cause lenders to scrutinize Greenway very carefully. Therefore, we must be certain that debt financing will indeed be better than sale of stock for Mr. Greenway, the little Greenways, and the rest of the shareholders. How about the shareholders? Which would they prefer? Which alternative will create more value?

2. Income

One of the obvious impacts of financing on shareholder value is its effect on their income—the I in RICHS. If a particular form of financing increases the riskiness of the firm, the risk should be offset by increased income. New funds are generally invested in productive assets, with the benefits from investment accruing to the investors. Because the debtholders' claim, although senior, is fixed, the residual benefits belong to the common shareholders. That is why management should analyze income or value from the shareholders' point of view. Such an analysis is also consistent with the concept that management should maximize value for the shareholders.

In determining the impact the financing decision will have on the income of shareholders, two general costs need to be considered: first, the explicit cost of the financing—the impact on the earnings and cash flow per share, and second, the implicit cost—the impact on the market price of the stock.

Earnings-per-share impact. To determine explicit cost, as reflected in earnings and cash flow per share, Greenway managers will estimate the effects that each financing alternative would have on the company's earnings per share. This analysis is similar to the coverage analysis that was undertaken to estimate the impact of risk on the company.

The analysis starts with the assumption that earnings before interest and taxes will be the same regardless of the method used to finance the company, and that earnings are a good proxy for the value the investor will obtain. Exhibit 7–14 shows how each financing alternative—debt, or equity in the form of common stock—would affect Greenway with and without the new earnings. The only changes in the results from those before financing (the first column) are caused by the alternative financing plans. Note that the new plant, working-capital, and depreciation charges associated with the added capital have not yet been included, which makes the columns comparable.

Comparing the impact of the two alternatives indicates that the equity alternative, the issuance of common stock, lowers earnings per share for 1989 more than the debt alternative, with and without new earnings. Although total earnings for Greenway are expected to increase to $5.3 million from $4.5 million as the company uses its new capital, the additional shares issued dilute the impact of increased earnings on individual shares. Each owner now holds a smaller piece of the company, although the total size of the company has increased. A reduction in earnings per share is a common occurrence as additional common stock dilutes the benefits of stock ownership.

The higher the EBIT, the more attractive debt will look; because once the debt's fixed cost (interest) is covered, the residual goes to the shareholders. As EBIT rises, shareholders will find the debt financing increasingly attractive.

There is one more thing to notice about this analysis before we use it to help Greenway management decide between debt and equity financing. Notice that we focused on the impact of the financing alternatives on earnings per share, not cash flow, by looking at a range of earnings before interest and taxes. Why the focus on EBIT and earnings per share, not cash flow and cash flow per share, our focus in valuing investment strategies in Chapters 4 and 6?

The reason is that we can save ourselves some trouble. It is true that Greenway Corporation's net earnings will change as a result of the different financings; however, the changes in PP&E, working capital, and depreciation that are added and subtracted from those earnings to create the cash flow are identical for the two options. Therefore, we can use earnings per share as an indication of cash flow.

The effects on the shareholders of different financing methods are often shown graphically in an EPS-EBIT chart. Exhibit 7–15 shows this comparison for Greenway. Each line shows earnings per share (EPS) for a financing alternative under different EBIT levels. Since the relationships are linear, only two points are necessary to plot each of the lines. Typically, analysts determine the **breakeven point**—that is, the EBIT level at which the EPS figures are equivalent for the financing alternatives—and one other point. For Greenway, at any EBIT level above $4.3 million, the debt alternative will provide greater earnings per share. The earnings per share at the breakeven point are $2.05, calculated by using this formula:

$$\frac{(EBIT - I_n - I_o)(1 - t) - P}{CS_d} = \frac{(EBIT - I_n - I_o)(1 - t) - P}{CS_e}$$

where

$$
\begin{aligned}
EBIT &= \text{Breakeven EBIT level} \\
I_o &= \text{Interest payments on old debt} \\
I_n &= \text{Interest payments on new debt} \\
t &= \text{Tax rate} \\
P &= \text{Preferred dividends applicable} \\
&\quad \text{to the alternative under consideration} \\
CS_d &= \text{The number of common shares outstanding} \\
&\quad \text{with the debt alternative} \\
CS_e &= \text{The number of common shares outstanding} \\
&\quad \text{with the equity alternative}
\end{aligned}
$$

The breakeven formula can be solved for the EBIT level, as follows:

$$EBIT = \frac{(CS_d \times I_o) - (CS_e \times I_o) - (CS_e \times I_n)}{CS_d - CS_e} + \frac{P}{(1 - t)}$$

Although earnings (and cash flow) are higher with debt financing, it is important to consider that Greenway surpassed the breakeven EBIT and EPS level, above which debt is preferable, only in one of the past years, 1988. While debt financing does provide higher EPS for the projected growth range of the company, Greenway has recently passed the point at which debt financing would have resulted in lower earnings per share.

The EPS-EBIT chart, Exhibit 7–15, demonstrates the results of leverage. As can be seen, the slope of the debt financing line is greater than the slope of the equity financing line. In other words, for the same growth in EBIT, the growth in earnings per share under debt financing exceeds the EPS growth with common stock financing. This increased rate of change is the primary advantage of using leverage, or increased debt, in financing a firm. The bigger the difference in the slopes of the two lines, the faster the rate of change and the greater the impact of leverage on earnings.

Although our focus has been on the benefits of leverage, it is important to note that below the breakeven point, leverage works against shareholders. When the EBIT falls below this point, the impact of the leverage will be reversed and shareholders will suffer. The same analysis can be used to study the effect of financing alternatives on dividends per share at different EBIT levels when the payout ratio is kept constant.

Risk to shareholders.   We have seen that income increases with debt. We also concluded that lenders should see that Greenway can afford debt— that the probability of bankruptcy is not large, even with a proportion of

EXHIBIT 7–14   Impact on Greenway's Earnings and Cash Flow of Proposed Financing Schemes, 1989 (dollars in thousands except per share data)

		Old EBIT	
		Proposed Financing	
	Before Financing	Debt	Equity
EBIT	$4,500	$4,500	$4,500
Old interest	(700)	(700)	(700)
New interest	0	(720)	0
Profit before taxes	3,800	3,080	3,800
Taxes	(1,292)	(1,047)	(1,292)
Profit after taxes	2,508	2,033	2,508
Depreciation	1,800	1,800	1,800
Change in property, plant, and equipment and in working capital	(1,800)	(1,800)	(1,800)
Cash flow	$2,508	$2,033	$2,508
Number of shares	926	926	1,157
Earnings per common share	$ 2.71	$ 2.19	$ 2.17
Earnings dilution	0	19%	20%
Cash flow per share	$ 2.71	$ 2.19	$ 2.17

		New EBIT	
		Proposed Financing	
	Before Financing	Debt	Equity
EBIT	$5,300	$5,300	$5,300
Prior interest	(700)	(700)	(700)
New interest	0	(720)	0
Profit before taxes	4,600	3,880	4,600
Taxes	(1,564)	(1,319)	(1,564)
Profit after taxes	3,036	2,561	3,036
Depreciation	2,120	2,120	2,120
Change in property, plant, and equipment and in working capital	(2,120)	(2,120)	(2,120)
Cash flow	$3,036	$2,561	$3,036
Number of shares	926	926	1,157
Earnings per common share	$ 3.28	$ 2.76	$ 2.62
Earnings dilution	0	16%	20%
Cash flow per share	$ 3.28	$ 2.76	$ 2.62

EXHIBIT 7–15   EPS-EBIT Chart, Greenway Corporation

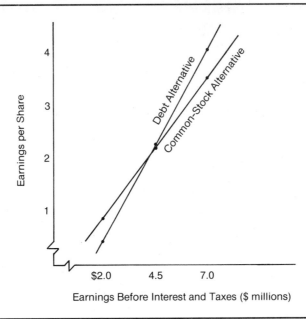

Earnings Before Interest and Taxes ($ millions)

debt to total capital of 31.8 percent. How will Greenway's shareholders see the increase in risk?

Leverage certainly affects shareholders' risk. Greenway will have higher fixed costs; and while its EBIT will not be any more sensitive to changes in economic conditions after financing costs than before, earnings and thus cash flows will certainly be affected. These changes will in turn affect the safety of the shareholders' returns.

Earlier in this section we saw that effect when we looked at the three scenarios for Greenway in Exhibit 7–3 and saw that the value of the equity rose and fell more with each increase in leverage. The impact of leverage on shareholders' value is that risk to the shareholders' position rises with leverage, and so should their required return. Let's look at the effect of leverage on Greenway shareholders' required return using the two models of equity valuation that we used in Chapter 4: the capital asset pricing model and the dividend discount model.

How would changes in leverage affect the factors used in the capital asset pricing model? Regardless of what happens to Greenway, or how much leverage it takes on, the estimated nominal risk-free rate of return and market premium used in the capital asset pricing model will not change: they depend on overall economic conditions. What will change is Greenway's beta. If Greenway takes on this fixed-rate debt, the beta will change. It will increase, because the after-tax earnings of the company will become more volatile. The increased volatility comes from deducting a fixed charge, interest, from the potentially volatile EBIT. As a result, any change in EBIT will be magnified by the time it reaches net income.

The beta for Greenway with a proportion of 31.8 percent debt in its total capital will be expected to change unless shareholders fail to see the potential increase in risk. We can estimate the size of this change using the capital asset pricing model and the following hypothetical relationship.

β of leveraged firm = β of unleveraged firm $\times$
$$(1 + [\text{Debt} / \text{Equity} \times (1 - \text{Tax rate})])$$

Greenway has a beta of 1.30 at its current debt-to-equity level of 25.5 percent. Without debt, its beta would be 1.11; and with 26.9 percent debt, it would be 1.46. Since lenders are willing to lend Greenway $6 million for 12 percent, with a 7-year Treasury security rate of 7.54 percent and the risk premium at a low of 6 percent, Greenway's cost of equity would be 16.3 percent and its cost of capital would be 13.6 percent. Before seeing how this would affect the company's and its shareholders' value, let's double-check our capital asset pricing model estimate using the dividend discount model:

$$\text{Shareholders' required return} = \frac{\text{Dividends}}{\text{Market price}} + \text{Growth}$$

Because of the increase in leverage, Greenway will have to pay more interest. This fixed cost can affect the company's ability to raise its dividend, so investors' estimates of dividend growth should change. Currently Greenway pays $2.40 per share in dividends. This dividend is very high relative to earnings, but Greenway is mature and has had few uses for its profitability inside the company. Furthermore, the Greenway family has expressed a need for the money. Before the financing, earnings growth was expected to be 5.2 percent, as shown in Exhibit 7–16. After financing, growth will increase to 6.8 percent with debt financing and 6 percent with equity financing. Thus shareholders might expect that management will increase dividends at about the earnings and cash flow growth rate of 6.9 percent. With debt financing and using this figure as the growth rate in the dividend discount model, we find the cost of equity to be:

$$\text{Shareholders' required return} = \frac{\text{Dividends}}{\text{Market price}} + \text{Growth}$$

$$= \frac{\$2.40}{\$25.50} + 6.9$$

$$= 16.3\%$$

which is the same as the cost of equity we calculated using the capital asset pricing model. The weighted-average cost of capital that results is 13.6

EXHIBIT 7–16   Greenway Corporation EBIT Forecasts

	1989	1990	1991	1992	1993	Compound Rate of Growth
EBIT (millions)	$5.30	$5.58	$5.87	$6.17	$6.49	5.2%
Earnings and cash flow per share:						
Without financing	$3.28	$3.48	$3.69	$3.90	$4.63	5.9%
Debt financing	$2.77	$2.97	$3.17	$3.39	$3.61	6.8%
Equity financing	$2.62	$2.78	$2.95	$3.12	$3.30	6.0%

percent. Combining the cost of capital with the forecasted cash flows shown in Exhibit 7–9, we can determine the value of Greenway.

We do have to make some other assumptions that are reasonable in light of our analysis. First, the company will grow at 6.9 percent. Second, there will be no changes in working capital, and depreciation will be reinvested in new plant and equipment. Using the perpetuity method of valuation and a cost of capital of 13.6 percent, the value of Greenway, debt financed, is:

$$\text{Company value} = \frac{\text{Annual cash flow}}{\text{Cost of capital} - \text{Constant growth}}$$

$$= \frac{\$3,498}{13.6\% - 6.9\%}$$

$$= \frac{\$3,498}{6.7\%}$$

$$= \$52,209$$

Remember to use the after-tax cash flow *without* deducting any financing costs. Those costs are included in the cost of capital.

If equity is used to finance the $6 million need, debt will constitute 17.4 percent of capital; and with a cost of equity of 15.3 percent (beta of 1.30), the cost of capital will be 14.2 percent. Assuming that earnings and cash flows grow at 6.0 percent, as shown in Exhibit 7–16, the value under equity financing is:

$$\text{Company value} = \frac{\$3,498}{14.2\% - 6.0\%}$$

$$= \frac{\$3,498}{8.2\%}$$

$$= \$42,659$$

EXHIBIT 7–17   Greenway Value: Alternative Financing (in thousands except per share value)

	Debt Financing	Equity Financing
Value of company	$52,209	$42,659
Debt value:		
Old	(7,200)	(7,200)
New	(6,000)	(0)
Equity value	$39,009	$35,458
Number of shares	926	1,157
Value per share	$ 42.13	$ 30.65

This cannot simply be compared to the $52,209, the value under debt financing. We are looking at the value of the total company, not the value to equity holders. We must reduce the total company value by the value of the debt, as shown in Exhibit 7–17, and compare values per share.

Debt financing increases shareholders' returns. Since the increase in income is not fully offset by increased risk, the value of Greenway increases. Thus, given our analysis, the best alternative appears to be debt financing. A debt-to-total-capital ratio of 31.8 percent should not be considered too extreme by lenders, the cost of capital should decline, and shareholder value should increase, with the addition of debt. The result will be an increased price for the shareholders' stock; and the price/earnings ratio, often a measure of the relative value of a company, should increase under debt financing, as shown in Exhibit 7–18.

3. Control

Equity Financing.   In addition to diluting earnings per share, issuing equity involves a potential loss of ownership control—the C in RICHS. An issue of new common stock can expand the existing ownership and dilute

EXHIBIT 7–18   Impact of Financing on Greenway's Price/Earnings Ratio

		New Plant	
	No New Plant	Debt Financing	Equity Financing
Earnings per share	$ 2.71	$ 2.77	$ 2.62
Market price per share	$27.17	$42.13*	$30.20*
Implied price/earnings ratio	10.1	15.2	11.5

*From Exhibit 7-17.

voting control of the company. Whether this dilution is important depends on the distribution of ownership of the company. For companies with a significant proportion of ownership in the hands of an individual or a small group of shareholders, the issue of ownership dilution may be critical. If the existing owners wish to maintain a dominant voting position without buying the new stock, then an equity issue may not be appropriate. Typically, the dilution issue is critical at three levels: when the ownership bloc will be reduced below 100, below 50, and below 25 percent.

Considering the first level, 100 percent, the problem of introducing outside owners for the first time is usually more a psychological problem than a managerial one. If the original owners can still maintain an ownership position greater than 50 percent, they are in a position to continue control of the affairs of the company. The primary change will be that outside owners now have an interest in the operations of the company and may require additional accounting, reporting, and legal efforts.

There may be compelling reasons for issuing outside equity. Not the least of these is the need to develop a market for the equity to provide for liquidity in the owners' holdings. Another factor that may force a company to admit outside owners is rapid growth accompanied by capital needs that exceed the company's debt capacity. For these or other reasons, the owner or ownership bloc may believe that selling equity to outsiders is necessary. This decision is usually not easy to make, however.

Once outside owners are involved, the original owners can maintain operating control only so long as they own 50 percent of the voting common stock. Thus the 50 percent hurdle is a difficult one for many owners to pass. Usually the need for outside equity must be severe before the controlling owners will relinquish their 50 percent equity control.

For publicly held companies with a widely distributed ownership position, effective control can usually be maintained with an ownership bloc of 20 to to 25 percent. Through solicitation of proxy votes, an insider group with a significant minority position can dominate managerial decisions and control the operations of the company. Because dilution of this bloc through the issuance of additional shares could eliminate effective control, dilution below this level is another critical point in evaluating the equity control issue.

There have been recent instances of companies' using equity dilution as a means of thwarting unwanted takeover bids. Through issuing new stock, the company dilutes the ownership an unfriendly suitor may have gained, thereby making the takeover more difficult.

Other than at these critical points, the dilution of control is not usually a significant issue. Obviously, for the company with a widely dispersed ownership and no significant ownership blocs, the control issue is typically moot.

Debt Financing.   Although the control issue is more easily assessed for equity financing, debt financing may also impose some control issues. Frequently lenders impose restrictions on company operations in the form of debt covenants. These covenants may specify certain actions the company may or may not undertake or may limit other actions. For example, loan covenants may require the company to maintain specific levels of working capital, to limit additional borrowings, or to limit the amount of dividends. The purpose of the covenants is to protect the lender's investment, but their effect may be to restrict the ability of managers to operate the company as they believe necessary.

Jim Greenway and the Greenway family own 30 percent of the stock of Greenway Corporation. Since the rest of the shares are held by a large number of people, the Greenway family effectively controls the company. They certainly will be concerned about what happens to their control under different financing alternatives.

Greenway has 926,376 shares outstanding. If the company were to finance its needs with equity, 230,769 new shares would be sold. Jim Greenway and his family would then own:

$$\text{New proportion} = \frac{\text{Old proportion} \times \text{Old shares}}{\text{New shares}}$$

$$= \frac{30\% \times 926,376}{1,157,145}$$

$$= 24\%$$

Even if one person were to buy all the new shares, he or she would only control 20 percent of the company. The family would not, apparently, lose effective control. Even so, this issue, added to the value created by debt financing, should encourage management to consider debt the more attractive alternative.

4. Hedging/Speculating

Hedging and speculating, the final factors in the RICHS analysis, are actions that most of us think of in connection with commodities or securities markets. When investors want to insulate themselves from a change in price, they may hedge. One way to hedge is in the futures markets. A futures contract is a contract to deliver a particular quantity of a commodity (including Treasury bills and bonds, and stock market indices) at a particular time at a given price. A producer or owner of the commodity can lock in the price at which it will be sold (hedge) by selling a futures contract large enough to cover the commodity held, such as the crop expected to be harvested. Regardless of what happens to the price between the time the future is sold and the date the commodity is to be delivered, the hedger has a guaranteed price—has "hedged his or her risk."

The same futures contract can be used to speculate. For example, a speculator, believing a commodity price will decline in the future, can sell a futures contract (without owning the commodity) and, if the price declines, cover the obligation to deliver with another, less expensive futures contract. The speculator gains the difference between the price at which the first contract was sold and the price for which the covering contract was bought.

These are just two examples of ways futures can be used to hedge and speculate. Investors who are satisfied with the current price can hedge by locking in the price and eliminating price volatility. Investors willing to bet on the upward or downward direction of prices speculate.

Corporate managers do the same thing every time they make a financing decision. Implicitly or explicitly, they bet on the direction in which interest rates and stock market levels will move, and they either hedge or speculate. In the past, managers have used a simple rule of thumb: match the maturity of the need (e.g., new plant) with that of the financing instrument (e.g., long-term debt or equity). Thus, financing decisions were made by default. While the rule of thumb is reasonable in environments where interest rates and the stock market are relatively stable, management must decide whether to speculate or hedge when markets are not stable. Decisions by default can be costly.

Risk-averse managers can use options and futures contracts to protect a company if they believe interest rates are going to change. Change is the operative word because, if the manager believes there will be a change in either direction, the potential change can be hedged—can be insured against. This insurance is bought in the futures or options markets.

A risk-taking manager might decide to try to capture gains that cheaper financing later on might bring. For instance, Greenway's managers might choose to finance the needed $6 million with short-term money—like commercial paper or an existing bank line of credit—and refinance later, deliberately mismatching the lives of the asset and the liability for a short time. If the managers' bet is wrong, however, and rates go up, the speculating managers will be forced to borrow later at higher rates, rather than making the expected profit.

Managers deciding to finance with equity face the same dilemma. Should they issue stock at the going price, or wait until the market rises and fewer shares need to be issued to raise the same money? Typically, managers are tempted to delay issuing new equity as long as possible because they believe that, in a growing company, earnings will steadily increase. In that case, a stock issue should be delayed to take advantage of the impact of increased profitability on the stock price.

The dilemma must be faced. Forecasting interest rates and market prices is difficult, and the consequences of incorrect forecasts are especially severe in planning capital structure. If forced to raise capital in unfavorable markets, a company will bear the impact of that decision for several years. Exhibit 7–19 shows the rapidity with which short-term rates can change. Rate changes in the 1970s and 1980s have been especially severe and rapid. For most growing companies, the problem is not whether to issue debt or

EXHIBIT 7–19   Interest Rates for Debt of Different Maturities

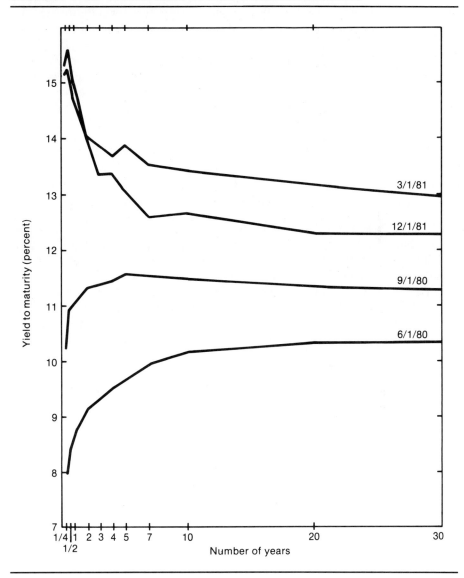

SOURCE: Salomon Bros., "An Analytical Record of Yields and Yield Spreads," May 1981.

equity, but when to do so. Growth brings with it a continuous need for funds, and most companies find that they are unable to finance growth solely through internal sources. Recognizing that the use of external capital is inevitable, companies should seek the most opportune time to enter the markets.

In considering whether to hedge or speculate, management has two primary concerns: (1) the use of long-term versus short-term financing, and (2) the sequencing of financing methods over time when the company needs money continuously.

A complete discussion of hedging and speculating is well beyond the purposes of this chapter. However, you have learned to use multiscenario analysis to see what would happen *if* changes occurred. For example, for the risk-taking manager who wants to issue debt but believes that rates will decline, there will be at least three scenarios:

1. Interest rates do not decline and the money must be renegotiated later at the same cost.
2. Interest rates decline and the money is borrowed later at the lower rate.
3. Interest rates rise and the money is borrowed later at a higher rate.

Each of the three scenarios would result in a different value for the company. Managers must balance the value gained if rates decline against the value lost if rates rise. In addition, the probability that each scenario will occur must be considered. This analysis can be quite sophisticated.

The implicit and explicit speculating and hedging activities involved in financing corporations today are increasingly complex. A wise manager will call on experts inside the firm and at the company's bank and investment bank to explore hedging and speculating in:

1. The general level of interest rates.
2. The level of the stock market.
3. The company's stock price.
4. The quality rating of the company's debt.

5. Greenway's Financing Decision

Now back to Greenway. On the basis of Risk, Income, Control, Hedging, and Speculating, what should Greenway use to finance its needs? Since good managers create value—they add to their shareholders' RICHS—Greenway management should borrow: value will be created for its shareholders, without subjecting them to undue risks.

Greenway managers decided to use debt to finance their $6 million need. Since the company was growing slowly, management did not believe it would need much new financing in the near future and thus did not feel the need to retain much debt capacity for future use. In addition, management believed that interest rates, lower than they had been in the recent past, were unlikely to drop much further. Management concluded that the shareholders would prefer debt and that the risk the added debt created was not excessive.

6. Leasing

Greenway considered one other way to finance a part of its needs: it could lease new equipment for the fabrication operation in the new plant. It may seem peculiar to be discussing leasing in a chapter on financing, but leasing is a form of financing. There are some who believe that the question management should answer is whether to lease or to buy equipment. That is not the question. The question is: Once you have decided to get the equipment, should you use equity or debt financing to purchase the equipment or should you lease it?

Greenway's new equipment would amount to $446,975 of the total $4.5 million needed for the new plant. Greenway could, of course, borrow this amount at 12 percent, but the equipment manufacturer's salesperson suggested that the company might want to lease the equipment for $90,910 a year for 10 years. Should management lease the equipment?

While there is considerable disagreement about the best way to analyze the lease-borrow decision, we will use a straightforward net present value analysis and a 7.92 percent discount rate (12 percent after taxes) to reflect the cost of debt. We could, of course, use the cost of capital, as we have in other valuations, but both the lease and the debt will use similar amounts of Greenway's debt capacity. Thus, if the lease is superior at the cost of debt, it would be so at the cost of capital. If leasing provides a better net present value, Greenway should lease the equipment. If borrowing yields a superior NPV, borrowing is the way it should be financed.

Exhibit 7–20 illustrates an analysis of the alternative financing schemes. By buying the equipment and borrowing the money, Greenway gets tax shields from depreciation and interest. By leasing the equipment, Greenway benefits from the fact that lease payments are tax-deductible expenses. The present value of the lease payments is $16,890 greater than borrowing to buy the equipment. Thus it should not be leased.

7. Leverage and Corporate Value

We began this long chapter by discussing whether leverage can create value for shareholders, and if so, where that value comes from. Unused debt capacity reduces shareholder value. Companies that do not fully use their debt capacity are less risky for their shareholders, but they provide lower returns. These companies are also prey for acquirers willing to take more risk and use unused debt capacity.

In Chapter 6 we discussed the valuation of acquisitions and divestitures. What we did not discuss was the value of debt capacity in making an acquisition. Leveraged buyouts are examples of acquisitions in which value is created when the acquirer permanently or temporarily increases the leverage of the target.

EXHIBIT 7–20 Lease Versus Borrow and Buy Analysis

	Borrow and Buy						
Year	Loan Payment (1)	Interest (2)	Depreciation (3)	Tax Shield [(2)+(3)]×.34	After-Tax Cash Cost (1)−(4)	Lease Payment (5)	After-Tax Lease Cash Cost (5)×.66
1	$88,492	$60,000	$100,000	$54,400	$ 34,092	$90,909	$ 60,000
2	88,492	56,581	80,000	46,438	42,055	90,909	60,000
3	88,492	52,752	64,000	39,696	48,797	90,909	60,000
4	88,492	48,463	51,200	33,885	54,607	90,909	60,000
5	88,492	43,659	40,960	28,771	59,722	90,909	60,000
6	88,492	38,279	32,768	19,709	68,783	90,909	60,000
7	88,492	32,254	32,768	17,667	70,825	90,909	60,000
8	88,492	25,505	32,768	15,373	73,119	90,909	60,000
9	88,492	17,947	32,768	12,803	75,689	90,909	60,000
10	88,492	9,481	32,768	9,925	78,567	90,909	60,000
Net present value at 7.92%					$387,172		$404,062

In Chapter 6 we discounted cash flows to all capital providers by the cost of capital to determine the value of an investment. This approach is appropriate so long as there will be *no major change in the capital structure or costs of debt.* In a leveraged buyout, there is a change in the capital structure.

Let's look at Zeus, the company we analyzed in Chapter 6. Zeus had no debt. It could raise debt at a cost of 10.8 percent and, using industry averages as a guide, could raise 30 percent of its capital in the form of debt. Exhibit 7–21 shows the analysis that a potential acquirer might make of Zeus in valuing it as an acquisition. Notice that we have included a line for interest cost in the expenses, and the principal in- and outflows in the cash flows, even though Zeus has no long-term debt. When we use this approach, the resulting net cash flows belong to the equity shareholders alone. Thus these cash flows must be discounted at the required return, the cost of equity, 13.8 percent.

The leveraged value of Zeus is $4.4 million or $43.68 per share. Without the increase in leverage to 70 percent, the value of the company is $3.3 million or $30.30 per share—an obvious illustration of how leverage can create value.

III. SUMMARY

In this section you have discovered that there is an optimal capital structure, at least in a world where interest is tax-deductible. You learned how to analyze the choice between debt financing and equity financing by looking at risk, income, control, hedging, and speculating. Although Greenway's financing decision involved only two alternatives, the RICHS framework of analysis can be used to evaluate multiple alternative methods of financing. It is simply an analytical framework for examining the capital-structure decision. The purpose of the analysis is to determine whether shareholder value has been created, whether managers are making shareholders RICH or just tricking investors, or themselves. Value is created only when returns are larger than required for the risk being taken, or when the risk is less than the size of the returns warrants.

Up to a point, leverage can create value for shareholders; at least it appears to do so. However, determining that point, the optimal capital structure, the point at which the cost of capital is lowest and the value of the company highest, is hard. We had to use all our tools—historical analysis, forecasting, cost of capital analysis, and valuation—to determine whether Greenway should issue debt or equity. It is a complex problem.

The task of the financial manager is to assess various factors and scenarios and determine the capital structure that will yield the optimum value for the company. Unfortunately, there is no simple formula that can be used to make the best decision. For the time being, capital structure analysis, like all financial analysis, will remain a managerial art.

EXHIBIT 7–21 Zeus Industries: Leveraged Valuation at 5% Real Growth and 70% Debt/Total Capital
(in thousands except per share value)

	1988	1989	1990	1991	1992	1993
Sales	$9,147	$9,605	$10,085	$10,589	$11,118	$11,674
Operating expenses	(8,415)	(8,836)	(9,278)	(9,742)	(10,229)	(10,740)
Depreciation	(50)	(53)	(55)	(58)	(61)	(64)
Interest	0	(107)	(107)	(107)	(107)	(107)
Income before taxes	682	609	645	682	721	763
Taxes (34%)	(232)	(207)	(219)	(232)	(245)	(259)
Income after taxes	450	402	426	450	476	504
Depreciation	50	53	55	58	61	64
Increase in property, plant and equipment	(50)	(53)	(55)	(58)	(61)	(64)
Increase in working capital	0	(91)	(96)	(101)	(106)	(111)
Payment of principal	0	(90)	(100)	(111)	(123)	(136)
Principal inflow*	990	90	100	111	123	136
Residual cash flow	1,440	311	330	349	370	393
Terminal value†	0	0	0	0	0	4,466
Total residual cash flow	$1,440	$ 311	$ 330	$ 349	$ 370	$ 4,859

Net present value = $4,368
Net present value per share = $43.68

*Principal inflow in 1988 is $0.99 million with new debt of 30% of capital. Capital is 90% of total assets of $3.6 million.
†The perpetuity value at a discount rate of 13.8% and with 5% inflation.

SELECTED REFERENCES

For a more detailed examination of value creation through capital structure, see:
Fruhan, William E., Jr. *Financial Strategy.* Homewood, Ill.: Richard D. Irwin, 1979.
Shapiro, Alan C. "Guidelines for Long-Term Corporate Financing Strategy." *Midland Corporate Finance Journal,* Winter 1986, pp. 6–19.

For additional information on assessing debt capacity, see:
Donaldson, Gordon. "Strategy for Financial Emergencies." *Harvard Business Review,* November-December 1969, pp. 67–79.
————. "New Framework for Corporate Debt Policy." *Harvard Business Review,* September-October 1978, pp. 149–64.

For other discussions of capital structure, see:
Bowen, Robert M.; Lane A. Daley; and Charles C. Huber, Jr.; "Leverage Measures and Industrial Classification: Review and Additional Evidence." *Financial Management,* Winter 1982, pp. 10–20.
Brealey, Richard, and Stewart Myers. *Principles of Corporate Finance.* 3d ed. New York: McGraw-Hill, 1988, chaps. 13–15, 17–18.
Pringle, John J., and Robert S. Harris. *Essentials of Managerial Finance.* Glenview, Ill.: Scott, Foresman, 1984, chaps. 13–14.
Myers, Stewart. "The Capital Structure Puzzle." *Midland Corporate Finance Journal* 3 (Fall 1985), pp. 6–18.
————. "The Search for the Optimal Capital Structure," *Midland Corporate Finance Journal* 1 (Spring 1983), pp. 6–11.
Ross, Steven and Randolph Westerfield. *Corporate Finance.* St. Louis, Mo.: Times Mirror/Mosby, 1988, chap. 21.
Scott, David F., Jr, and Dana J. Johnson. "Financing Policies and Practices in Large Corporations." *Financial Management,* Summer 1982, pp. 51–59.
VanHorne, James C. *Financial Management and Policy.* 6th ed. Englewood Cliffs, N.J.: Prentice-Hall, 1983, chaps. 9–10.
Weston, J. F., and Eugene Brigham. *Essentials of Managerial Finance.* 8th ed. Hinsdale, Ill.: Dryden Press, 1987, chap. 22.

The seminal articles on the irrelevance of capital structure are:
Modigliani, Franco, and Merton H. Miller. "The Cost of Capital, Corporation Finance, and the Theory of Investment." *American Economic Review,* June 1958, pp. 261–97.
————. "Corporate Income Taxes and the Cost of Capital: A Correction." *American Economic Review,* June 1963, pp. 433–43.

For discussion of leveraged buyouts, see:
Ferenbach, C. "Leveraged Buyouts: A New Capital Market Evolution." *Midland Corporate Finance Journal* 1 (Winter 1983), pp. 56–62.

For additional information about leasing analysis, see:
Bayless, Mark E., and J. David Diltz. "An Empirical Study of the Debt Displacement Effects of Leasing." *Financial Management,* Winter 1986, pp. 53–60.
Brick, Ivan E.; William Fung; and Marti Subrahmanyam. "Leasing and Financial Intermediation: Comparative Tax Advantages." *Financial Management,* Spring 1987, pp. 55–59.
Schall, L. "The Evaluation of Lease Finance Options," *Midland Corporate Finance Journal* 3 (Spring 1985), pp. 48–65.

STUDY QUESTIONS

1. Management at Zumar, Inc., a chain of gourmet food stores located primarily in New York, was planning to expand its main store in Manhattan. By expanding, Zumar management could add an imported beer and wine section. This $15 million addition, management believed, would increase sales by 20 percent, to $120 million in the next year, 1988. The new EBIT would be the same as Zumar had on its current product lines, 13 percent, and once the new beer and wine lines were established, management expected overall growth to go back to its traditional 2 percent. Taxes were expected to be 34 percent. Zumar currently had $40 million in 7 percent coupon long-term debt. While principal payments on this debt were $2.8 million per year, management expected to keep debt at this level and thus borrowed whenever principal payments were due. In addition to the debt, Zumar had 2 million shares of stock outstanding, with a par value of $2. The current balance sheet for the company is shown below.

Zumar, Inc.
(in millions)

Assets

Cash.	$ 54
Long-term assets	80
Total assets.	$134

Liabilities and Equity

Current liabilities.	$ 40
Long-term debt	40
Common stock ($2 par)	4
Retained earnings	50
Total debt and equity.	94
Total liabilities and equity	$134

   To finance the $15 million needed for expansion, management had two alternatives:
   a. Borrowing $15 million of 10-year 10 percent coupon debt with annual principal payments beginning after 5 years.
   b. Issuing equity of 750,000 common shares, netting, after issue costs, $20 per share.
   Prepare an EPS-EBIT table and chart using the existing and proposed levels of EBIT. What is the breakeven EBIT? How do you interpret these data?

2. Zumar management currently had a policy of increasing dividends about 5 percent per year. In 1987 the dividend per share was $0.75. Analyze

and compare the present dividend coverage with that likely under both debt and equity financing schemes at the projected level of sales.

3. Analyze the effect of both financing schemes on the company's risk and return. The company's current beta is 1.05. Seven-year U.S. Treasury bonds are yielding 8 percent and common stocks are expected to yield 6 percent above Treasury bonds. Several ratios for others in Zumar's industry are shown below.

Ratio	Zumar	Fallio's	Carston's Fine Foods
Assets/equity	248.2%	292.0%	100.0%
Return on sales	6.7	6.2	7.1
Total asset turnover	74.6	101.1	140.6
Return on equity	12.4	18.3	9.9
Dividend payout	22.4	80.0	85.0
EBIT/interest	464.3	150.0	NAp.

4. Which of the two financing schemes is expected to create more value for Zumar's shareholders? [Note: There will be no changes in net working capital, and corporate expenditures will be equal to depreciation. These aspects are typical of a low-growth company.]

APPENDIX A
Financial Modeling

It has long been recognized that forecasting performance—whether it is estimating the effect of marketing plans, predicting the cost savings from introducing new production methods, or forecasting future cash needs—is an art rather than a science. Although sophisticated statistical and mathematical techniques have been developed to aid in forecasting, these procedures have only *assisted* managers in dealing with uncertainty; they have not *eliminated* it.

An additional technique that has been developed to help managers in coping with uncertainty is financial modeling. Modeling consists of determining the variables that affect the results in a situation and defining the relationships between these variables in mathematical terms. Because the results of such models are typically stated in financial terms, the technique has come to be known as financial modeling. If properly used, the modeling process will provide insights that will assist managers in making better-informed decisions.

I. INTRODUCTION TO MODELING

One reason for the usefulness of models is that the technique provides a means for managers to examine the effects of the uncertainty of forecasts through sensitivity or "what if" analysis. Using this approach, managers develop forecasts and then change the values of the variables used in estimating the future results. Managers can then determine what the results would be if the values for the variables were to differ from those originally projected. By evaluating the sensitivity of the results to these changes, they are able to examine the riskiness or uncertainty of the projections. In addition, managers are able to determine which variables have the greatest impact on the results and therefore warrant the greatest scrutiny if the plans are implemented.

Despite the managerial value of this approach, it has typically been used to evaluate only plans or projects that would have a significant impact on the company. The primary reason for restricting its use has been the cost of developing the projections and recalculations needed for sensitivity analysis. Before the development of computers, the necessity of hand calculations obviously limited the practicality of sensitivity analysis. Even using computers, it was usually necessary to develop a specific computer program for each model. This meant that the manager needed to explain the project to a systems analyst or programmer, wait for the program to be written, and then—working with the programmer or analyst—evaluate the results.

Using the computer to perform the calculations for sensitivity analysis has been greatly facilitated in recent years with the development of "modeling languages." These computer languages are specialized computer programs designed to simplify the creation of models or forecasted relationships. Once the manager has specified the relationships between the variables in a model, the computer then goes through the laborious process of performing the calculations. Because the languages are user friendly, managers can use them without the assistance of computer programmers. Modeling languages allow the manager to do what he or she does best—think—and the computer to do what it does best—calculate.

Originally, these languages were developed to run on large mainframe systems. Now, many modeling programs have been created for use on microcomputers. The best known of these programs are generically called electronic spreadsheets because of their similarity to the spreadsheets used in manual projections. Appendix B provides an introduction to one of the most popular spreadsheet programs, Lotus 1-2-3. In addition, the mainframe modeling languages have been adapted to the microcomputer environment. The combination of these spreadsheet and modeling programs has made computer-based modeling available for all levels of management.

II. THE MODELING PROCESS

Regardless of the type of modeling approach used, either a spreadsheet or modeling language, the general process of developing a model is similar. The procedure for creating a model can be summarized in the following six steps.

1. Determine the Objectives

Before starting to create the model, it is important to understand what information the model is expected to provide. In other words, what is the purpose of the model? The answer to this question will provide the manager with the objectives for the model and the detail the model should include.

If the manager does not have a good idea of what the model should accomplish before the development process commences, there is obviously no way of knowing whether it is doing what it is supposed to do. Managers who don't know where they are going won't know what direction to go in, nor will they know if they have arrived.

Although this step seems obvious, many modeling projects start with managers deciding to "build a model." Such general approaches are unlikely to provide useful results. Unless the manager has a specific use in mind and constructs the model to fit that use, the model will not be a useful managerial tool.

2. Specify the Variables

After deciding what the model is supposed to do, the manager can then determine which variables or factors are important to include. The number of different variables and detail of the data depend on the nature and objectives of the model. For example, if the objective is to provide information about required inventory levels, the model will require detailed forecasts about expected orders, delivery times, production capacities, throughput times, and so on. On the other hand, a pro forma financial statement model might require only a few general income, expense, and balance sheet accounts.

The time horizons will also affect the level of detail required for the model. Monthly cash account projections for the next year would require more detail for the relevant variables than would an annual cash account projection for a five-year model.

The general approach is to match the detail of the input with the required detail of the output. If the objectives of the model are to provide detailed results, it should include all variables, stated as specifically and in as much detail as possible. If the objectives are broad and general, the variables needed are accordingly more general and less detailed.

3. Define the Relationships

After determining the relevant variables to include in the model, the next step is to define the relationships between the variables. These relationships are stated in mathematical terms. For example, if maintenance expense for a particular machine is expected to be $100 for each 500 hours of operation, the relationship could be expressed as:

$$\text{Maintenance expense} = \$100 \times (\text{Operating Hours}/500)[1]$$

In determining the relationships, most managers start with historical relationships. If the cost of goods sold for a company has been 85 percent of sales revenue, this would be a good starting relationship for the model. There may, however, be relationships that are expected to differ from historical patterns, or the model may contain relationships with which the company has not had previous experience. In these cases, the manager must rely on expectations for the model specifications. In any case, the relationships could, and should, be altered and the results examined using sensitivity analysis.

---

[1] The procedures for naming the variables and the mathematical operations used to specify the relationships vary between different modeling systems.

4. Construct the Model

Having defined the relationships among the relevant variables, these relationships are then combined to form the model. The specific procedures for combining these mathematical statements will depend on the modeling system being used. (See Appendix B for instructions on entering model statements using Lotus 1-2-3.) Different systems require the model to be constructed in different ways. Some systems are almost "free form," with no particular order required. Other systems are more procedural in nature and require that the statements be placed in a specific order. The instruction manual for the particular system being used must obviously be referenced for the proper procedures.

Too often managers undertake the model construction step as the first stage rather than the fourth stage in the modeling process. As a result, the model requires extra time to develop or may never provide meaningful results. As in any other type of construction project, having a plan and assembling the materials (the variable relationships) facilitates the final construction.

5. Validate the Model

Having constructed the model, it is critical to test it to ensure that it is working correctly. Mistakes do occur. There is no failure in making mistakes; the failure comes in neglecting to find and correct them. Too often managers accept the results of the model without verifying the accuracy of the output. This can lead to disastrous results.[2]

In examining the model, unusual results are an immediate clue that a mistake may have been made. Other than this obvious method, the only reliable way to ensure that the model is providing reliable results is to manually work through each step in the model to verify its accuracy.

This manual verification is naturally much easier with simple models. Therefore, it is a good procedure when developing complicated models to separate the model into simpler pieces and validate each piece. The model can then be expanded by including each piece after it has been tested. This approach simplifies the building and testing of the model.

6. Document the Model

Unfortunately most modelers stop once the model has been constructed and tested. The problem with ending at this stage is that few if any models are self-explanatory. The explanation of what the model is doing and of the nature of the relationships is not critical when the manager uses the model

---

[2] See "How Personal Computers Can Trip Up Executives," *Business Week,* September 24, 1984, pp. 94–102.

immediately. The problem occurs when others use it or when the manager returns to it after a lapse in time. There may be subsequent questions about how the model was constructed or what it does. For this reason, it is important to provide documentation explaining the variables and relationships used, critical assumptions, and other relevant factors. This documentation becomes an invaluable reference for understanding the model and greatly facilitates its use.

The documentation process begins with the construction of the model itself. The interpretation of the model can be increased by using variable names whenever possible. SALES IN YEAR 1 or SALES1 is more understandable than B3. Most spreadsheet programs allow the assigning of names to ranges or blocks of variables. Most modeling systems allow the inclusion of comments. The use of these features provides a type of self-documentation for the model.

The usefulness of the model is greatly increased if other managers can understand and use it. If it is only to be used occasionally, a well-documented model will save the manager time each time it is used.

III. SENSITIVITY ANALYSIS

The process of planning, constructing, and testing a model is a labor-intensive and often time-consuming task. If the manager has no intention of evaluating any of the relationships included in the model, then the use of a computer-based modeling system may not be required. However, since the relationships between variables are rarely known with certainty, the ability to change the relationships and observe the results is an important managerial tool. It is in this process of sensitivity analysis that computer-based modeling excels.

Sensitivity analysis is often called "what if" analysis because it allows the manager to ask the question, "What if the value of a relationship or a variable were changed?" Since the computer can quickly recompute the model following changes in any of the variables, it is a simple task for the manager to vary any of the relationships. Obviously, if the recalculations were to be done manually, every change would require a significant amount of time. Use of the computer reduces recalculation time to seconds.

This ease of recalculating the model with changed assumptions has its dangers, however. Because it is so easy to make changes in the variables, it is possible to become overwhelmed with numbers. When calculations were done by hand, managers made only the changes in relationships that were believed to be realistic and possible. Although computer modeling systems have removed the time constraint, they should not be used to replace managerial deliberation. Changing variables over unrealistic ranges may result in more data than the manager can assimilate and use. Instead of providing too much data, which leads to "analysis paralysis," the modeling approach should lead to better managerial analysis and decision making.

The crucial skill is to determine which variables to analyze. The manager should be seeking insights and understanding of the problem, not simply a vast array of numbers. Although these critical variables will differ from model to model, a few general comments can be made.

Most models are based on a few key assumptions, such as a sales forecast or a cost level. Sensitivity analysis should be performed on these "keystone" variables to determine how sensitive the results are to changes in these key assumptions.

If variable relationships were based on changes from historical results or were forecast for areas where the company had no previous experience, the manager should examine the effects of changes in these relationships. An efficient means of doing this is through an iterative approach. The manager makes several runs or iterations of the model, changing the value for one or more of the variables for each iteration. The more uncertainty surrounding any relationship, the greater the need for sensitivity analysis of the relationship.

In addition to this "what if" sensitivity analysis, accomplished by changing the value of one or more relationships, the manager may also wish to determine what the relationship between certain variables would need to be to achieve a certain specific or optimum value for another variable. For example, the manager could alter sales expense values to achieve a certain net profit margin level. If the sales expense figure is reasonable, the manager can use it as a planning or performance objective. This process is called optimization or goal seeking.

Some modeling systems are designed to allow the manager to easily perform optimization or goal-seeking analysis. On any system, it is possible to do the analysis through a trial-and-error process of changing the value of one variable and observing the effect on the goal or target variable. This process is repeated until the target or optimum results occur. Although a more laborious process, this approach may provide useful results.

Another approach to sensitivity analysis is to develop various sets of relationships based on different scenarios. The manager determines possible future events or combinations of events and runs the model using the appropriate relationships for each of these scenarios.[3] For example, in modeling a new product introduction, the manager may develop scenarios for possible competitive reactions, different economic environments, and alternative marketing strategies.

Some modeling systems also allow the manager to use probability distributions. Instead of a specific relationship between variables, the manager can include a range of values for the relationship with a probability distribution for the values in the range. The modeling system would then ran-

---

[3] See Robert E. Linneman and John D. Kennell, "Shirt-Sleeve Approach to Long-Range Plans," *Harvard Business Review*, March-April, 1977, pp. 141–150.

domly select one value from the range, calculate the results of the model using that value, select another value, calculate the results, and so forth for a specified number of iterations. This approach, known as Monte Carlo simulation, provides the manager with a distribution of outcomes instead of a specific or "point estimate" of the results.[4]

Monte Carlo simulation provides useful information about the range of possible results and therefore the riskiness of the outcomes. Unlike goal seeking, however, if simulation capabilities are not available on the modeling system, it is difficult to duplicate the process through successive recalculations of the model.

IV. SUMMARY

The purpose of all these analytical techniques is to provide the manager with useful information to aid in decision making. The advantage of using a modeling system is that the manager can directly examine the results of various decisions before having to implement them. The manager can examine the results of various alternatives and test the effects of changing relationships or variable values. Such testing enables the manager to better understand the risks of the alternatives and provides useful information for monitoring critical variables.

The power of the modeling approach is now available to all managers with the development of microcomputers and modeling systems that run on these systems. The proper use of financial models will provide for better decision making by managers.

---

[4] See David B. Hertz, "Risk Analysis in Capital Investment," *Harvard Business Review,* September-October, 1979, pp. 169–181.

APPENDIX B

Using Lotus 1–2–3

As discussed in Appendix A, computer-based financial modeling (or decision support systems, as the programs are sometimes called) has revolutionized the use of computers in business applications. Many different modeling programs are available for both large, mainframe computers and microcomputers such as IBM personal computers. The programs vary in price, ease of use, and level of sophistication.

A popular approach to financial modeling on microcomputers has been the development of electronic spreadsheets. These programs simulate the familiar matrix or spreadsheet format used in accounting. Their popularity is due to the ease with which managers can make changes in the spreadsheet. This, along with their flexibility, facilitates their use in sensitivity analysis.

One of the most popular spreadsheet programs is Lotus 1-2-3. This program follows the current trend in software development in that it includes several different capabilities in one integrated package. In addition to a well-developed spreadsheet program, Lotus 1-2-3 also includes a graphics program and data management system. The advantage of this integrated approach is that it allows the user to shift easily from one type of data analysis to another.

This appendix provides an introduction to the spreadsheet and graphics capabilities of 1-2-3 Release 2. For a description of other capabilities, refer to the 1-2-3 User's Manual. This appendix is not intended as a replacement for the manual. The following instructions are designed to provide only the bare essentials necessary to begin the program.

I. GETTING STARTED

1. After the computer operating system (DOS) has been loaded and the A> prompt appears on the computer screen, remove the DOS diskette from the A drive, the one on the left or top, and insert the Lotus 1-2-3 diskette. Make sure that the label side is up and that the end with the label enters last. Close the door of the disk drive.

2. Type LOTUS and press the [ENTER] key. The computer will then load the 1-2-3 program.

3. When the program is loaded, the 1-2-3 access menu will appear on the screen, resembling the diagram in Exhibit B–1. The words in

EXHIBIT B–1   1-2-3 Access Command Menu

```
1-2-3   PrintGraph   Translate   Install   View   Exit
Enter 1-2-3—LOTUS Spreadsheet/Graphics/Database program
```

the second row on the screen indicate alternate functions of 1-2-3. By selecting from this menu of commands, the user is able to perform various tasks. This multilevel command menu concept is used throughout the program.

4. The highlighted section of the screen is called the cursor. It is currently over the 1-2-3. You can move the cursor by using the four arrow keys located on the cursor control pad or the 2, 4, 6, and 8 keys on the numeric keypad section of the keyboard. By pressing the right arrow key, you can scroll through each of the menu alternatives. When the cursor reaches the last function, Exit, if you press the right arrow key again it will return to the first item in the menu, 1-2-3. Notice that as you scroll through the commands, the descriptions on the second line change. The second line shows a description of the particular command that is highlighted by the cursor.

5. The 1-2-3 has a built-in Help capability. If at any time you are unsure what to do, press the F1. The program will provide some clarifying instructions as well as a menu to access further help messages.

The other function keys have specific uses in 1-2-3. Not all of the functions will be described in this appendix. Consult the User's Manual for details on the uses of the function keys.

6. To cancel a command, press the Esc key. This will cause 1-2-3 to go back to the previous command menu.

7. To save spreadsheets that you develop with 1-2-3, you need a disk prepared for this purpose. You cannot save spreadsheets on the 1-2-3 program disk. The process of disk preparation needs to be done only once. After the disk has been prepared, it can be used over and over again to store spreadsheets. The process of preparing a disk is called formatting. You must exit the 1-2-3 program and return to the operating system to format a disk. When you are in the operating system, the computer screen will show the A> prompt. Consult the manual for your computer's operating system for help in formatting a disk.

1. Cautions

A. Handle disks carefully. Do not touch the magnetic surface. Do not place disks on top of your monitor; this can damage them. When writing on the labels on the disks, use only a felt-tip pen.

B. Do not turn off the computer when there is a disk in the drive and the red light is on. This could damage the disk.

C. While you are using the 1-2-3 program, do not remove the program disk from disk drive A. The system must frequently access data that is stored on the system disk.

2. Stopping

If you wish to stop using 1-2-3, move the cursor to the Exit command on the 1-2-3 access menu and press [ENTER]. Remember, do not turn off the computer if the red light on a disk drive is on.

II. ENTERING A MODEL

To enter the spreadsheet program of 1-2-3, move the cursor to 1-2-3 on the access command menu and press [ENTER]. The system will load the spreadsheet program and the 1-2-3 logo will be momentarily displayed on the monitor. The logo will disappear, leaving only a blank worksheet resembling Exhibit B-2.

1-2-3 can be looked at as an electronic worksheet with 256 columns and 8,192 rows. The columns are lettered A, B, C, and so on out to IV. The rows are designated by the numbers 1 through 8,192. Each position on the worksheet is identified by the column and row number; e.g., A1, BB45, and so on.

If you have followed the starting steps described above, your worksheet should now show columns A through H and rows 1 through 20. To see other parts of the worksheet, you must move the cursor.

1. Moving the Cursor

The cursor is at position A1. The cursor is always in position A1 when a new worksheet is started. The position of the cursor determines where entries are made on the worksheet. Note that the position of the cursor is indicated in the upper-left corner of the screen above the worksheet on what is called the cell contents line, as shown on Exhibit B-2.

The cursor can be moved in five ways:

A. Arrow keys.   The four arrow keys located on the numeric or cursor control keypad are probably the most used method of moving the cursor. Pressing on one of the arrow keys moves the cursor one cell in that direction. To increase the speed of movement while using arrow keys, just depress and hold down the key.

B. End key and arrow keys.   Pressing the End key (also the number 1 key on the numeric keypad) followed by one of the arrow keys will move

EXHIBIT B–2   The 1-2-3 Worksheet

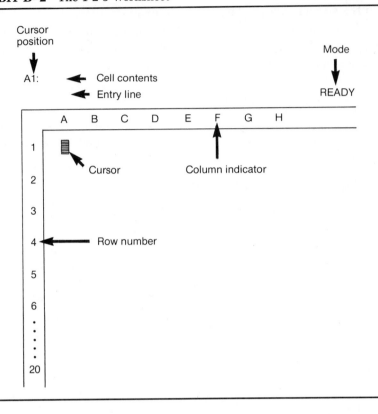

the cursor to the next "break" cell. If the cursor is on a cell with an entry, it will move to the cell preceding the next blank cell. If the cursor is on a blank cell, the break cell will be one with an entry.

C. Pg Up, Pg Dn, and Tab keys.   Pressing either the Pg Up or Pg Dn key will move the worksheet one page, 20 rows, up or down. Pressing the tab key (⇆) will move the worksheet one screen width to the right or left. To access the left tab key (⇆), you must depress the shift key (↑) while pressing the tab key (⇆).

D. F5 (Go To) key.   Pressing the F5 key invokes the Go To command. When you press this key, the words "Enter address to go to: A1" appear on the entry line. A1 is the current cursor position. Type in the coordinates of the position where you would like the cursor to be and then press [ENTER]. The cursor will move to the entered position.

E. The Home key.   Pressing the Home key (also the number 7 key on the numeric keypad) will move the cursor to the upper leftmost position on the worksheet.

If at any time you try to move the cursor to a position outside the limits of the worksheet, you will hear a beep. Don't worry, this does no harm. It is just a signal that you are doing something unacceptable.

2. Entering Words and Numbers

Now that you have familiarized yourself with the movement of the cursor, you can begin to enter words and numbers. As you make an entry, it appears on the screen on the entry line above the worksheet. The column width is nine characters, so longer entries will show only the first nine characters when entered on the worksheet. Column size can be increased or decreased, as will be explained later.

There are three types of entries:

A. Labels.   A label is a word or some combination of letters, symbols, and numbers. Examples of labels that might be used are SALES, COGS1, ASSETS, MAR★.

B. Values.   Values are numbers that remain fixed or constant. 1-2-3 assumes that all numbers are positive (+) unless indicated. If the number is negative, you must first type a minus sign (−) and then the numeric value.

C. Relationships.   Relationships include all formulas or mathematical expressions. They define the relationships between various cells on the worksheet. In developing relationships, the typical mathematical operators for addition (+), subtraction (−), multiplication (*), and division (/) are used. Other operators described in the User's Manual can also be used. The following are examples of valid relationships:

+ B3 + B4 (add the contents of positions B3 and B4)

+ A40*B20 (multiply the contents of A40 by B20)

+ BE10/1.5 (divide the contents of BE10 by 1.5)

3. Things to Remember in Entering Values and Labels

When making an entry, the first character struck tells 1-2-3 whether the entry is a value or label. Once the first character is struck, either VALUE or LABEL will be displayed on the mode indicator in the upper right-hand corner of the screen. The characters you have entered will be displayed on the entry line above the worksheet.

Labels usually begin with letters, and values begin with numbers. Ordinarily this shouldn't cause any problem except when you want to start a label with a number or a symbol such as (+), (−), or (.), which 1-2-3 assumes are the first characters of a value. To avoid this problem, first type ("); everything after that is assumed to be a label. No quotation marks are needed at the end of the label; just press [ENTER]. Thus, if you wish to rule a line on the worksheet, you can type "------ and then press [ENTER].

The (") entry will result in the labels being right-aligned in the column. If you wish the label to be left-aligned, precede the entry with ('). To center the label in the column, use the (^) entry.

Another interpretation problem occurs with position indicators such as A3 and FV256. When the first character is struck, 1-2-3 assumes that you are entering a label. However, you may be attempting to enter a relationship such as A3*FV256. To eliminate this problem, precede the first position indicator with a (+), as in +A3*FV256. The (+) sign indicates to 1-2-3 that you are entering a value or relationship.

Parentheses may be used to change the normal right-to-left calculation order used by 1-2-3. Suppose the following is true:

Position	Contains the Value
A6	10
A7	2
A8	5

If you enter the expression +A6+A7*A8, the result will be 20. 1-2-3 would calculate $2 * 5 = 10$ then $10 + 10 = 20$. If you want the calculation performed as (+A6+A7)*A8, then you must enter it that way.

On computers without a separate cursor control pad, it is easier to enter numbers with the keys on the top row of the keyboard. This is because the numeric keypad on those computers also contains the cursor control keys. If you want to use the numeric keypad to enter numbers, you must press the Num Lock key. To return the keypad to its alternative uses, you must press the Num Lock key again.

After you have typed an entry, you must press the enter key [ENTER] or one of the arrow keys to put the entry on the worksheet. Depressing one of these keys indicates that the entry is complete. Once the entry has been included on the worksheet, you will see the entry on the cell contents line.

4. Mistakes and Typographical Errors

Before the [ENTER] is pressed, errors may be corrected using the right and left arrow keys and the ← and Del keys. Pressing the ← key erases the character to the left of the current entry position, the small highlighted underline. The Del key deletes the character at the underline position. Using the arrow keys, move the highlighted underline to the appropriate position and then delete the desired character or characters.

After [ENTER] has been depressed, there are two methods of making changes. You can position the cursor at the cell position you want to change and type a new entry. This will replace the old entry. You can also use the

F2 key to enter the edit function and, using the arrow ← and Del keys, make changes as described above. In the edit mode, you may insert characters by positioning the cursor at the appropriate place and typing the new entry. The insertion occurs automatically without deleting any of the previous characters. In any case, when you are finished, put the entry on the worksheet by pressing [ENTER].

5. A Simple Income Statement

Now that you know how to move the cursor and make entries, let's try to enter a simple income statement.

Assume that for ABC Manufacturing Company:

Sales = $100,000
Cost of goods sold (COGS) = 65% of Sales
Selling, general, and administrative expense (SG&A) = 15% of Sales
Interest expense = $5,000
Tax rate = 35%

Move the cursor to position A1 and begin to make entries in the appropriate columns and rows, as shown below. These entries will result in an income statement for ABC Manufacturing that is consistent with the assumptions listed above. The labels for subtotals stand for gross margin (MARGIN), profit before taxes (PBT), and profit after taxes (PAT).

```
ROWS                    COLUMNS
              A                 B
1            SALES        100000
2            COGS         .65*B1 or +B1*.65
3                         "_____
4            MARGIN       +B1-B2
5            SG&A         .15*B1 or +B1*.15
6            INTEREST     5000
7                         "_____
8            PBT          +B4-B5-B6
9            TAXES        .35*B8 or +B8*.35
10                        "_____
11           PAT          +B8-B9
```

When you are finished your screen should look like this:

```
SALES         100000
COGS           65000
              ------
MARGIN         35000
SG&A           15000
INTEREST        5000
              ------
PBT            15000
TAXES           5250
              ------
PAT             9750
```

As you were typing, you may have noted several things.

A. There are no commas in numbers; i.e., 100,000 is typed as 100000. If you enter a comma, the computer will beep and will not accept the entry. If you would like the numbers to be displayed with commas, you can change the numeric formatting as will be described later.

B. Relationships or formulas are not displayed on the worksheet (foreground); however, the formula or relationship is saved in the background. 1-2-3 can thus be thought of as a matrix that is 256 columns wide by 8,192 rows long and 2 deep, as shown in Exhibit B–3.

One cannot immediately ascertain by looking at a particular position on the worksheet whether that number is a constant or whether it is the result of a computation involving values in other positions, i.e., that it is related to some other figures on the sheet. The only way to discover how a particular number was derived is to place the cursor at that position. The top line of the 1-2-3 screen above the worksheet, the cell contents line, will then display the cell address together with the entry. In other words, the background for that position will be displayed.

For example, observe the value 65000 in position B2 of your worksheet. If the cursor is placed at B2, the cell contents line (topmost line on the screen) will read as illustrated in Exhibit B–4. This tells you that in position B2 there is a value that is .65 times the entry in position B1.

What happens if there is a change in ABC's income statement? For example, suppose ABC's cost of sales increases to 68%. To determine the

EXHIBIT B–3   The 1-2-3 Concept

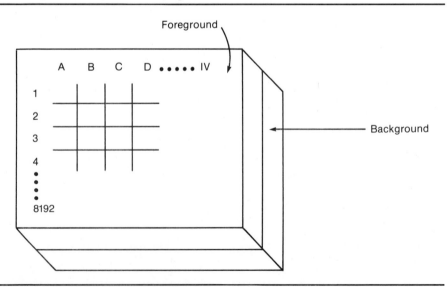

EXHIBIT B–4   1-2-3 Screen with Cell Contents Line

B2:   0.65*B1   READY

---

effect of this change on the statement, move the cursor to position B2 and type .68*B1 [ENTER]. You will see that 1-2-3 automatically recalculates the margin, profit before tax, and profit after tax.

Changes in other values can be accomplished similarly. This ease of change is what makes 1-2-3 and other modeling programs so useful.

6. Printing the Model

Now that you have completed the income statement, you may wish to print a copy. Most printers used with microcomputers only print 80 columns across a page. This means that if you have a model with a large number of columns, for example 20 columns each nine characters in width, the program will print one part of the model on one page and continue on a second and third page until it is completed. The same continuation procedure is followed for models with more than the 56 rows that can be printed on one page.

1-2-3 is designed to print any contiguous block of the foreground of the worksheet. You simply indicate the upper leftmost position and the lower right position. The block that is to be printed will be highlighted on the screen.

To print the income statement model, follow these steps:

A. Make sure the printer is turned on and set for on-line.

B. Position the cursor on the upper left position of the block, in this case A1.

C. Type /. This is the keystroke that starts all commands. The entry line will read as shown in Exhibit B–5. Each of the words represents different sets of commands or functions that 1-2-3 can perform. You need to select a command from this menu.

D. Move the cursor to the Print command and press [ENTER]. The entry line now shows a subset of commands for printing.

E. Move the cursor to Printer and press [ENTER]. This command tells the system that you want the worksheet printed. 1-2-3 next provides another submenu of commands for printing on a printer.

EXHIBIT B–5   1-2-3 Modeling Commands

Worksheet Range Copy Move File Print Graph Data System Quit

F. Move the cursor to Range and press [ENTER]. This command enables you to enter the block or range of positions you would like printed in two ways. First, you may type in the range, with the beginning and ending cell labels separated by a period, e.g., A1.B11. You may also use the cursor to point to the range. Since the cursor was already on position A1, this position is shown. To note it is the range beginning, press the period key [.].

G. You may change the block to be printed by moving the cursor. As you do, you will notice the range of positions will be highlighted on the screen, and the ending range position on the entry line will change. When the cursor is positioned at the lower right position, B11, press [ENTER]. The print submenu will again appear on the entry line.

H. Move the cursor to Go and press [ENTER]. The printout should now begin.

I. When the printout is completed, select Quit from the menu to exit from the Print submenu.

7. Saving the Model

Having printed the model, you may now wish to save it for future use. In order to do this, you need a formatted diskette, as described in the section on GETTING STARTED. We will call this the model file disk. It should be placed in disk drive B, the right-hand or bottom drive, and the door closed. Then take the following steps:

A. Type /. Remember, this accesses the modeling commands.

B. Move the cursor to File and press [ENTER]. It is also possible to just type F. Either method displays the File command submenu.

C. Move the cursor to Save or press S and press [ENTER]. The 1-2-3 will ask for the name you wish to give the model.

D. Type FILENAME [ENTER]. You may give the model any name you like. File names can use any combination of eight letters or numbers. No spaces or special characters may be used.

The system will first check the file names already stored on the model file disk in drive B for duplicate names and then store the file. The red light on drive B will be on while the program is being stored.

8. Ending a Session

After you have completed a model and printed it for further study, you may want to exit from 1-2-3.

A. Type /.

B. Select Quit from the menu and press [ENTER].

C. Since exiting 1-2-3 will result in losing all worksheet data unless it has previously been saved, the system will ask you to confirm that you want to exit. Press Y to end the session and return to the Access System menu. You may exit from the Access system using the procedure described previously.

III. MORE COMPLEX MODELS

In the preceding section, you learned how to enter a simple income statement for one year. The same principles can be applied to writing more complex income statements, balance sheets, cash flow statements, or other financial models. This section will demonstrate how to use 1-2-3 for financial forecasting and planning. In order to do this, let's go back to the ABC Manufacturing Company income statement model already developed.

A. Load the 1-2-3 worksheet program as described in the GETTING STARTED section. Put the model file disk in the B drive.

B. Type /. Move the cursor to File and press [ENTER].

C. Since the cursor is already on the Retrieve subcommand, press [ENTER].

D. The program will display a menu of the file names that have been saved on the model file disk. Move the cursor to the file you would like to retrieve and press [ENTER].

While the system is loading the file you specified, the mode indicator in the upper right corner of the screen will change from READY to WAIT. When the model is loaded, the READY status will reappear.

1. Clearing a Worksheet

If you have been working on one model and wish to start a different one, you may want to begin with a blank worksheet. To clear a worksheet from the screen, type /W. The W is the first letter of the Worksheet command. Press E or move the cursor in the Worksheet command submenu to Erase and press [ENTER]. The system will ask if you want to erase the worksheet. Enter Y. The confirmation is used because erasing the worksheet will cause all of the data to be lost unless it has previously been saved on a disk.

2. Copy Command

In order to use 1-2-3 for financial modeling, you will want to use the copy command. The copy command enables you to copy or duplicate relationships, values, or labels across many columns or down many rows. The relationship, value, or label that you wish to copy is called the source position, and the location into which you wish to copy it is the target position.

The source position can be replicated into another position;

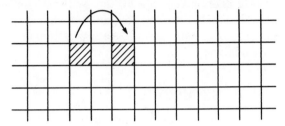

into a range of positions across a row;

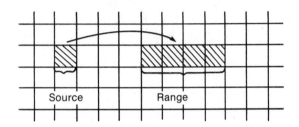

or into a range of positions down a column.

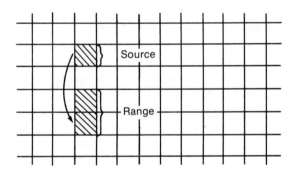

It is also possible to copy a range of source positions into a range of target positions.

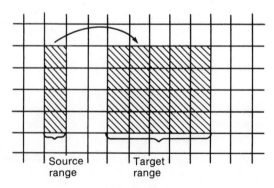

The copy command facilitates quickly expanding a model across a number of time periods once the basic relationships in the source range are established. Obviously, it would be possible to expand the model without using the copy command by laboriously retyping all of the relationships for each time period.

3. Absolute versus Relative Relationships

In defining relationships, cell positions are often used. For example, in the ABC Manufacturing income statement, the entry in position B5 is .15*B1. 1-2-3 interprets this to mean that the value for B5 is calculated by multiplying the value four rows above in the same column by .15. If this relationship were copied into the C column, it would appear as .15*C1. Therefore, in calculating the value for C5, 1-2-3 would look for a value four rows above in the same column, which would now be position C1. This is known as a relative relationship, and it is the nature of most relationships in a model.

Absolute or fixed relations are those where a specific value is accessed regardless of where it may appear in the model. For example, if you wish the model to utilize the specific value in B1, the relationship in B5 would be written as .15*$B$1. The $ signs indicate an absolute cell address.

When a fixed position is copied, the specified position does not change. For example, if .15*$B$1 were to be copied to C5, the relationship would remain .15*$B$1. You may indicate an absolute relationship by typing in $ or striking F4 after the cell address.

4. Copying One Position

To copy the label SALES from position A1 into position A15:

A. Move the cursor to position A1.

B. Type /.

C. Move the cursor in the command menu to Copy and press [ENTER].

D. The entry line reads "Enter range to copy FROM: A1..A1" with A1 being the current cursor position. Press [ENTER] to indicate that only the A1 position is to be copied.

E. The entry line will read "Enter range to copy TO: A1" with A1 still the current cursor position. However, we do not want to copy A1 to itself, so move the cursor to the desired position, in this case A15, or type A15 and press [ENTER]. The word sales will now appear in position A15.

5. Copying a Range of Positions

Now that you have copied one label, let's try copying the rest of the labels in one step.

A. Move the cursor to A2. This will be the beginning of the range we wish to copy.

B. Type /C.

C. Type a period (.). The period is necessary to separate the beginning position of the range from the ending position. Although you only typed one period, the entry line will show two periods and now reads "Enter range to copy FROM: A2..A2."

D. Move the cursor to A11, the end of the source range. As you move the cursor, the highlighted positions will increase and the last position indicator in the source range prompt will change to reflect the current cursor location. Press [ENTER].

E. Move the cursor to A16 or type A16. The prompt line will now read "Enter range to copy TO: A16." Press [ENTER]. 1-2-3 will now copy the contents of the source range to the target range beginning in position A16.

6. Copying Relationships

Although copying labels indicated the usefulness of the Copy command in saving typing, it did not demonstrate the ability of Copy to deal with changing relationships. For example, suppose that sales of ABC Manufacturing are increasing at 10% per year and you want an income statement for the next five years. To accomplish this with 1-2-3, you:

A. Move the cursor to C1.

B. Type the relationship for a 10% sales growth; e.g., 1.1*B1 [ENTER].

C. Type /C.

D. The source range shows C1. Press [ENTER].

E. 1-2-3 is now prompting for the target range. Move the cursor to D1 and press period (.). Then move the cursor to G1 and press [ENTER]. Alternatively, you could type D1. G1[ENTER]. This specifies that C1 should be copied to the target range D1 to G1 to provide the last four years of the forecast.

Since the original expression in C1 was specified as a relative relationship, the formula in D1 will read 1.1*C1. The formula in E1 reads 1.1*D1 and so forth. The sales row on the worksheet should now increase by 10% per year for five years.

It is now possible to copy the rest of the income statement using the same relationships that were used in the original model.

A. Move the cursor to B2.

B. Type /C.

C. Type a period (.) and move the cursor to B11. Press [ENTER].

D. Type C2.G2 [ENTER] or use the cursor as previously described. This tells 1-2-3 to copy the range from B2 to B11 in columns C through G.

You should now have an original income statement and forecasts for five additional years. What happens if you want to change one term and see what the impact is? For example, what happens if COGS changes to 70% of sales? Move the cursor back to B2. Type .7*B1 [ENTER]. Only the profit for that year will change. You must use the Copy command to copy the new relationship in position B2 to the other columns before the income statements for the other years are changed.

IV. CHANGING THE WORKSHEET

In the previous sections, you learned the basics of using 1-2-3; however, there are a number of modeling commands that will allow you to alter the display or change the model you have entered without retyping it.

1. Changing the Column Width

You may change the column width for the entire model, for a range of columns, or for a single column.

To change the column width for the entire model, key / and then select Worksheet from the command menu. The Worksheet submenu will then appear as follows:

EXHIBIT B–6 Worksheet Command Submenu

Global Insert Delete Column Erase Titles Window Status Page

Move the cursor to Global and press [ENTER]. This will display the Global command submenu.

EXHIBIT B–7 Global Command Submenu

```
        Label-  Column-
Format  Prefix  Width     Recalculation  Protection  Default  Zero
```

Select Column-Width from the menu and press [ENTER]. You can then adjust the column width by specifying a number or by pressing the right and left arrow keys and observing the changing column width on the high-lighted cursor on the screen.

To change the column width for a single column, type /W and select the Column-Width command from the Worksheet submenu. Select Set-Width from the next submenu. You set the column width either by specifying a number or by using the horizontal arrow keys. When the column is at the desired width, press [ENTER].

2. Changing the Numerical Format

The format used for displaying numbers can be changed for the entire worksheet, for a range of columns or rows, or for a single position.

To change the display format for the entire worksheet, first press /W to access the Worksheet command submenu. Then select the Global submenu, followed by the Format command. The Format command will further display a menu of ten alternative formats for your selection.

Fixed	This format allows you to specify a fixed number of decimal places that will be displayed.
Scientific	This format displays the numbers in scientific notation; e.g., $1.2E5$.
Currency	This displays numbers in a dollar and cents format of $x,xxx.xx. You are allowed to specify the number of decimal places to be displayed.
	This format is the common format for numbers, xxx,xxx. You may specify the number of decimal places to be shown. This format also displays negative numbers in parentheses.
General	This is the default format, which allows a floating decimal position to be displayed.
+/-	This is a low-level graphics format that displays the appropriate number of + or - signs for the number in that position.
Percent	Numbers are displayed in a percent format of x.xx%. You may indicate the number of decimal positions to be shown.
Date	The command provides three alternatives for displaying a date.
Text	The text command will display the background formula rather than the calculated value.
Hidden	Cell contents are not displayed. Subsequently selection of any other format will redisplay the cells.

To change the format for a specific position or a range of positions, select the Range command from the modeling commands menu. The Range submenu consists of:

EXHIBIT B–8 Range Command Submenu

```
                                 Pro- Unpro-               Trans-
Format Label Erase Name Justify tect tect   Input Value pose
```

Selecting the Format command provides the same choices as above, with the addition of a Reset command. The Reset command changes the format for the specified range to the global format that was specified for the worksheet.

After choosing the format, you will be asked to specify the range of positions that should use that format. The range can be a single position, a range of rows, or a range of columns. You specify the range in the same manner used for entering ranges for the Copy command.

3. Inserting or Deleting a Row or Column

Often it is necessary to add a column or row in the middle of a 1-2-3 model. To add a column in the model, place the cursor wherever the new column is needed. The cursor can be placed anywhere in the column. Key /W and then select the Insert subcommand from the menu. Next select Column from the menu. You may insert several columns at once, so the system will prompt for a range to be inserted. You may specify a single column or a range of columns. When you are finished entering the range, press [ENTER] and 1-2-3 will insert the specified blank columns.

Inserting rows is done similarly. Select Row from the Insert subcommand menu and specify the row or range of rows to be inserted.

To delete rows or columns that are no longer needed, use the Delete command. You will be prompted to indicate whether rows or columns are to be deleted and then to specify the range to be deleted. After entering the range, press [ENTER], and the relevant range will be removed from the program. Since the deletions are irretrievable, you should be careful when using this command.

4. Blanking a Position or Range

If you have a position or a range with entries that you would like to change to blanks, this can be done by selecting the Range command followed by the Erase subcommand. You will be asked to specify a range to be erased. When you finish entering the range, press [ENTER]. The range will still be on the worksheet, but it will now be blank. Again, caution in using this command is warranted since the contents are lost once the range is erased.

5. Keeping Titles on Your Monitor

When the cursor is moved to the right beyond the first few columns, the contents of column A disappear, then column B, and so on. A similar thing happens when you scroll down beyond row 20; row 1 disappears and then row 2, and so on. Often the leftmost columns and/or topmost rows contain labels or values you would prefer to fix on the screen for constant reference. The Titles command does this.

A. Move the cursor to the row below or column to the right of that which you would like to fix on the screen.

B. Type /.

C. Select Worksheet from the menu and press [ENTER].

D. Select Titles from the submenu and press [ENTER].

E. If you want to set a horizontal title (a row), select Horizontal from the menu. For a vertical title (a column), choose Vertical. You may fix both a horizontal and vertical title by using the Both command.

Once you have fixed the titles, the cursor cannot be moved into the title area(s) except by using the F5 (Go To) key. To remove any Title command that is in effect, select the Clear command from the Title submenu.

6. Built-In Functions

Some mathematical relationships are used so frequently that they have been built into 1-2-3. To specify one of the functions, you should first type (@), then the function, followed by the required value or range for that function. When it is necessary to specify a value, you may indicate either a numeric value or a cell position in the worksheet. If a range of values is required, the standard procedure of indicating the first position followed by a period and the last position should be used.

Some of the available functions are:

@ABS(x)	Absolute value of x
@EXP(x)	Exponential value of x
@INT(x)	Integer part of the value of x
@LN(x)	Log on the base e for x
@LOG(x)	Log on the base 10 for x
@RAND	Random number between 0 and 1
@ROUND(x,n)	Round the number x to decimal places
@SQRT(x)	Square root of x
@NPV(x,range)	Net present value of the range using the discount rate x

```
@IRR(x,range)     Internal rate of return for the range, enter
                  a trial rate for x
@TODAY            Today's date
@COUNT(range)     Counts the number of items in range
@SUM(range)       Sums the values of all items in the range
@AVG(range)       Averages the values of all items in the
                  range
@MIN(range)       Selects the minimum of all items in the
                  range
@MAX(range)       Selects the maximum of all items in the
                  range
@STD(range)       Standard deviation of all items in the range
@VAR(range)       Variance of all items in the range
```

V. USING GRAPHICS

The graphics facility of Lotus 1-2-3 allows you to present data so that it is attractive and easily understood. The Graphics section of the Lotus 1-2-3 package displays data that have been entered into or generated by the worksheet. You must specify which data are to be displayed and how they are to be displayed, then 1-2-3 does the rest. To illustrate how to use the graphics, you can create a graph using the data from the simple six-year income statements you created in the previous sections.

1. Selecting Graphics

To enter the Graphics subprogram, you:

A. Type /.

B. Select Graphics from the menu. You will see the following submenu.

EXHIBIT B–9   Graphics Command Submenu

```
Type  X  A  B  C  D  E  F  Reset  View  Save  Options  Name  Quit
```

C. Press T to select the type of graph. You may choose between a line chart, bar graph, X-Y graph, stacked bar graph, or a pie chart. Select the line chart.

D. Select A to set the first data range. You will see the prompt "Enter first data range:". You may specify any row or column of data to be graphed. For our example, you should enter B11..G11, the profit after tax.

E. Select View from the menu. If you have a graphics monitor, you should now see the following graph:

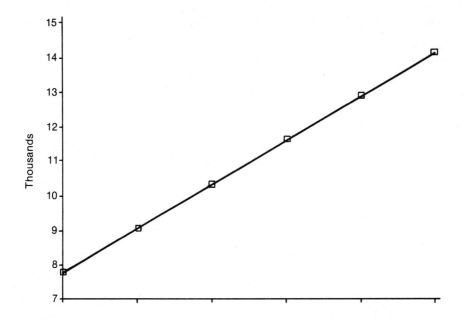

Press any key to return to the worksheet text.

Some monochrome monitors do not display graphs. You can still create graphs and then print them, as will be explained later.

2. Adding Additional Data Ranges

The graph is not very impressive with just one line of data. You may include up to six different data ranges to be graphed. To add more ranges, do the following:

A. Select B from the graphics submenu. You will then be prompted for the second data range. Enter B4..G4, the margin. You could of course specify data ranges for C through F.

B. Press V to view the graph. You will see the graph at the top of the next page. Notice that the left-hand axis (Y-axis) has been automatically rescaled.

3. Adding Labels

With two lines on the graph, it is confusing as to what each line represents. To eliminate confusion, which is of course the purpose of using graphs, you should label the lines. To do this:

A. Select Options. Then select L for Legends from the submenu.

B. Press A. The entry line now reads "Enter legend for A-range:". Since the A-range is the profit after tax, you enter PAT.

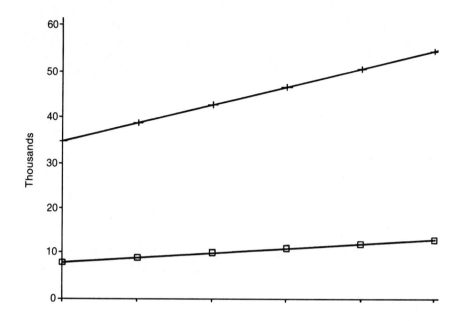

C. Press L and then B. You now enter the legend for the B-range. This is the gross margin, so enter MARGIN.

D. Select Quit and press V. You will see the following graph.

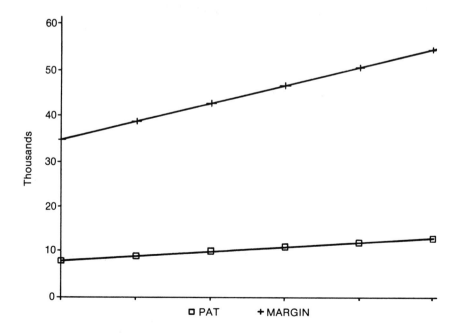

Once a graph has been created, you can return to the ready mode of the worksheet, change any data you like, and then view the results by pressing the F10 key. It is not necessary to access the graphics submenu to view the graph, only to change any of the graphics specifications.

4. Saving the Graph

In order to print the graph, you must first name and save it. This can be done through the following steps.

A. Select Name from the Graphics submenu.

B. Select Create from the submenu. You will see the prompt "Enter graph name". Type in the name you would like for the graph.

C. Select Save. Again you will be prompted "Enter graph name". The names of all previously saved graphics files will be displayed. Type in the name you just created, and the graph will be saved on the disk in the B drive.

5. Printing a Graph

The program to print a graph can only be accessed from the 1-2-3 Access menu.

A. Press the Esc key until you return to the ready mode of the worksheet with a clear prompt line.

B. Press / and then Q to exit from the worksheet. Press Y at the prompt to return to the Access menu.

C. Select PrintGraph from the Access menu. You will be prompted to remove the 1-2-3 Systems disk and insert the PrintGraph disk. When you have done that, press [ENTER]. You will see the PrintGraph menu shown in Exhibit B–10.

EXHIBIT B–10   PrintGraph Command Menu

Image–Select	Settings	Go	Align	Page	Exit

D. Press I to select the file you would like printed. A directory of the graphics files will be displayed. Scroll through the directory using the up and down arrow keys. Mark the file you would like printed by pressing the space bar when the highlighted cursor is on the file. Then press [ENTER].

E. Select Settings from the menu. Then select Hardware from the submenu, followed by Printer. This allows you to select the type of printer you have. Scroll through the list of printers and select the appropriate one by marking it with the space bar. Press [ENTER].

F. Press Q twice to exit from the Hardware and Settings submenus.

G. Make sure the printer is on and connected. Select Go for printing to commence. If the graphics are not printing, consult the 1-2-3 User's Manual for more detailed instructions.

VI. CREATING DATA TABLES

One of the features of using Lotus 1-2-3, or any other spreadsheet program, is the ability to easily change the value of a variable and determine the impact on the results. This process is known as "what if" or sensitivity analysis. Typically, the user changes the value of a specific variable, such as the selling price, and then observes the effect this change has on another variable, such as net income.

It is easy to change the value of a variable and have the computer recompute the model. Often the user would like to change the value using a range of several possible values. This could be done by changing the values one at a time and then manually writing down the results. Rather than using this labor-intensive process, it is possible to have 1-2-3 automatically make changes in the values and record the results. The procedure that accomplishes this is called using data tables. A data table can also be called a sensitivity analysis table.

A data table consists of two parts: a range of input values that will be used to change the value of a specific variable in a specific cell, and the resulting values for each change. The data table is illustrated by a matrix with the user-specified values (input cells) on the left and the resulting values (output cells) on the right. When Lotus 1-2-3 calculates the data table, one value is selected from the input cells, the model is recalculated using this value, the resulting value for a specified variable or variables is recorded in the output cell.

For example, suppose we want to evaluate the effect that changing the sales amount would have on the profitability of a product. The relationships could be defined as in our simple income statement for the ABC Manufacturing Company.

	A	B
1	SALES	100000
2	COGS	65000
3		-------
4	MARGIN	35000
5	SG&A	15000
6	INTEREST	5000
7		-------
8	PBT	15000
9	TAXES	5250
10		-------
11	PAT	9750

To determine the effect of changing the sales revenue over the range $80,000, $90,000, $100,000, $110,000, and $120,000, we create a data table by entering the values we wish to use for sales revenue in cells A15 to A19. Since we are interested in the results for profit after tax, we enter that cell reference (+B11) in cell B14. Using the format command for text, you can change the cell display in B14 from 9750 (the value in B11) to B11. The annotated table looks like this:

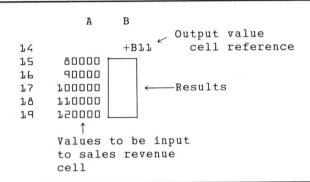

After entering these values, we need to tell Lotus that these data should be used as input in a data table. This is called defining a data table. To do this:

A. Type /.

B. Select Data from the menu.

C. You will see the following submenu.

EXHIBIT B–11   Data Command Submenu

Fill Table Sort Query Distribution Matrix Regression Parse

D. Press T to select Table from the submenu.

E. From the next submenu, select 1, which means that there will be only one input variable.

F. You will be prompted to enter the data table range. In this case, the range is A14..B19. This range includes the input value cells, the output cell reference (B14), and the cells that will show the output values (B15 to B19).

G. Next you will be prompted to enter the input cell, the cell where the input values should be used. In this case, you want sales revenue to be input, so enter the sales revenue cell, B1.

Lotus 1-2-3 substitutes the values from the input cells in the sales revenue cell and calculates the output values. These values are shown in the output range, B15..B19. The data table will look like this:

	A	B
14		+B11
15	80000	7150
16	90000	8450
17	100000	9750
18	110000	11050
19	120000	12350

The table shows that the profit after tax varies from $7,150 to $12,350 depending on the sales revenue achieved. It is possible to expand the data table by specifying additional output values. To do so, merely add additional columns to the data table and specify the output cell reference for each column of output values. You may also change the values for the input variable, to determine the effects of a different set of values, by replacing the input values as appropriate and pressing the F8 key. This will recompute the output values in the data table.

With the data table completed, it may be useful to show the results graphically. This can easily be done using the graphics functions of Lotus 1-2-3. Specify the input value range as the X-axis values and the output value range as the A data range.

It is also possible to create a data table with two input values, termed a two-way data table. For this table, 1-2-3 takes a value for each of the two input ranges and calculates a resulting value. This value is then shown in the output range.

Using our example, a two-way data table with two input variable values, sales revenue and interest, would appear as follows:

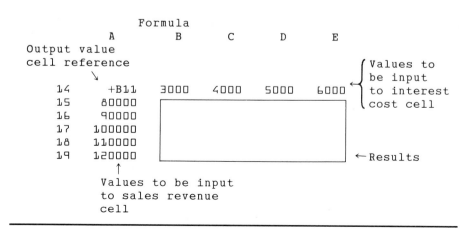

The output cell reference, profit after tax, is in the upper left corner of the data table range. The values for the first variable to be changed are in the first column of the data table and the values for the second variable are in the top row.

To perform a two-way data table analysis, you should:

A. Select Data from the main menu, followed by Table, and then 2 to indicate two variable values to be changed.

B. In response to the data range prompt, enter A14..E19.

C. You will be prompted to enter the input cell for the first range of values to be changed. The first range of input values is the left column of the data table. Since these values correspond to sales revenue, you enter B1, the sales revenue cell.

D. You must next enter the input cell for the second range of values to be changed. The second range is the top row of the data table. In this case, the values are for interest cost, so enter B6.

1-2-3 then calculates the results based on each pair of values from the table. The data table will appear as follows:

	A	B	C	D	E
14	+B11	3000	4000	5000	6000
15	80000	8450	7800	7150	6500
16	90000	9750	9100	8450	7800
17	100000	11050	10400	9750	9100
18	110000	12350	11700	11050	10400
19	120000	13650	13000	12350	11700

The output range shows the resulting profit after tax amount for each combination of input values for sales revenue and interest cost. The profits vary between $8,450 and $13,650. This sensitivity analysis could be duplicated by running the one-way data table four times; however, the two-way approach simplifies the work. That, of course, is the purpose of using spreadsheet programs.

VII. OTHER MODELING SYSTEMS

While Lotus 1-2-3 is a powerful and popular spreadsheet program, many other similar programs are also available. These include SuperCalc 4, Multiplan, VP-Planner, Twin, Quattro, and Excel. In addition, several so-called integrated programs such as Enable, Symphony, and Framework include spreadsheet programs.

Another approach to modeling is presented by programs such as IFPS/ Personal, ENCORE! and Javelin. They allow the user to specify relationships between variables using English language-like statements. Rather than requiring specific cell references, as with the spreadsheet programs, these programs generate the matrix of cells based on the model relationships.

A detailed review of all of these programs is beyond the scope of this book. However, a wide variety of different types of modeling programs are available. We believe that, wisely used, these programs are an effective managerial tool.

Solutions to Study Questions

This appendix consists of two parts. The first section has detailed solutions to the questions. The second section explains the entries that could be used in creating Lotus 1-2-3 models for solving the study questions.

C–1 Manual Solutions to Study Questions

CHAPTER 1—SOLUTIONS

Problem 1.

a. The sustainable growth rate for CSX has remained fairly constant over the years with the exception of 1985, when CSX had a large loss. The calculations are as follows:

$$1982 \text{ SGR} = \frac{\text{Net income}}{\text{Total equity}} * (1 - \text{Payout}) = \frac{338}{3398} * (1 - .35) = .06 \text{ or } 6\%$$

$$1983 \text{ SGR} = \frac{272}{4526} * (1 - .48) = .03 \text{ or } 3\%$$

$$1984 \text{ SGR} = \frac{465}{4909} * (1 - .33) = .06 \text{ or } 6\%$$

$$1985 \text{ SGR} = \frac{-118}{4595} * (1 + 1.45) = -.06 \text{ or } -6\%$$

$$1986 \text{ SGR} = \frac{418}{4873} * (1 - .43) = .05 \text{ or } 5\%$$

b. The industry sustainable growth rate is 3.4 percent $\times$ $(1 - .75) = .85$ percent. The industry average is much lower than CSX's sustainable growth rate. This is due to the much higher industry average dividend payout as well as the lower return on equity for the industry.

Problem 2.

New Tech
Income Statement
(component percentage)

	Manufacturing			Chemicals		
	1986	1987	1988	1986	1987	1988
Sales	100.0%	100.0%	100.0%	100.0%	100.0%	100.0%
Cost of goods sold	(44.4)	(43.0)	(50.0)	(60.8)	(59.6)	(58.1)
Gross profit	55.6	57.0	50.0	39.2	40.4	41.9
Operating expense	(6.7)	(7.1)	(7.1)	(5.6)	(6.0)	(5.9)
EBIT	49.0	49.9	42.9	33.5	34.4	36.0
Interest	(14.7)	(13.0)	(12.4)	(11.5)	(10.7)	(10.0)
Taxes	(12.7)	(13.6)	(13.7)	(8.3)	(8.7)	(3.9)
Net income	21.6%	23.2%	16.8%	13.7%	15.0%	22.1%

New Tech
Income Statement
(percentage change)

	Manufacturing		Chemicals	
	1987	1988	1987	1988
Sales	4.9%	4.0%	3.9%	3.9%
Cost of goods sold . . .	1.6	20.9	1.8	1.3
Gross profit	7.5	(8.8)	7.2	7.8
Operating expense . . .	11.9	3.9	10.2	3.1
EBIT	6.9	(10.6)	6.7	8.6
Interest	(7.1)	(0.9)	(3.3)	(3.4)
Taxes	12.9	4.7	9.2	(53.5)
Net income	12.8%	(25.0)%	13.6%	53.5%

For the Manufacturing division, 1987 and 1988 were erratic years. Although net income increased in 1987, this was substantially the result of a decrease in interest expense and a small growth in sales. A sharp increase in cost of goods sold significantly reduced net income in 1988. Operating expense and taxes maintained the same percentage of sales in the three years.

Growth in sales for the Chemicals division was constant for the years in question. Operating expense and interest remained a fairly constant percentage of sales in the three years. The jump in net income in 1988 was primarily the result of a sharp decrease in taxes.

Problem 3.

Assumptions:

Dividend payout	40%
Market price	$75
Dividend yield	20%
Shares outstanding (millions)	10
ROE	15%
LTD/Equity	2.3
Current ratio	2.67
Acid test ratio	1.34
Profit margin	5%
Gross margin	20%
ROA	4%
Inventory turnover	6
Profit as percentage of gross profits	90%
Accounts receivable collection period	24 days
Accounts payable collection period	61 days
Tax rate	50%

The financial statements that follow were determined using the following steps (dollars are in millions except per share amounts):

1. Dividend yield = 20 percent
   Market price = $75
   Dividend per share = $15

2. Dividend payout ratio = 40 percent
   Dividend per share = $15
   Earnings per share = $37.5

3. Earnings per share = $37.5
   Shares outstanding = 10 million
   Net income = $375

4. Profit margin = 5 percent
   Net income = $375
   Total revenue = $7,500

5. Gross margin = 20 percent
   Total revenue = $7,500
   Cost of goods sold = $6,000

6. Total revenue = $7,500
   Cost of goods sold = $6,000
   Gross profit = $1,500

7. Operating profit = 90 percent of gross profit
   Operating profit = $1,350

8. Operating expense = Gross profit − Operating profit
   Operating expense = $150

9. Tax rate = 50 percent
   Net income = $375
   Earnings before taxes = $750

10. Earnings before taxes = $750
    Operating profit = $1,350
    Interest = $600

11. Earnings before taxes = $750
    Tax rate = 50 percent
    Taxes = $375

12. Return on equity = 15 percent
    Net income = $375
    Owners' equity = $2,500

13. Long-term debt to equity = 230 percent
    Owners' equity = $2,500
    Long-term debt = $5,750

14. Return on assets = 4 percent
    Net income = $375
    Total assets = $9,375

15. Total liabilities and owners' equity = $9,375
    Owners' equity = $2,500
    Long-term debt = $5,750
    Current liabilities = $1,125

16. Current ratio = 267 percent
    Current liabilities = $1,125
    Current assets = $3,004

17. Inventory turnover = six times
    Cost of goods sold = $6,000
    Inventory = $1,000

18. Accounts receivable collection period = 24 days
    Sales = $7,500
    A/R = $500

19. Acid-test ratio = 134 percent
    Current liabilities = $1,125
    A/R = $500
    Cash = $1,008

20. Other current assets = Current assets − Cash − A/R − Inventory
    Other current assets = $4,976

21. Net property, plant, and equipment (PPE) = Total assets − Current assets
    Net PPE = $6,371

22. Payables payment period = 61 days
    Cost of goods sold = $6,000
    Accounts payable = $1,007
    Other current liabilities = $108

Income Statement
(in millions)

Sales	$7,500
Cost of goods sold	(6,000)
Gross profit	$1,500
Operating expense	(150)
Operating profit	$1,350
Interest	(600)
Taxes	(375)
Net income	$ 375

Balance Sheet
(in millions)

Cash	$1,007
Accounts receivable (360-day year)	500
Inventory (360-day year)	1,000
Other current assets	497
Current assets	$3,004
Net PP&E	6,371
Total assets	$9,375
Accounts payable (360-day year)	$1,007
Other current liabilities	108
Current liabilities	$1,125
Total long-term debt	5,750
Total liabilities	$6,875
Owners' equity	2,500
Total liabilities & owners' equity	$9,375

Problem 4.

a. Based on analysis of the ratios calculated on the next page, Peterson's
   Chemicals faces two major problems: (1) high costs, and (2) working-
   capital problems. Because the chemical industry has such low profit margins (5 percent), the average 10 percent increase in raw materials and
   the 4 percent increase in operating expenses results in negative profit
   margins for the company. Operating expenses declined slightly in 1986,
   but the cost of goods sold jumped 5 percent, slimming gross profits to 20

Peterson's Chemicals
Income Statement Compared with Industry
(percent of sales)

	Peterson 1985	Industry 1985	Peterson 1986	Industry 1986
Sales	100%	100%	100%	100%
Cost of goods sold . . .	(75)	(67)	(80)	(68)
Gross profit	25	33	20	32
Operating expense . .	(31)	(27)	(30)	(26)
Operating profit	(6)	6	(10)	6
Interest	(2)	(1)	(2)	(2)
Net income	(8)%	5%	(12)%	4%

Peterson's Chemicals (Ratio Analysis)

	1985	1986	Industry
Current ratio	164%	113%	15%
Acid-test ratio	101	68	9
Accounts receivable (days)	110	105	65
Accounts payable (days)	138	152	60
Profit margin	(8)%	(12)%	5%
Debt to equity	75	79	110
Return on equity	(29)%	(77)%	19%
Return on assets	(10)%	(14)%	7%

percent of sales instead of the industry average of 32 percent. Costs must decrease if Peterson is ever going to be profitable.

Working capital is the second area Peterson's Chemicals needs to manage. Days' sales outstanding (A/R days) are 60 percent higher than the industry average. Collections must be more rigorously enforced. The payables payment period is also too high. Reducing this period might result in suppliers reducing costs.

b. Had management made these changes, the 1986 loss would have decreased by 62 million. ROE and ROA would still be negative but vastly improved over the current ROE of − 77 percent and ROA of − 14 percent.

New Management Decisions:

Reduce receivables to	78 days
Reduce sales by	3%
Reduce payables to	69 days
Reduce COGS by	9%
Debt to equity	100%

Peterson's Chemicals
Income Statement
(in millions)

	1986
Sales	$ 1,434
Cost of goods sold	(1,076)
Gross profit	358
Operating expense	(443)
Operating profit	(85)
Interest	(27)
Net income	($112)

Peterson's Chemicals
Balance Sheet
(in millions)

Assets	1986	Liabilities & Equity	1986
Cash and equivalents	$120	A/P	$206
A/R (net)	311	Other current	310
Inventory	324		
Other current assets	37	Current liabs.	516
		Long-term debt	288
Current assets	792		
		Total Liabs.	804
Net PP&E	300	Owners' equity	288
Total assets	$1,092	Liabs. & equity	$1,092

Resulting Ratios:	1986
Current	1.54
Quick	0.84
Debt to equity	1.00
Return on equity	−39%
Return on assets	−10%

CHAPTER 2—SOLUTIONS

Problem 1.

Assumptions for 1989:

Sales growth	60%
COGS	75%
Operating expense growth	10%
Tax rate	40%
Minimum cash/sales	20%
Accounts receivable (360-day year)	45 days
Accounts payable (360-day year)	30 days
Inventory turnover	3 times
Change in property, plant, and equipment	0
Depreciation	$ 8,000
Long-term debt	$125,000
Common stock	$100,000

Chateau Royale International
Income Statements
For the Periods Ending December 31, 1987, 1988

	1988	Forecast 1989
Sales	$375,000	$600,000
Cost of goods sold	(276,150)	(450,000)
Gross profit	98,850	150,000
Operating expenses	(75,000)	(82,500)
Depreciation	(5,100)	(8,000)
Operating profit	18,750	59,500
Taxes	(7,500)	(23,800)
Net profit	$ 11,250	$ 35,700

Chateau Royale International
Balance Sheets

	1988	Forecast 1989
Assets		
Cash	$ 75,000	$120,000
Accounts receivable	46,233	75,000
Inventory	93,750	150,000
Current assets	214,983	345,000
Net PP&E	115,000	107,000
Total assets	$329,983	$452,000

Chateau Royale International
Balance Sheets (concluded)

	1988	Forecast 1989
Liabilities & Equity		
Accounts payable.	$ 23,116	$ 37,500
Other short-term debt	51,867	123,800
Current liabilities	74,983	161,300
Long-term debt	125,000	125,000
Common stock.	100,000	100,000
Retained earnings	30,000	65,700
Total equity	130,000	165,700
Total liabilities & equity	$329,983	$452,000
Current assets.	$214,983	345,000
Current liabilities	74,983	161,300
Net working capital.	$140,000	$183,700
Current ratio	287%	214%

Problem 2.

Assumptions for 1989:

Sales growth.	60%
COGS	75%
Operating expense growth	10%
Tax rate.	40%
Minimum cash/sales	15%
Accounts receivable (360-day year)	45 days
Accounts payable (360-day year).	45 days
Inventory turnover	4 times
Change in property, plant, and equipment	0
Depreciation.	$ 8,000
Long-term debt.	$125,000
Common stock.	$100,000

Chateau Royale International
Income Statements

	1988	Forecast 1989
Sales	$375,000	$600,000
Cost of goods sold	(276,150)	(450,000)
Gross profit	98,850	150,000
Operating expenses.	(75,000)	(82,500)
Depreciation.	(5,100)	(8,000)
Operating profit	18,750	59,500
Taxes.	(7,500)	(23,800)
Net profit.	$ 11,250	$ 35,700

Chateau Royale International
Balance Sheet

	1988	Forecast 1989
Assets		
Cash	$ 75,000	$ 90,000
Accounts receivable.	46,233	75,000
Inventory.	93,750	112,500
Current assets	214,983	277,500
Net PP&E	115,000	107,000
Total assets	$329,983	$384,500
Liabilities & Equity		
Accounts payable	$ 23,116	$ 56,250
Other short-term debt	51,867	37,550
Current liabilities.	74,983	93,800
Long-term debt.	125,000	125,000
Common stock	100,000	100,000
Retained earnings.	30,000	65,700
Total equity	130,000	165,700
Total liabs. & equity	$329,983	$384,500
Current assets	$214,983	$277,500
Current liabs..	74,983	93,800
Net working capital.	$140,000	$183,700
Current ratio	287%	296%

The working-capital policy changes brought the current ratio closer to the industry average of 3.2. This is the result of keeping a lower cash balance and a higher movement of inventory, as well as the longer payment period for creditors. Chateau Royale will have to be aware that delayed payment may result in higher supplier costs as interest, either explicit or implicit, is included in the prices. Management should also be aware of possible stockouts and the reduced liquidity caused by the $30,000 drop in the cash balance.

Problem 3.

a.

Assumptions:

	Options	
	Dine	*Triano*
Sales growth	20%	50%
COGS (% of sales)	75%	75%
Operating expense growth.	0%	0%
Tax rate	35%	35%
Minimum cash balance (% of sales)	15%	20%
Accounts receivable (360-day year).	30 days	60 days
Accounts payable (360-day year)	30 days	30 days
Inventory turnover.	5	7
Fixed assets.	$130,000	$130,000
Long-term debt	$110,000	$110,000
Common stock	75,000	75,000
Bad debt	0%	2%

Kurz Corporation
Income Statement

		Options	
	1988	*Dine*	*Triano*
Sales	$505,000	$606,000	$757,500
Bad debt expense	(5,000)	0	(15,150)
Net sales.	500,000	606,000	742,350
Cost of goods sold.	(375,000)	(454,500)	(568,125)
Gross profit	125,000	151,500	174,225
Operating expenses	(90,900)	90,900	(90,900)
Operating profit.	34,100	60,600	83,325
Taxes	(11,935)	(21,210)	(29,164)
Net profit	$ 22,165	$ 39,390	$ 54,161

Kurz Corporation
Balance Sheets

	1988	Options Dine	Triano
Cash	$ 90,000	$ 90,900	$151,500
Accounts receivable.	61,644	50,500	126,250
Inventory.	62,500	90,900	81,161
Current assets	214,144	232,300	358,911
Net property, plant, and equipment. . . .	130,000	130,000	130,000
Total assets	$344,144	$362,300	$488,911
Accounts payable	$ 30,822	$ 37,875	$ 47,344
Other short-term debt	86,322	58,035	160,406
Current liabilities.	117,144	95,910	207,750
Long-term debt.	110,000	110,000	110,000
Common stock	75,000	75,000	75,000
Retained earnings.	42,000	81,390	96,161
Total equity	117,000	156,390	171,161
Total liabs. & equity	$344,144	$362,300	$488,911
Current assets	$214,144	$232,300	$358,911
Current liabs.	117,144	95,910	207,750
Net working capital.	$ 97,000	$136,390	$151,161
Current ratio	183%	242%	173%

b. Ms. Brittain should implement Mr. Triano's plan. Despite the higher costs, Mr. Triano's plan results in a higher net profit and higher asset growth. Ms. Brittain should be aware, however, that this policy change will result in higher short-term leverage, thereby increasing the risk of financial distress should sales decline.

CHAPTER 3—SOLUTIONS

Problem 1.

Assumptions for 1989 (dollars in thousands):

Beginning balances:

Cash	65	Cash sales	25%
Accounts receivable	184	Selling, general, and	
Accounts payable	173	administrative expenses	19%
Inventory	50	Safety stock	6%
Equity	471	Cost of goods sold	75%
PPE (net)	345	Lease and interest expense	$24
Accounts receivable	30 days	Depreciation	$12
Accounts payable	30 days		

Mary's Ski Chalet
Monthly Cash Budget for 1989
(in thousands)

	Jan.	Feb.	Mar.	Apr.	May	June	July	Aug.	Sept.	Oct.	Nov.	Dec.
Sales	$210	$175	$160	$140	$50	$30	$30	$75	$90	$125	$165	$230
Receipts:												
Accounts receivable (beginning)	184	158	131	120	105	38	23	23	56	68	94	124
Credit sales	158	131	120	105	38	23	23	56	68	94	124	173
Less: Collections	184	158	131	120	105	38	23	23	56	68	94	124
Accounts receivable (end)	$158	$131	$120	$105	$38	$23	$23	$56	$68	$94	$124	$173
Collections	$184	$158	$131	$120	$105	38	$23	$23	$56	$68	$94	$124
Cash sales	52	44	40	35	12	7	7	19	22	31	41	57
Total receipts	$236	$202	$171	$155	$117	$45	$30	$42	$78	$99	$135	$181
Disbursements:												
Accounts payable (beginning)	$173	$170	$142	$130	$113	$41	$24	$24	$61	$73	$101	$134
Purchases	170	142	130	113	41	24	24	61	73	101	134	186
Less: Payments	173	170	142	130	113	41	24	24	61	73	101	134
Net accounts payable (end)	$170	$142	$130	$113	$ 41	$24	$24	$61	$73	$101	$134	$186
Payments	$173	$170	$142	$130	$113	$41	$24	$24	$61	$73	$101	$134
Selling, general, and administrative exp.	40	33	30	27	10	6	6	14	17	24	31	44
Lease and interest	2	2	2	2	2	2	2	2	2	2	2	2
Total disbursements	$215	$205	$174	$159	$125	$49	$32	$40	$80	$99	$134	$180
Net receipts	21	(3)	(3)	(4)	(8)	(4)	(2)	2	(2)	0	1	1
Cum. cash flow	21	18	15	11	3	(1)	(3)	(1)	(3)	(3)	(2)	(1)
Chg. in monthly cash:												
Beginning cash	$ 65	$ 86	$ 83	$ 80	$ 76	$68	$64	$62	$64	$ 62	$ 62	$ 63
Chg. in cash	21	(3)	(3)	(4)	(8)	(4)	(2)	2	(2)	0	1	1
Ending cash	$ 86	$ 83	$ 80	$ 76	$ 68	$64	$62	$64	$62	$ 62	$ 63	$ 64

Although Ms. Turnbull will have negative net receipts for nine months, she will not need additional financing due to the $65,000 balance in the cash account from previous years.

Problem 2.

Mary's Ski Chalet
Income Statement
(in thousands)

	1989
Sales	$1,480
Cost of goods sold	(1,110)
Gross margin	$ 370
Selling and general expense	(282)
Depreciation	(12)
Lease and interest	(24)
Net income	$ 52

Mary's Ski Chalet
Balance Sheets
(in thousands)

	1988	*Forecast 1989*
Assets		
Cash	$ 65	$ 64
Accounts receivable	184	173
Inventory	50	139
Current assets	$299	$376
Net property, plant, and equipment	345	333
Total assets	$644	$709
Liabilities & Equity		
Accounts payable	$173	$186
Current liabilities	173	186
Equity	471	523
Total liabilities & equity	$644	$709

Problem 3.

Assumptions:

	Actual	Projected				
	1987	1988	1989	1990	1991	1992
Sales growth	20%	20%	10%	11%	12%	13%
Gross margin (% of sales)	38%	48%	50%	50%	50%	50%
Selling, general, and administrative (% of sales)	13%	13%	13%	13%	13%	13%
Tax rate	50%	50%	50%	38%	38%	38%
Cash (% of sales)	14%	14%	14%	14%	14%	14%
Days' sales outstanding	80	43	43	43	43	43
Inventory turnover	3	4	8	8	6	6
Payables payment period (days)	75	60	60	60	60	60

ARIES CORPORATION
Income Statements
For the Periods 1986 through 1992
(in thousands)

	Actual		Projected				
	1986	1987	1988	1989	1990	1991	1992
Sales	$221	$266	$319	$351	$390	$437	$493
Cost of goods sold	(145)	(166)	166	176	195	218	247
Gross profit	76	100	153	176	195	219	247
Selling, general, and administrative expense . .	(38)	35	41	46	51	57	64
Operating profit	38	65	112	130	144	162	183
Tax	(19)	33	56	65	55	62	70
Net income	$ 19	$ 32	$ 56	$ 65	$ 89	$100	$113

Aries Corporation
Balance Sheets
For the Periods 1986 through 1992
(in thousands)

	Actual		Projected				
	1986	1987	1988	1989	1990	1991	1992
Assets							
Cash	$22	$37	$45	$49	$55	$61	$69
Accounts receivable	49	31	38	42	47	51	59
Inventory	47	45	21	22	24	36	41
Current assets	118	113	103	113	126	149	169
Fixed assets	70	122	265	291	323	403	513
Total assets	$188	$235	$368	$404	$449	$552	$682
Liabilities & Equity							
Notes payable, financing							
required	$ 0	$ 0	$ 84	$ 52	$ 4	$ 4	$ 16
Accounts payable	19	34	28	30	33	37	42
Current liabilities	19	34	112	82	37	41	58
Equity	169	201	257	322	411	511	624
Total liabilities & equity . . .	$188	$235	$368	$404	$449	$552	$682

CHAPTER 4—SOLUTIONS

Problem 1.

Marvel Corporation's investment will pay back in 3.3 years. The benefit/cost ratio is 5.74. Since the payback ratio is lower than the four years required, the project should be accepted. The following forecasts were used in calculating these numbers:

PROBLEM 1 (continued)

	Years						
	0	*1*	*2*	*3*	*4*	*5*	*6*
Income statement changes:							
Sales		$1,250.0	$1,250.0	$1,250.0	$1,250.0	$1,250.0	$1,250.0
Raw materials		(462.5)	(462.5)	(462.5)	(462.5)	(462.5)	(462.5)
Operating costs		(10.0)	(10.0)	(10.0)	(10.0)	(10.0)	(10.0)
Wages		(450.0)	(450.0)	(450.0)	(450.0)	(450.0)	(450.0)
Gross margin		327.5	327.5	327.5	327.5	327.5	327.5
Depreciation		(80.0)	(72.0)	(64.8)	(58.3)	(52.5)	(47.2)
Profit before taxes		247.5	255.5	262.7	269.2	275.0	280.3
Taxes		(84.2)	(86.9)	(89.3)	(91.5)	(93.5)	(95.3)
Profit after taxes		163.3	168.6	173.4	177.7	181.5	185.0
Noncash charges:							
Depreciation		80.0	72.0	64.8	58.3	52.5	47.2
Capital investments:							
Machinery	($800.0)						
Net cash flow	($800.0)	$ 243.3	$ 240.6	$ 238.2	$ 236.0	$ 234.0	$ 232.2
Payback = 3.33							
Benefit/cost ratio = 5.74							
Depreciation Analysis:							
Double-declining balance	$800	$ 80.0	$ 72.0	$ 64.8	$ 58.3	$ 52.5	$ 47.2
Undepreciated balance		720.0	648.0	583.2	524.9	472.4	425.2
Straight-line for remaining life		40.0	37.9	36.0	34.3	32.8	31.5

PROBLEM 1 (continued)

	Years						
	7	8	9	10	11	12	13
Income statement changes:							
Sales	$1,250.0	$1,250.0	$1,250.0	$1,250.0	$1,250.0	$1,250.0	$1,250.0
Raw materials	(462.5)	(462.5)	(462.5)	(462.5)	(462.5)	(462.5)	(462.5)
Operating costs	(10.0)	(10.0)	(10.0)	(10.0)	(10.0)	(10.0)	(10.0)
Wages	(450.0)	(450.0)	(450.0)	(450.0)	(450.0)	(450.0)	(450.0)
Gross margin	327.5	327.5	327.5	327.5	327.5	327.5	327.5
Depreciation	(42.5)	(38.3)	(34.4)	(31.0)	(27.9)	(27.9)	(27.9)
Profit before taxes	285.0	289.2	293.1	296.5	299.6	299.6	299.6
Taxes	(96.9)	(98.3)	(99.6)	(100.8)	(101.9)	(101.9)	(101.9)
Profit after taxes	188.1	190.9	193.5	195.7	197.7	197.7	197.7
Noncash charges:							
Depreciation	42.5	38.3	34.4	31.0	27.9	27.9	27.9
Capital Investments:							
Machinery							
Net cash flow	$ 230.6	$ 229.2	$ 227.9	$ 226.7	$ 225.6	$ 225.6	$ 225.6
Payback = 3.33							
Benefit/cost ratio = 5.74							
Depreciation Analysis:							
Double-declining balance	$ 42.5	$ 38.3	$ 34.4	$ 31.0	$ 27.9	$ 25.1	$ 22.6
Undepreciated balance	382.6	344.4	309.9	278.9	251.0	225.9	203.3
Straight-line for remaining life	30.4	29.4	28.7	28.2	27.9	27.9	27.9

243

PROBLEM 1 (concluded)

	Years						
	14	15	16	17	18	19	20
Income statement changes:							
Sales	$1,250.0	$1,250.0	$1,250.0	$1,250.0	$1,250.0	$1,250.0	$1,250.0
Raw materials	(462.5)	(462.5)	(462.5)	(462.5)	(462.5)	(462.5)	(462.5)
Operating costs	(10.0)	(10.0)	(10.0)	(10.0)	(10.0)	(10.0)	(10.0)
Wages	(450.0)	(450.0)	(450.0)	(450.0)	(450.0)	(450.0)	(450.0)
Gross margin	327.5	327.5	327.5	327.5	327.5	327.5	327.5
Depreciation	(27.9)	(27.9)	(27.9)	(27.9)	(27.9)	(27.9)	(27.9)
Profit before taxes	299.6	299.6	299.6	299.6	299.6	299.6	299.6
Taxes	(101.9)	(101.9)	(101.9)	(101.9)	(101.9)	(101.9)	(101.9)
Profit after taxes	197.7	197.7	197.7	197.7	197.7	197.7	197.7
Noncash charges:							
Depreciation	27.9	27.9	27.9	27.9	27.9	27.9	27.9
Capital investments:							
Machinery							
Net cash flow	$ 225.6	$ 225.6	$ 225.6	$ 225.6	$ 225.6	$ 225.6	$ 225.6
Payback = 3.33							
Benefit/cost ratio = 5.74							
Depreciation Analysis:							
Double-declining balance	$ 20.3	$ 18.3	$ 16.5	$ 14.8	$ 13.3	$ 12.0	$ 10.8
Undepreciated balance	183.0	164.7	148.2	133.4	120.1	108.1	97.3
Straight-line for remaining life	27.9	27.9	27.9	27.9	27.9	27.9	27.9

244

Problem 2.

The net present value for the SUN Company investment is $60,750 and the investment should be made. The major component of the cash flows are the high depreciation allowances. The analysis is done as follows.

SUN Company
Alternative Investments
(in thousands)

	0	1	2	3	4	5
				Years		
Income statement changes:						
Sales		$120.0	$138.0	$158.7	$182.5	$209.9
Costs		(46.8)	(53.8)	(61.9)	(71.2)	(81.9)
Depreciation - 1		(80.0)	(48.0)	(28.8)	(21.6)	(21.6)
Depreciation - 2				(40.0)	(13.3)	(6.7)
Profit before taxes		(6.8)	36.2	28.0	76.4	99.7
Taxes		2.3	(12.3)	(9.5)	(26.0)	(33.9)
Profit after taxes		(4.5)	23.9	18.5	50.4	65.8
Noncash charges:						
Depreciation - 1		80.0	48.0	28.8	21.6	21.6
Depreciation - 2		0	0	40.0	13.3	6.7
Capital investments:						
Investment - 1	($200.0)					
Investment - 2			(60.0)			
Net cash flow	($200.0)	$75.5	$11.9	$87.3	$85.3	$94.1

Discount rate = 10%
Net present value = $60.750
The net present value is the sum of the present value of each cash flow:
($200.00) + 68.64 + 9.83 + 65.59 + 58.26 + 58.43

Problem 3.

Of the two projects Kertin management is considering, project 1 is better if payback or net present value is used. However, if benefit/cost ratio is the criterion, they are equal. Since net present value is the best criterion, project 1 should be accepted.

	Year			
	0	*1*	*2*	*3*

Project 1

Income statement changes:				
Sales		$500	$500	$500
Cost of goods sold		(245)	(245)	(245)
Gross margin		255	255	255
Advertising		(50)	(50)	(50)
Depreciation		(160)	(128)	(102)
Profit before taxes		45	77	103
Taxes		(15)	(26)	(35)
Profit after taxes		30	51	68
Noncash charges:				
Depreciation		160	128	102
Capital investments:				
Machinery	($800)			
Cash flow	($800)	$190	$179	$170

Net present value = $218
Benefit/cost = 2.03
Payback = 4.62

	Year			
	0	*1*	*2*	*3*

Project 2

Income statement changes:				
Sales		$350	$385	$424
Cost of sales		(175)	(192)	(212)
Gross margin		175	193	212
Advertising		(88)	(96)	(106)
Depreciation		(120)	(96)	(77)
Training	($200)			
Profit before taxes	(200)	(33)	0	29
Taxes	68	11	0	(10)
Profit after taxes	(132)	(22)	0	19
Noncash charges:				
Depreciation		120	96	77
Capital investments:				
Production facilities	(600)			
Cash flow	($732)	$ 98	$ 96	$ 96

Net present value = $133
Benefit/cost = 2.12
Payback = 6.29

Note: The $100,000 market research expense is a sunk cost and not included in the analysis.

			Year			
4	5	6	7	8	9	10

Project 1

4	5	6	7	8	9	10
$500	$500	$500	$500	$500	$500	$500
(245)	(245)	(245)	(245)	(245)	(245)	(245)
255	255	255	255	255	255	255
(50)	(50)	(50)	(50)	(50)	(50)	(50)
(82)	(66)	(52)	(52)	(52)	(52)	(52)
123	139	153	153	153	153	153
(42)	(47)	(52)	(52)	(52)	(52)	(52)
81	92	101	101	101	101	101
82	66	52	52	52	52	52
$163	$158	$153	$153	$153	$153	$153

			Year			
4	5	6	7	8	9	10

Project 2

4	5	6	7	8	9	10
$466	$536	$616	$708	$779	$857	$943
(233)	(268)	(308)	(354)	(390)	(429)	(472)
233	268	308	354	389	428	471
(100)	(100)	(100)	(100)	(100)	(100)	(100)
(61)	(49)	(39)	(39)	(39)	(39)	(39)
72	119	169	215	250	289	332
(24)	(40)	(57)	(73)	(85)	(98)	(113)
48	79	112	142	165	191	219
61	49	39*	39	39	39	39
$109	$128	$151	$181	$204	$230	$258

	Project 1	Project 2
Benefit/cost	2.03	2.12
Payback	4.62	6.29
Net present value	$218	$133

CHAPTER 5—SOLUTIONS

Problem 1.

Bakelite's cost of capital is slightly different using each method for calculating the cost of equity. The range is 14.0 percent to 14.6 percent.

Cost of capital:

Cost of debt $14.5\% \times (1-40\%) = 8.7\%$

Cost of equity

CAPM: $R_e = R_f + B \times (R_m - R_f)$

$\qquad = 8.9\% + 1.32 * 6\%$ (using 7-year bill yield)

$\qquad = \quad 16.82\%$

$\qquad = 6.5\% + 1.32 \times 8.5\%$ (using 90-day bill yield)

$\qquad = \quad 17.72\%$

Dividend growth model: $R_e =$ Dividend/Price + Growth

$\qquad\qquad\qquad = \$3/\$25 + 4.9\%$

$\qquad\qquad\qquad = \quad 16.90\%$

Cost of capital (weighted average) = $(D \times Rd + E*Re)/(D+E)$

$\qquad$ D = \$1.3, E = \$2.4, D + E = \$3.7

A) Using 7-year bond yield:

$\qquad R_{WACC} = [(1.3 \times 8.7\%) + (2.4 \times 16.82\%)]/3.7 = 13.98\%$

B) Using 90-day bond yield:

$\qquad R_{WACC} = [(1.3 \times 8.7\%) + (2.4 \times 17.72\%)]/3.7 = 14.56\%$

C) Dividend growth model:

$\qquad R_{WACC} = [(1.3 \times 8.7\%) + (2.4 \times 16.9\%)]/3.7 = 13.03\%$

Problem 2.

The marginal weighted-average cost of capital for Select Company is calculated as follows:

A. Capital structure: 35% debt, 65% equity.
B. Cost of debt:
   Before tax 11.75%.
   After tax $11.75 \times (1 - .34) = 7.75\%$
C. Cost of equity:
   1. *Dividend discount model:* $R_e = \dfrac{D_1}{P_0} + g$

   a. To calculate the dividend yield: $\dfrac{D_1}{P_0}$

   Projected earnings = \$554,400.
   Dividend payout = $.24 \times \$554,400 = \$133,056$.
   Dividend/share = \$133,056/300,000 shares = \$0.44
   Current market price/share = \$18.50

   $D_1/P_0 = \$0.44/\$6.90 = .0638$ or 6.4%.

b. To calculate the growth (g):
   $g = (1 - \text{Payout})(\text{ROE})$.
   $g = (1 - .24) \times .12 = .091$.
c. To calculate the weighted-average cost:
   Cost of equity $= .064 + .091 = .155$ or 15.5%.
   Weighted cost of equity $= .65 \times .115 = .101$.
   Weighted cost of debt $= .1175 \times .35(1 - .34)$
   $\qquad\qquad\qquad\qquad\qquad = .027$.
   Weighted-average cost of capital $= .027 + .101 = .128$ or 12.8%.
2. *CAPM:* $R_{ej} = R_f + \beta_j(R_m - R_f)$
   $R_{ej} = .101 + 0.98(.16 - .101) = .159$.
   Weighted cost of equity $= .65 \times .159 = .103$.
   Weighted-average cost of capital $= .103 + .027 = .130$ or 13.0%.

CHAPTER 6—SOLUTIONS

Problem 1.

	Net Cash Flow/Year (EPS/Number of Shares)	
	X Company	Y Company
1981	$700,000	$501,000
1982	756,000	561,200
1983	816,000	625,000
1984	880,000	701,950
1985	952,000	785,850
Increase in EPS	Average 8% per year	Average 12% per year

If the Single-Firm Company is interested primarily in growth, it should pursue the Y Company. Before it does, however, it should get more information.

Problem 2.

a. Book value of Klick $= \$543,000 - (\$137,000 + \$111,000) = \$295,000$. This is the lowest of any of the values identified and, based on the nature of the assets involved, should be the minimum price acceptable to Klick's management. If the assets have appreciated in value since their purchase (e.g., land), this price might be unacceptable. In such a case, the minimum acceptable price might be based on a market appraisal of the assets' value.
b. Current market price $= 50,000$ shares $\times \$6.00 = \$300,000$.
c. PV of Klick's net cash flow $= \$40,000/.1125 = \$355,556$.

d. Klick's implied P/E = PV/Earnings
   $355,556/$30,000 = 11.85 times.
e. Price of indifference to Kupp:
   [PV combined − (PV Kupp + PV Klick)] = (Price − PV Klick)
   [$1,000,000 − ($480,000 + $355,556)] = (X − $355,556)
   Breakeven price X = $520,000.

This is the price at which Kupp should be indifferent about acquiring Klick. Unless Kupp felt they had underestimated Klick's future potential or value, they should not pay more than $520,000 for the company.

Klick management should expect, *at a minimum,* the present value of the cash flows, $355,556. The fact that this is above the book value indicates that the company has potential not reflected on the balance sheet.

Problem 3.

Valuation of Smyth, Robinson, and the combined company can be done with the discounted cash flow formulation.

$$P = CF/(k - g)$$

Using this approach, the calculations are as follows:

A. Value of Smyth:
   $6.45/(.122 − .04) = $78.66 million.
B. Value of Robinson:
   $2.2/(.105 − .04) = $33.85 million.
C. Value of combined company:
   $9.45/(.11 − .04) = $135 million.

Since there are no debtholder claims on Robinson, Smyth could offer up to $56.34 million ($135 − $78.66), and Robinson should accept any offer above $33.85 million.

Problem 4.

To maximize shareholders' return, Mr. Santiago should sell for not less than $301 million. At any price below that, the shareholders' value will be destroyed.

Projected Cash Flows
(in millions)

	1988	1989	1990	1991	1992	1993	1994	1995
Sales	$257.5	$265.2	$273.2	$281.4	$289.8	$298.5	$307.5	$316.7
Cost of goods sold	(193.1)	(198.9)	(204.9)	(211.0)	(217.4)	(223.9)	(230.6)	(237.5)
Selling, general, and administrative	(25.8)	(26.5)	(27.3)	(28.1)	(29.0)	(29.9)	(30.7)	(31.7)
Depreciation	(7.0)	(7.0)	(7.0)	(7.0)	(7.0)	(7.0)	(7.0)	(7.0)
Profit before taxes	31.6	32.8	34.0	35.3	36.4	37.7	39.2	40.5
Taxes	(10.8)	(11.1)	(11.6)	(12.0)	(12.4)	(12.8)	(13.3)	(13.8)
Profit after taxes	20.8	21.7	22.4	23.3	24.0	24.9	25.9	26.7
Depreciation	7.0	7.0	7.0	7.0	7.0	7.0	7.0	7.0
Terminal value	0.0	0.0	0.0	0.0	0.0	0.0	0.0	411.0
Net cash flow	$ 27.8	$ 28.7	$ 29.4	$ 30.3	$ 31.0	$ 31.9	$ 32.9	$444.7

Net present value = $330.3

Cost of debt $(R_d) = 10.1\% \ (1 - 34\%) = 6.67\%$

Cost of equity $(R_e) = 12\%$

Cost of capital = 11.22%

Terminal value = $33.7/(11.2\% - 3\%) = \$411$

CHAPTER 7—SOLUTIONS

Problem 1.

If Zumar can gain more than $8.1 million in earnings before interest and taxes, the debt alternative will result in larger EPS.

Zumar, Inc. Earnings with Existing and Expected Revenues (in millions except per share amounts)

	Debt Financing		Equity Financing	
	Old Revenues	New Revenues	Old Revenues	New Revenues
Revenues	$100.0	$120.0	$100.0	$120.0
Earnings before Interest & Taxes	13.0	15.6	13.0	15.6
Interest:				
Old	(2.8)	(2.8)	(2.8)	(2.8)
New	(1.5)	(1.5)	0.0	0.0
Profit before taxes	8.7	11.3	10.2	12.8
Taxes	(3.0)	(3.8)	(3.5)	(4.4)
Profit after taxes	$ 5.7	$ 7.5	$ 6.7	$ 8.4
Number of shares	2.0	2.0	2.8	2.8
Earnings per share	$ 2.85	$ 3.75	$ 2.40	$ 3.00

Problem 2.

Dividends can be covered no matter how Zumar finances its needs.

Zumar, Inc. Dividend Coverage with Existing and Expected Revenues (in millions except per share amounts)

	Debt Financing		Equity Financing	
	Old Revenues	New Revenues	Old Revenues	New Revenues
Revenues	$100.0	$120.0	$100.0	$120.0
Earnings before Interest & Taxes	13.0	15.6	13.0	15.6
Interest:				
Old	(2.8)	(2.8)	(2.8)	(2.8)
New	(1.5)	(1.5)	0.0	0.0
Profit before taxes	8.7	11.3	10.2	12.8
Taxes	(3.0)	(3.8)	(3.5)	(4.4)
Profit after taxes	$ 5.7	$ 7.5	$ 6.7	$ 8.4
Number of shares	2.0	2.0	2.8	2.8
Earnings per share	$ 2.85	$ 3.75	$ 2.40	$ 3.00
Dividends per share	$ 0.75	$ 0.75	$ 0.75	$ 0.75
Dividend coverage	380%	500%	319%	400%

Problem 3.

The weighted-average cost of capital would rise to 13.5 percent with an equity issue and would be 12.9 percent with debt. Risk for the shareholders, as proxied by beta, rises more with debt than equity, even though the risk of the firm does not change. The following steps were used to determine these conclusions.

a. The capital structure will change.

	Current	Debt Alternative	Equity Alternative
Debt	$40	$55	$40
Equity	$54	$54	$69
Debt/equity	74%	102%	58%

b. The beta without leverage is .89 calculated using:

$$B_L = B_U\left[1+\left(\left(\frac{D}{E}\right)\times(1-t)\right)\right]$$

With a debt issue and D/E of 102 percent, the beta rises to 1.48, and with new equity and D/E of 58 percent, the beta would be 1.23.

c. The weighted-average costs of capital (WACC) are

	Debt Cost*	Debt Proportion	Equity Cost	Equity	WACC
Debt issued	10.0%(1−t)	50.5%	16.9%	49.5%	11.7%
Equity issued	10.0%(1−t)	36.7	15.4	63.7	12.1
*t=taxes of .34%.					

Problem 4.

Since the value per share of the equity is greater with the debt alternative, that alternative should be accepted.

Zumar, Inc. Shareholder Value-Creation with Financing from Debt Sources

	1988	1989	1990
Sales	$120.0	$122.4	$124.8
Earnings before interest & taxes	15.6	15.9	16.2
Interest:			
Old	(2.8)	(2.8)	(2.8)
New	(1.5)	(1.5)	(1.5)
Earnings before taxes	11.3	11.6	11.9
Taxes	(3.8)	(3.9)	(4.0)
Profit after taxes	7.5	7.7	7.9
Depreciation	4.8	4.8	4.8
New PP&E	(4.8)	(4.8)	(4.8)
Annual cash flow	7.5	7.7	7.9
Terminal value			52.7
Net cash flow	$ 7.5	$ 7.7	$ 60.6

Net present value = $49.9
NPV per share = $24.95
*At the cost of equity of 16.9%.

Zumar, Inc. Shareholder Value-Creation with Financing from Equity Sources

	1988	1989	1990
Sales	$120.0	$122.4	$124.8
Earnings before interest & taxes	15.6	15.9	16.2
Interest:			
Old	(2.8)	(2.8)	(2.8)
New	0.0	0.0	0.0
Earnings before taxes	12.8	13.1	13.4
Taxes	(4.4)	(4.5)	(4.6)
Profit after taxes	8.4	8.6	8.8
Depreciation	4.8	4.8	4.8
New PP&E	(4.8)	(4.8)	(4.8)
Annual cash flow	8.4	8.6	8.8
Terminal value			66.2
Net cash flow	$ 8.4	$ 8.6	$ 75.1

Net present value = $62.7
NPV per share = $22.80
*At the cost of equity of 15.4%.

C–2 Lotus 1-2-3 Models for Study Questions

This section shows examples of solutions to chapter problems using Lotus 1-2-3 and is provided to allow the user of this financial planning tool to practice.

For each of the models, the entries for the rows and columns are stated. The results of these models may differ slightly from the manual solutions to the study questions because of differences in rounding.

CHAPTER 1—SOLUTIONS

Problem 1.

	-A-	-B-	-C-	-D-	-E-	-F-
1	'1-1					
2		[]	+B2+1	+C2+1	+D2+1	+E2+1
3						
4	'Sales	[$4,409]	[$5,787]	[$7,934]	[$7,320]	[$6,345]
5	'Net Income	[$338]	[$272]	[$465]	[($118)]	[$418]
6	'Div Payout	[35%]	[48%]	[33%]	[-145%]	[43%]
7	'Total Assets	[$8,109]	[$10,835]	[$11,636]	[$11,494]	[$12,661]
8	'Total Equity	[$3,398]	[$4,526]	[$4,909]	[$4,595]	[$4,873]
9						
10	'ROS	+B5/B4	+C5/C4	+D5/D4	+E5/E4	+F5/F4
11	'ROA	+B5/B7	+C5/C7	+D5/D7	+E5/E7	+F5/F7
12	'ROE	+B5/B8	+C5/C8	+D5/D8	+E5/E8	+F5/F8
13	'1-PO	1-B6	1-C6	1-D6	1-E6	1-F6
14						
15	'SGR	(B5/B8)*(1-B6)	(C5/C8)*(1-C6)	(D5/D8)*(1-D6)	(E5/E8)*(1-E6)	(F5/F8)*(1-F6)

CSX appears to be outperforming the industry averages.

Problem 2.

	-A-	-B-	-C-	-D-	-E-	-F-	-G-	-H-
1	'1-2							
2								
3					'NewTech			
4								
5			'Manufacturing				'Chemicals	
6								
7		[]	+B7+1	1+C7		[]	+F7+1	1+G7
8								
9	'Sales	[$2,384]	[$2,500]	[$2,600]		[$1,562]	[$1,623]	[$1,687]
10	'COGS	[(1,058)]	[(1,075)]	[(1,300)]		[(950)]	[(967)]	[(980)]
11		"-------	"-------	"-------		"-------	"-------	"-------
12	'Gross	+B9+B10	+C9+C10	+D9+D10		+F9+F10	+G9+G10	+H9+H10
13	'Oper Exp	[(159)]	[(178)]	[(185)]		[(88)]	[(97)]	[(100)]
14		"-------	"-------	"-------		"-------	"-------	"-------
15	'EBIT	+B12+B13	+C12+C13	+D12+D13		+F12+F13	+G12+G13	+H12+H13
16	'Interest	[(350)]	[(325)]	[(322)]		[(180)]	[(174)]	[(168)]
17	'Taxes	[(302)]	[(341)]	[(357)]		[(130)]	[(142)]	[(66)]
18		"-------	"-------	"-------		"-------	"-------	"-------
19	'Net Inc	+B15+B16+B17	+C15+C16+C17	+D15+D16+D17		+F15+F16+F17	+G15+G16+G17	+H15+H16+H17
20								
21								
22								
23					'NewTech			

PROBLEM 2   *(continued)*

	-A-	-B-	-C-	-D-	-E-	-F-	-G-	-H-
24								
25			'Manufact uring				'Chemical s	
26								
27		[]	+B27+1	1+C27		[]	+F27+1	1+G27
28								
29	'Componen t							
30								
31	'Sales	+B9/B9	+C9/C9	+D9/D9		+F9/F9	+G9/G9	+H9/H9
32	'COGS	+B10/B9	+C10/C9	+D10/D9		+F10/F9	+G10/G9	+H10/H9
33								
34	'Gross	+B31+B32	+C31+C32	+D31+D32		+F31+F32	+G31+G32	+H31+H32
35	'Oper Exp	+B13/B9	+C13/C9	+D13/D9		+F13/F9	+G13/G9	+H13/H9
36								
37	'EBIT	+B15/B9	+C15/C9	+D15/D9		+F15/F9	+G15/G9	+H15/H9
38	'Inter	+B16/B9	+C16/C9	+D16/D9		+F16/F9	+G16/G9	+H16/H9
39	'Taxes	+B17/B9	+C17/C9	+D17/D9		+F17/F9	+G17/G9	+H17/H9
40								
41	'Net Inc	+B19/B9	+C19/C9	+D19/D9		+F19/F9	+G19/G9	+H19/H9
42								
43					'NewTech			
44								
45			'Manufact uring				'Chemical s	

PROBLEM 2 *(concluded)*

	-A-	-B-	-C-	-D-	-E-	-F-	-G-	-H-
46								
47		[]	+B47+1	1+C47		[]	+F47+1	1+G47
48	'Changes							
49								
50	'Sales		+C9/B9-1	+D9/C9-1			+G9/F9-1	+H9/G9-1
51	'COGS		+C10/B10-1	+D10/C10-1			+G10/F10-1	+H10/G10-1
52								
53	'Gross		+C12/B12-1	+D12/C12-1			+G12/F12-1	+H12/G12-1
54	'Oper Exp		+C13/B13-1	+D13/C13-1			+G13/F13-1	+H13/G13-1
55								
56	'EBIT		+C15/B15-1	+D15/C15-1			+G15/F15-1	+H15/G15-1
57	'Inter		+C16/B16-1	+D16/C16-1			+G16/F16-1	+H16/G16-1
58	'Taxes		+C17/B17-1	+D17/C17-1			+G17/F17-1	+H17/G17-1
59								
60	'Net Inc		+C19/B19-1	+D19/C19-1			+G19/F19-1	+H19/G19-1

The manufacturing division has had erratic performance. The chemicals division has been much more stable.

Problem 3.

	-A-	-B-	
1	'1-3	'Given:	
2			
3	'Dividend payout	[ ]	
4	'Market price	[ ]	
5	'Dividend yield	[ ]	
6	'Shares out	[ ]	
7	'ROE	[ ]	
8	'LTD/Equity	[ ]	
9	'Current ratio	[ ]	
10	'Acid-test ratio	[ ]	
11	'Profit margin	[ ]	
12	'Gross margin	[ ]	
13	'ROA	[ ]	
14	'Inv turnover	[ ]	
15	'Op profit/gross	[ ]	
16	'AR collection	[ ]	
17	'AP period	[ ]	
18	'Tax rate	[ ]	
19			
20	'Income Stmt		
21			
22	'Sales	+B32/B11	
23	'Cost	+B22-B25	
24			

PROBLEM 3   *(concluded)*

	-A-	-B-
25	'Gross Margin	+B22*B12
26	'Op Expenses	(1-B15)*B25
27		
28	'Op Profit	+B15*B25
29	'Interest	+B28-B30-B32
30	'Taxes	+B32
31		
32	'Net Income	((B5*B4)*B6)/B3
33		
34		
35	'Balance Sheet	
36		
37	'Cash	(B10*B49)-B38
38	'AR	(B16/360)*B22
39	'Inventory	+B23/B14
40	'Other	+B41-B38-B39-B37
41	'CA	+B9*B49
42	'PPE	+B44-B41
43		
44	'Total Assets	+B32/B13
45		
46	'AP	(B17/360)*B23
47	'Other	+B49-B46
48		
49	'CL	+B55-B53-B50
50	'LTD	+B8*B53
51		
52	'Total Liab	+B49+B50
53	'Equity	+B32/B7
54		
55	'Liab & Equity	+B44

Problem 4.

a.

	-A-	-B-	-C-	-D-	-E-	-F-	-G-
1	'1-4a						
2							
3			'Peterson's Chemicals				
4							
5			|[]		|[]		
6	'Income Stmt						
7							
8	'Sales		|[$1,435]		|[$1,478]		
9	'Cost		|[(1,076)]|		|[(1,182)]|		
10			"------		"------		
11	'Gross Margin		+C8+C9		+E8+E9		
12	'S&A		|[(445)]		|[(443)]		
13			"------		"------		
14	'Op Profit		+C11+C12		+E11+E12		
15	'Interest		|[(29)]		|[(27)]		
16			"------		"------		
17	'Net Income		+C14+C15		+E14+E15		
18							
19							
20							
21			|'Peterson				

PROBLEM 4a   *(continued)*

	-A-	-B-	-C-	-D-	-E-	-F-	-G-
			's Chemic als				
22							
23		"1985	"1986			"1985	"1986
24	'Bal Shee t						
25							
26	'Cash	[$76]	[$120]		'AP	[]	[]
27	'AR	[]	[]		'Other	[]	[]
28	'Inv	[]	[]			"------	"------
29	'Other	[]	[]		'CL	+F26+F27	+G26+G27
30		"------	"------		'LTD	[]	[]
31	'CA	@SUM(B26. .B29)	@SUM(C26. .C29)			"------	"------
32					'Tot Liab	+F29+F30	+G29+G30
33	'PPE	[]	[]		'Equity	[]	+F33+E17
34		"------	"------			"------	"------
35	'Tot Asse t	+B31+B33	+C31+C33		'Total L& E	+F32+F33	+G32+G33
36							
37							
38							
39							
40							
41			'Peterson	'Industry		'Peterson	'Industry
42			[]	[]		[]	[]

PROBLEM 4a (*continued*)

	-A-	-B-	-C-	-D-	-E-	-F-	-G-
43	'Income S tmt						
44							
45	'Sales		+C8/C8	[100%]		+E8/E8	[100%]
46	'Cost		+C9/C8	[-67%]		+E9/E8	[-68%]
47							
48	'Gross Ma rgin		+C11/C8	[33%]		+E11/E8	[32%]
49	'S&A		+C12/C8	[-27%]		+E12/E8	[-26%]
50							
51	'Op Profi t		+C14/C8	[6%]		+E14/E8	[6%]
52	'Interest		+C15/C8	[-1%]		+E15/E8	[-2%]
53							
54	'Net Inco me		+C17/C8	[5%]		+E17/E8	[4%]
55							
56							
57							
58			'Peterson 's Chemic als				
59							
60			[]	[]		'Industry	
61	'Ratios						
62	'Current		+B31/F29	+C31/G29		[]	
63	'Acid		(B26+B27)	(C26+C27)		[]	

PROBLEM 4a   *(concluded)*

	-A-	-B-	-C-	-D-	-E-	-F-	-G-
			/F29	/G29			
64	'Rec Coll		(B27/C8)* 360	(C27/E8)* 360		[]	
65	'Pay		(+F26/-C9)*360	(+G26/-E9)*360		[]	
66	'Inv Turn		-C9/B28	-E9/C28		[]	
67	'Gross		+C11/C8	+E11/E8		[]	
68	'Profit		+C17/C8	+E17/E8		[]	
69	'D/E		+F30/F33	+G30/G33		[]	
70	'ROE		+C17/F33	+E17/G33		[19%]	
71	'ROA		+C17/B35	+E17/C35		[7%]	

Peterson's Chemicals faces two major problems : (1) high costs, and (2) working capital concerns.

Problem 4.

b.

	-A-	-B-	-C-	-D-	-E-	-F-	-G-
74							
75	'New Mana gement De cisions						
76							
77	'AR colle ction per iod			[]			
78	'Sales re duction			[]			
79	'AP payme nt period			[]			
80	'COGS red uction			[]			
81	'Debt/equ ity ratio			[]			
82							
83							
84							
85							
86							
87							
88							
89		'Peterson 's Chemic als					
90							
91				|[]			
92	'Income S						

PROBLEM 4b   *(continued)*

	-A-	-B-	-C-	-D-	-E-	-F-	-G-
	tmt						
93							
94	'Sales			+E8*(1-D7 8)	+D94/D94		
95	'Cost			+E9*(1-D8 0)	+D95/D94		
96							
97	'Gross			+D94+D95	+D97/D94		
98	'S&A			+E12	+D98/D94		
99							
100	'Op Prft			+D97+D98	+D100/D94		
101	'Int			+E15	+D101/D94		
102							
103	'Net Inc			+D100+D10 1	+D103/D94		
104							
105							
106							
107							
108				'Peterson 's Chemic als			
109							
110			[]			[]	
111							
112	'Bal Shee t						

PROBLEM 4b (*concluded*)

	-A-	-B-	-C-	-D-	-E-	-F-	-G-
113							
114	'Cash		[$120]		'AP		-@ROUND(((D79/360) *D95),0)
115	'AR		@ROUND(((D77/360)* D94),0)		'Other		+G117-G11 4
116	'Inventor y		[324]				
117	'Other		[37]		'CL		+G120-G11 8
118					'LTD		+G121*D81
119	'CA		@SUM(C114 ..C117)				
120					'Total Li ab		+G123-G12 1
121	'PPE		[300]		'Equity		400+D103
122							
123	'Total As sets		+C119+C12 1		'Total L& E		+C123
124							
125							
126							
127			'Peterson	'Industry			
128	'Ratios						
129	'Current		+C119/G11 7	[]			
130	'Acid		(C114+C11 5)/G117	[]			
131	'Rec Coll		(C115/D94)*360	[]			
132	'Payables		(+G114/-D 95)*360	[]			
133	'D/E		+G118/G12 1	[]			
134	'ROE		+D103/G12 1	[19%]			
135	'ROA		+D103/C12 3	[7%]			

Had management made the changes, the 1986 loss would have been lower.

CHAPTER 2—SOLUTIONS

Problem 1.

	-A-	-B-	-C-	-D-
1	'2-1			
2				
3	'Assumptions:			
4				
5	'Sales growth		[60%]	
6	'COGS		[75%]	
7	'Op expense growth		[10%]	
8	'Tax rate		[40%]	
9	'Cash to sales		[20%]	
10	'AR		[]	
11	'AP		[]	
12	'Inv turnover		[]	
13	'Depr		[$8,000]	
14	'LTD		[$125,000]	
15	'Common stock		[$100,000]	
16				
17				
18				
19		'Chateau Royale International		
20				
21		[]		[]
22	'Income Stmt			
23				

PROBLEM 1 *(continued)*

	-A-	-B-	-C-	-D-	
24	'Sales	[$375,000]		+B24*(1+C5)	
25	'Cost	[276,150]		+C6*D24	
26		"-------		"-------	
27	'Gross	+B24-B25		+D24-D25	
28	'Op Exp	[75,000]		(1+C7)*B28	
29	'Depr	[5,100]		+C13	
30		"-------		"-------	
31	'Op Prft	+B27-B28-B29		+D27-D28-D29	
32	'Taxes	[7,500]		+C8*D31	
33		"-------		"-------	
34	'Net Inc	+B31-B32		+D31-D32	
35					
36					
37					
38					
39		'Chateau Royale International			
40					
41		[]		[]	
42					
43	'Bal Sheet				
44					
45	'Cash	[$75,000]		+C9*D24	
46	'AR	[46,233]		(C10/360)*D24	

PROBLEM 1 (concluded)

	-A-	-B-	-C-	-D-
47	'Inv	[93,750]		+D25/C12
48		"-------		"-------
49	'CA	@SUM(B45..B47)		@SUM(D45..D47)
50				
51	'PPE	[115,000]		+B51-D29
52		"-------		"-------
53	'TA	+B49+B51		+D49+D51
54				
55				
56				
57	'AP	[23,116]		(C11/360)*D25
58	'STD	[51,867]		+D69-D65-D64-D62 -D57
59		"-------		"-------
60	'CL	[74,983]		+D57+D58
61				
62	'LTD	[125,000]		+C14
63				
64	'CS	[100,000]		+C15
65	'RE	[30,000]		+B65+D34
66		"-------		"-------
67	'Tot Eq	+B64+B65		+D64+D65
68		"-------		"-------
69	'Tot L&E	@SUM(B60..B65)		+D53
70				
71				
72	'CA	+B49		+D49
73	'CL	+B60		+D60
74		"-------		"-------
75	'NWC	+B72-B73		+D72-D73
76				
77	'C Ratio	+B72/B73		+D72/D73

Problem 2.

	-A-	-B-	-C-	-D-
1	'2-2			
2				
3	'Assumptions:			
4				
5	'Sales growth		[60%]	
6	'COGS		[75%]	
7	'Op expense growth		[10%]	
8	'Tax rate		[40%]	
9	'Cash to sales		[15%]	
10	'AR		[]	
11	'AP		[]	
12	'Inv turnover		[]	
13	'Depr		[$8,000]	
14	'LTD		[$125,000]	
15	'Common stock		[$100,000]	
16				
17				
18				
19		'Chateau Royale International		
20				
21		[]		[]
22	'Income Stmt			
23				

PROBLEM 2   *(continued)*

	-A-	-B-	-C-	-D-
24	'Sales	[$375,000]		+B24*(1+C5)
25	'Cost	[276,150]		+C6*D24
26		"-------		"-------
27	'Gross	+B24-B25		+D24-D25
28	'Op Exp	[75,000]		(1+C7)*B28
29	'Depr	[5,100]		+C13
30		"-------		"-------
31	'Op Prft	+B27-B28-B29		+D27-D28-D29
32	'Taxes	[7,500]		+C8*D31
33		"-------		"-------
34	'Net Inc	+B31-B32		+D31-D32
35				
36				
37				
38				
39		'Chateau Royale International		
40				
41		[]		[]
42				
43	'Bal Sheet			
44				
45	'Cash	[$75,000]		+C9*D24
46	'AR	[46,233]		(C10/360)*D24

PROBLEM 2   *(concluded)*

	-A-	-B-	-C-	-D-
47	'Inv	[93,750]		+D25/C12
48		"-------		"-------
49	'CA	@SUM(B45..B47)		@SUM(D45..D47)
50				
51	'PPE	[115,000]		+B51-D29
52		"-------		"-------
53	'TA	+B49+B51		+D49+D51
54				
55				
56				
57	'AP	[23,116]		(C11/360)*D25
58	'STD	[51,867]		+D69-D65-D64-D62 -D57
59		"-------		"-------
60	'CL	[74,983]		+D57+D58
61				
62	'LTD	[125,000]		+C14
63				
64	'CS	[100,000]		+C15
65	'RE	[30,000]		+B65+D34
66		"-------		"-------
67	'Tot Eq	+B64+B65		+D64+D65
68		"-------		"-------
69	'Tot L&E	@SUM(B60..B65)		+D53
70				
71				
72	'CA	+B49		+D49
73	'CL	+B60		+D60
74		"-------		"-------
75	'NWC	+B72-B73		+D72-D73
76				
77	'C Ratio	+B72/B73		+D72/D73

The changes bring the company more in line with the industry.

Problem 3.

a.

	-A-	-B-	-C-	-D-
1	'2-3			
2			"Dine	"Triano
3	'Assumptions:			
4				
5	'Sales growth		[20%]	[50%]
6	'COGS		[75%]	[75%]
7	'Op expense growth		[0%]	[0%]
8	'Tax rate		[35%]	[35%]
9	'Cash to sales		[15%]	[20%]
10	'AR		[]	[]
11	'AP		[]	[]
12	'Inv turnover		[]	[]
13	'PPE		[$130,000]	[$130,000]
14	'LTD		[$110,000]	[$110,000]
15	'Common stock		[$75,000]	[$75,000]
16	'Bad debt		[0%]	[2%]
17				
18				
19				
20		'Kurz Corporation		
21				
22			"Dine	"Triano
23		[]		

PROBLEM 3 *(continued)*

	-A-	-B-	-C-	-D-
24	'Income Stmt		"-------	"-------
25				
26	'Sales	[$505,000]	+$B$26*(1+C5)	+$B$26*(1+D5)
27	'Bad Acct	[5,000]	[0]	+D26*D16
28		"-------	"-------	"-------
29	'Net	+B26-B27	+C26-C27	+D26-D27
30	'Cost	[375,000]	+C6*C26	+D6*D26
31		"-------	"-------	"-------
32	'Gross	+B29-B30	+C29-C30	+D29-D30
33	'Op Exp	[90,900]	[90,900]	[90,900]
34		"-------	"-------	"-------
35	'Op Prft	+B32-B33	+C32-C33	+D32-D33
36	'Taxes	[11,935]	+C8*C35	+D8*D35
37		"-------	"-------	"-------
38	'Net Inc	+B35-B36	+C35-C36	+D35-D36
39				
40				
41		'Kurz Corporation		
42				
43			"Dine	"Triano
44		[]		
45			"-------	"-------
46	'Bal Sheet			

PROBLEM 3   *(concluded)*

	-A-	-B-	-C-	-D-
47				
48	'Cash	[$90,000]	+C26*C9	+D26*D9
49	'AR	[61,644]	(C10/360)*C26	(D10/360)*D26
50	'Inv	[62,500]	+C30/C12	+D30/D12
51		"-------	"-------	"-------
52	'CA	@SUM(B48..B50)	@SUM(C48..C50)	@SUM(D48..D50)
53				
54	'PPE	[130,000]	+C13	+D13
55		"-------	"-------	"-------
56	'T Assets	+B52+B54	+C52+C54	+D52+D54
57				
58				
59	'AP	[30,822]	(C11/360)*C30	(D11/360)*D30
60	'STD	[86,322]	+C71-C67-C66-C64 -C59	+D71-D67-D66-D64 -D59
61		"-------	"-------	"-------
62	'CL	+B59+B60	+C59+C60	+D59+D60
63				
64	'LTD	[110,000]	+C14	+D14
65				
66	'CS	[75,000]	+C15	+D15
67	'RE	[42,000]	+$B$67+C38	+$B$67+D38
68		"-------	"-------	"-------
69	'Tot Eq	+B67+B66	+C67+C66	+D67+D66
70		"-------	"-------	"-------
71	'Tot L&E	@SUM(B62..B67)	+C56	+D56
72				
73				
74	'CA	+B52	+C52	+D52
75	'CL	+B62	+C62	+D62
76		"-------	"-------	"-------
77	'NWC	+B74-B75	+C74-C75	+D74-D75
78				
79	'C Ratio	+B74/B75	+C74/C75	+D74/D75

The Triano plan would result in higher net profits and asset growth.

CHAPTER 3—SOLUTIONS

Problem 1.

	-A-	-B-	-C-	-D-	-E-	-F-	-G-	-H-	-I-	-J-
1	'3-1									
2										
3	'Assumptions:									
4										
5	'Begin Cash	[]								
6	'Begin AR	[]								
7	'Begin AP	[]								
8	'Begin Inv	[]								
9	'Begin Eq	[]								
10	'Begin PPE	[]								
11	'AR (days)	[]								
12	'AP (days)	[]								
13	'Cash sales	[25%]								
14	'SG&A	[19%]								
15	'Safe stck	[6%]								
16	'COGS	[75%]								
17	'Lse & Int	[]								
18	'Depr	[]								
19										
20										
21					'Mary's Ski Chalet					

PROBLEM 1 *(continued)*

	-A-	-B-	-C-	-D-	-E-	-F-	-G-	-H-	-I-	-J-
22										
23										
24		'Jan	'Feb	'Mar	'Apr	'May	'June	'July	'Aug	'Sep
25										
26	'Sales	[]	[]	[]	[]	[]	[]	[]	[]	[]
27										
28	'Rec:									
29	'AR	[$184]	+B33	+C33	+D33	+E33	+F33	+G33	+H33	+I33
30	'Credit	@ROUND (0.75* B26,0)	@ROUND (0.75* C26,0)	@ROUND (0.75* D26,0)	@ROUND (0.75* E26,0)	@ROUND (0.75* F26,0)	@ROUND (0.75* G26,0)	@ROUND (0.75* H26,0)	@ROUND (0.75* I26,0)	@ROUND (0.75* J26,0)
31	'Coll	+B29	+C29	+D29	+E29	+F29	+G29	+H29	+I29	+J29
32										
33	'Net AR	+B29+B 30-B31	+C29+C 30-C31	+D29+D 30-D31	+E29+E 30-E31	+F29+F 30-F31	+G29+G 30-G31	+H29+H 30-H31	+I29+I 30-I31	+J29+J 30-J31
34										
35	'Coll	+B31	+C31	+D31	+E31	+F31	+G31	+H31	+I31	+J31
36	'Cash Sls	+B26-B 30	+C26-C 30	+D26-D 30	+E26-E 30	+F26-F 30	+G26-G 30	+H26-H 30	+I26-I 30	+J26-J 30
37										
38	'Tot Rec.	+B35+B 36	+C35+C 36	+D35+D 36	+E35+E 36	+F35+F 36	+G35+G 36	+H35+H 36	+I35+I 36	+J35+J 36
39										
40	'Disb:									
41	'AP	[$173]	+B45	+C45	+D45	+E45	+F45	+G45	+H45	+I45
42	'Pur	@ROUND (0.81*	@ROUND (0.81*	@ROUND (0.81*	@ROUND (0.81*	@ROUND (0.81*	@ROUND (0.81*	@ROUND (0.81*	@ROUND (0.81*	@ROUND (0.81*

PROBLEM 1 *(continued)*

	-A-	-B-	-C-	-D-	-E-	-F-	-G-	-H-	-I-	-J-
		B26,0)	C26,0)	D26,0)	E26,0)	F26,0)	G26,0)	H26,0)	I26,0)	J26,0)
43	'Pay	+B41	+C41	+D41	+E41	+F41	+G41	+H41	+I41	+J41
44										
45	'Net AP	+B41+B42-B43	+C41+C42-C43	+D41+D42-D43	+E41+E42-E43	+F41+F42-F43	+G41+G42-G43	+H41+H42-H43	+I41+I42-I43	+J41+J42-J43
46										
47	'Pay	+B43	+C43	+D43	+E43	+F43	+G43	+H43	+I43	+J43
48	'SGA	@ROUND(0.19*B26,0)	@ROUND(0.19*C26,0)	@ROUND(0.19*D26,0)	@ROUND(0.19*E26,0)	@ROUND(0.19*F26,0)	@ROUND(0.19*G26,0)	@ROUND(0.19*H26,0)	@ROUND(0.19*I26,0)	@ROUND(0.19*J26,0)
49	'Lease	[2]	[2]	[2]	[2]	[2]	[2]	[2]	[2]	[2]
50										
51	'Tot Disb	@SUM(B47..B49)	@SUM(C47..C49)	@SUM(D47..D49)	@SUM(E47..E49)	@SUM(F47..F49)	@SUM(G47..G49)	@SUM(H47..H49)	@SUM(I47..I49)	@SUM(J47..J49)
52										
53	'Net Rec	+B38-B51	+C38-C51	+D38-D51	+E38-E51	+F38-F51	+G38-G51	+H38-H51	+I38-I51	+J38-J51
54	'Cum CF	+B53	+B54+C53	+C54+D53	+D54+E53	+E54+F53	+F54+G53	+G54+H53	+H54+I53	+I54+J53
55										
56	'Chg Cash:									
57	'Beg Cash	[65]	+B60	+C60	+D60	+E60	+F60	+G60	+H60	+I60
58	'Chg	+B53	+C53	+D53	+E53	+F53	+G53	+H53	+I53	+J53
59										
60	'End Cash	+B57+B58	+C57+C58	+D57+D58	+E57+E58	+F57+F58	+G57+G58	+H57+H58	+I57+I58	+J57+J58

PROBLEM 1   *(continued)*

	-K-	-L-	-M-
1			
2			
3			
4			
5			
6			
7			
8			
9			
10			
11			
12			
13			
14			
15			
16			
17			
18			
19			
20			
21			
22			
23			
24	'Oct	'Nov	'Dec

PROBLEM 1 *(continued)*

	-K-	-L-	-M-
25			
26	[ ]	[ ]	[ ]
27			
28			
29	+J33	+K33	+L33
30	@ROUND (0.75* K26,0)	@ROUND (0.75* L26,0)	@ROUND (0.75* M26,0)
31	+K29	+L29	+M29
32			
33	+K29+K 30-K31	+L29+L 30-L31	+M29+M 30-M31
34			
35	+K31	+L31	+M31
36	+K26-K 30	+L26-L 30	+M26-M 30
37			
38	+K35+K 36	+L35+L 36	+M35+M 36
39			
40			
41	+J45	+K45	+L45
42	@ROUND (0.81* K26,0)	@ROUND (0.81* L26,0)	@ROUND (0.81* M26,0)
43	+K41	+L41	+M41
44			

PROBLEM 1   *(concluded)*

	-K-	-L-	-M-
45	+K41+K 42-K43	+L41+L 42-L43	+M41+M 42-M43
46			
47	+K43	+L43	+M43
48	@ROUND (0.19* K26,0)	@ROUND (0.19* L26,0)	@ROUND (0.19* M26,0)
49	[2]	[2]	[2]
50			
51	@SUM(K 47..K4 9)	@SUM(L 47..L4 9)	@SUM(M 47..M4 9)
52			
53	+K38-K 51	+L38-L 51	+M38-M 51
54	+J54+K 53	+K54+L 53	+L54+M 53
55			
56			
57	+J60	+K60	+L60
58	+K53	+L53	+M53
59			
60	+K57+K 58	+L57+L 58	+M57+M 58

Ms. Turnbull will not need additional financing due to the $65,000 beginning cash balance.

Problem 2.

	-A-	-B-	-C-
63			
64	'Inc Stmt	[]	
65			
66	'Sales	@SUM(B26..M26)	
67	'COGS	0.75*B66	
68		"-----	
69	'Gross	+B66-B67	
70	'SGA	@SUM(B48..M48)	
71	'Depr	[12]	
72	'Lease	@SUM(B49..M49)	
73		"-----	
74	'Net Inc	+B69-B70-B71-B72	
75			
76			
77			
78	'Bal Sheet	[]	[]
79			
80	'Cash	[65]	+M60
81	'AR	[184]	+M33
82	'Inv	[]	+B82+@SUM(B42..M42)-B67
83		"-----	"-----
84	'CA	@SUM(B80..B82)	@SUM(C80..C82)
85	'PPE	[]	+B85-B71
86		"-----	"-----
87	'TA	+B84+B85	+C84+C85
88			
89	'AP	[$173]	+M45
90		"-----	"-----
91	'CL	[173]	+C89
92	'Equity	[$471]	+B92+B74
93		"-----	"-----
94	'Tot L&E	+B91+B92	+C92+C91

Problem 3.

	-A-	-B-	-C-	-D-	-E-	-F-	-G-	-H-
1	'3-3		[1987]	+C1+1	+D1+1	+E1+1	+F1+1	+G1+1
2								
3	'Assumpti ons:							
4	'Sales gr owth		[0.2]	[0.2]	[0.1]	[0.11]	[0.12]	[0.13]
5	'Gross ma rgin		[0.38]	[0.48]	[0.5]	[0.5]	[0.5]	[0.5]
6	'SG&A		[0.13]	[0.13]	[0.13]	[0.13]	[0.13]	[0.13]
7	'Tax rate		[0.5]	[0.5]	[0.5]	[0.38]	[0.38]	[0.38]
8	'Cash to sales		[0.14]	[0.14]	[0.14]	[0.14]	[0.14]	[0.14]
9	'AR (days)		[80]	[43]	[43]	[43]	[43]	[43]
10	'Inv turn over		[3]	[4]	[8]	[8]	[6]	[6]
11	'AP (days)		[75]	[60]	[60]	[60]	[60]	[60]
12								
13								
14								
15				'Aries Co rporation				
16								
17		"Actual		"Projecte d				
18								
19		[1986]	[1987]	+C19+1	+D19+1	+E19+1	+F19+1	+G19+1

PROBLEM 3   (*continued*)

	-A-	-B-	-C-	-D-	-E-	-F-	-G-	-H-
20								
21	'Sales	[221]	[266]	+C21*(1+D4)	+D21*(1+E4)	+E21*(1+F4)	+F21*(1+G4)	+G21*(1+H4)
22	'COGS	[145]	[166]	+D21-D24	+E21-E24	+F21-F24	@ROUND(0.5*G21,0)	+H21-H24
23		"----	"----	"----	"----	"----	"----	"----
24	'Gross	+B21-B22	+C21-C22	@ROUND(D5*D21,0)	@ROUND(E5*E21,0)	@ROUND(F5*F21,0)	@ROUND(G5*G21,0)	@ROUND(H5*H21,0)
25	'SGA	[38]	[35]	+D6*D21	+E6*E21	+F6*F21	+G6*G21	+H6*H21
26		"----	"----	"----	"----	"----	"----	"----
27	'Op Profit	+B24-B25	+C24-C25	+D24-D25	+E24-E25	+F24-F25	@ROUND(G24-G25,0)	@ROUND(H24-H25,0)
28	'Taxes	[19]	[33]	+D7*D27	+E7*E27	+F7*F27	+G7*G27	+H7*H27
29		"----	"----	"----	"----	"----	"----	"----
30	'Net Inc	+B27-B28	+C27-C28	+D27-D28	+E27-E28	+F27-F28	@ROUND(+G27-G28,0)	@ROUND(+H27-H28,0)
31								
32								
33								
34								
35				'Aries Corporation				
36								
37		"Actual		"Projected				
38								
39		[1986]	[1987]	+C39+1	+D39+1	+E39+1	+F39+1	+G39+1

PROBLEM 3 (concluded)

	-A-	-B-	-C-	-D-	-E-	-F-	-G-	-H-
40								
41	'Cash	[22]	[37]	+D8*D21	+E8*E21	+F8*F21	+G8*G21	+H8*H21
42	'AR	[49]	[31]	@ROUND(D9 /360*D21, 0)	@ROUND(E9 /360*E21, 0)	@ROUND(F9 /360*F21, 0)	@ROUND(G9 /360*G21, 0)	@ROUND(H9 /360*H21, 0)
43	'Inv	[47]	[45]	+D22/D10	+E22/E10	+F22/F10	+G22/G10	+H22/H10
44		"----	"----	"----	"----	"----	"----	"----
45	'CA	@SUM(B41. .B43)	@SUM(C41. .C43)	@SUM(D41. .D43)	@SUM(E41. .E43)	@SUM(F41. .F43)	@SUM(G41. .G43)	@SUM(H41. .H43)
46								
47	'PPE	[70]	[122]	[265]	[291]	[323]	[403]	[513]
48		"----	"----	"----	"----	"----	"----	"----
49	'TA	+B45+B47	+C45+C47	+D45+D47	+E45+E47	+F45+F47	+G45+G47	+H45+H47
50								
51								
52	'L&E							
53	'Notes	[0]	[0]	+D56-D54	+E56-E54	+F56-F54	+G56-G54	+H56-H54
54	'AP	[19]	[34]	@ROUND(D1 1/360*D22 ,0)	@ROUND(E1 1/360*E22 ,0)	@ROUND(F1 1/360*F22 ,0)	@ROUND(G1 1/360*G22 ,0)	@ROUND(H1 1/360*H22 ,0)
55		"----	"----	"----	"----	"----	"----	"----
56	'CL	[19]	[34]	+D60-D58	+E60-E58	+F60-F58	+G60-G58	+H60-H58
57								
58	'Equity	[169]	[201]	+C58+D30	+D58+E30	+E58+F30	+F58+G30	+G58+H30
59		"----	"----	"----	"----	"----	"----	"----
60	'Tot L&E	[188]	[235]	+D49	+E49	+F49	+G49	+H49

CHAPTER 4—SOLUTIONS

Problem 1.

Marvel Corporation's investment will pay back in 3.3 years. The benefit cost ratio is 5.74. Since the payback ratio is lower than the four years required, the project should be accepted. The following forecasts were used in calculating the numbers.

	-A-	-B-	-C-	-D-	-E-	-F-	-G-
1	'4-1						
2					'Marvel Corporation		
3							
4					'Years		
5							
6			[0]	[1]	[2]	[3]	[4]
7							
8							
9	'Sales			[1,250.0]	[1,250.0]	[1,250.0]	[1,250.0]
10	'Raw Matls			-@ROUND(0.37*D9,1)	-@ROUND(0.37*E9,1)	-@ROUND(0.37*F9,1)	-@ROUND(0.37*G9,1)
11	'Op Costs			[(10.0)]	[(10.0)]	[(10.0)]	[(10.0)]
12	'Wages			[(450.0)]	[(450.0)]	[(450.0)]	[(450.0)]
13				"------	"------	"------	"------
14	'Gross			@SUM(D9..D12)	@SUM(E9..E12)	@SUM(F9..F12)	@SUM(G9..G12)
15	'Depr			-D38	-E38	-F38	-G38
16				"------	"------	"------	"------
17	'Profit BT			+D14+D15	+E14+E15	+F14+F15	+G14+G15
18	'Taxes			-@ROUND(0.34*D17,1)	-@ROUND(0.34*E17,1)	-@ROUND(0.34*F17,1)	-@ROUND(0.34*G17,1)
19				"------	"------	"------	"------
20	'Profit AT			+D17+D18	+E17+E18	+F17+F18	+G17+G18

PROBLEM 1   *(continued)*

	-A-	-B-	-C-	-D-	-E-	-F-	-G-
21	'Noncash						
22	'Depr			-D15	-E15	-F15	-G15
23							
24	'Cap Inv		[(800.0)]				
25			"------	"------	"------	"------	"------
26	'Net CF		+C20+C22+ C24	+D20+D22+ D24	+E20+E22+ E24	+F20+F22+ F24	+G20+G22+ G24
27							
28	'Payback		[3.3]				
29							
30	'B/C		@SUM(D26. .W26)/C36				
31							
32							
33							
34	'Deprecia tion Anal ysis						
35	'DDB			@DDB(800, 0,20,D6)	@DDB(800, 0,20,E6)	@DDB(800, 0,20,F6)	@DDB(800, 0,20,G6)
36	'Undepr A mt		[800.0]	+C36-D35	+D36-E35	+E36-F35	+F36-G35
37	'ST Line			+C36/20	@IF(D35>D 37,(D36/(20-D6)),D 37)	@IF(E35>E 37,(E36/(20-E6)),E 37)	@IF(F35>F 37,(F36/(20-F6)),F 37)
38	'Reported			@IF(D35>D 37,D35,D3 7)	@IF(E35>E 37,E35,E3 7)	@IF(F35>F 37,F35,F3 7)	@IF(G35>G 37,G35,G3 7)
39							

PROBLEM 1   *(continued)*

	-H-	-I-	-J-	-K-	-L-	-M-	-N-
1							
2							
3							
4							
5							
6	[5]	[6]	[7]	[8]	[9]	[10]	[11]
7							
8							
9	[1,250.0]	[1,250.0]	[1,250.0]	[1,250.0]	[1,250.0]	[1,250.0]	[1,250.0]
10	-@ROUND(0 .37*H9,1)	-@ROUND(0 .37*I9,1)	-@ROUND(0 .37*J9,1)	-@ROUND(0 .37*K9,1)	-@ROUND(0 .37*L9,1)	-@ROUND(0 .37*M9,1)	-@ROUND(0 .37*N9,1)
11	[(10.0)]	[(10.0)]	[(10.0)]	[(10.0)]	[(10.0)]	[(10.0)]	[(10.0)]
12	[(450.0)]	[(450.0)]	[(450.0)]	[(450.0)]	[(450.0)]	[(450.0)]	[(450.0)]
13	"------	"------	"------	"------	"------	"------	"------
14	@SUM(H9.. H12)	@SUM(I9.. I12)	@SUM(J9.. J12)	@SUM(K9.. K12)	@SUM(L9.. L12)	@SUM(M9.. M12)	@SUM(N9.. N12)
15	-H38	-I38	-J38	-K38	-L38	-M38	-N38
16	"------	"------	"------	"------	"------	"------	"------
17	+H14+H15	+I14+I15	+J14+J15	+K14+K15	+L14+L15	+M14+M15	+N14+N15
18	-@ROUND(0 .34*H17,1)	-@ROUND(0 .34*I17,1)	-@ROUND(0 .34*J17,1)	-@ROUND(0 .34*K17,1)	-@ROUND(0 .34*L17,1)	-@ROUND(0 .34*M17,1)	-@ROUND(0 .34*N17,1)
19	"------	"------	"------	"------	"------	"------	"------
20	+H17+H18	+I17+I18	+J17+J18	+K17+K18	+L17+L18	+M17+M18	+N17+N18
21							
22	-H15	-I15	-J15	-K15	-L15	-M15	-N15

PROBLEM 1   *(continued)*

	-H-	-I-	-J-	-K-	-L-	-M-	-N-
23							
24							
25	"------	"------	"------	"------	"------	"------	"------
26	+H20+H22+ H24	+I20+I22+ I24	+J20+J22+ J24	+K20+K22+ K24	+L20+L22+ L24	+M20+M22+ M24	+N20+N22+ N24
27							
28							
29							
30							
31							
32							
33							
34							
35	@DDB(800, 0,20,H6)	@DDB(800, 0,20,I6)	@DDB(800, 0,20,J6)	@DDB(800, 0,20,K6)	@DDB(800, 0,20,L6)	@DDB(800, 0,20,M6)	@DDB(800, 0,20,N6)
36	+G36-H35	+H36-I35	+I36-J35	+J36-K35	+K36-L35	+L36-M35	+M36-N35
37	@IF(G35>G 37,(G36/(20-G6)),G 37)	@IF(H35>H 37,(H36/(20-H6)),H 37)	@IF(I35>I 37,(I36/(20-I6)),I 37)	@IF(J35>J 37,(J36/(20-J6)),J 37)	@IF(K35>K 37,(K36/(20-K6)),K 37)	@IF(L35>L 37,(L36/(20-L6)),L 37)	@IF(M35>M 37,(M36/(20-M6)),M 37)
38	@IF(H35>H 37,H35,H3 7)	@IF(I35>I 37,I35,I3 7)	@IF(J35>J 37,J35,J3 7)	@IF(K35>K 37,K35,K3 7)	@IF(L35>L 37,L35,L3 7)	@IF(M35>M 37,M35,M3 7)	@IF(N35>N 37,N35,N3 7)
39							

PROBLEM 1   (*continued*)

	-O-	-P-	-Q-	-R-	-S-	-T-	-U-
1							
2							
3							
4							
5							
6	[12]	[13]	[14]	[15]	[16]	[17]	[18]
7							
8							
9	[1,250.0]	[1,250.0]	[1,250.0]	[1,250.0]	[1,250.0]	[1,250.0]	[1,250.0]
10	-@ROUND(0 .37*O9,1)	-@ROUND(0 .37*P9,1)	-@ROUND(0 .37*Q9,1)	-@ROUND(0 .37*R9,1)	-@ROUND(0 .37*S9,1)	-@ROUND(0 .37*T9,1)	-@ROUND(0 .37*U9,1)
11	[(10.0)]	[(10.0)]	[(10.0)]	[(10.0)]	[(10.0)]	[(10.0)]	[(10.0)]
12	[(450.0)]	[(450.0)]	[(450.0)]	[(450.0)]	[(450.0)]	[(450.0)]	[(450.0)]
13	"------	"------	"------	"------	"------	"------	"------
14	@SUM(O9.. O12)	@SUM(P9.. P12)	@SUM(Q9.. Q12)	@SUM(R9.. R12)	@SUM(S9.. S12)	@SUM(T9.. T12)	@SUM(U9.. U12)
15	-O38	-P38	-Q38	-R38	-S38	-T38	-U38
16	"------	"------	"------	"------	"------	"------	"------
17	+O14+O15	+P14+P15	+Q14+Q15	+R14+R15	+S14+S15	+T14+T15	+U14+U15
18	-@ROUND(0 .34*O17,1)	-@ROUND(0 .34*P17,1)	-@ROUND(0 .34*Q17,1)	-@ROUND(0 .34*R17,1)	-@ROUND(0 .34*S17,1)	-@ROUND(0 .34*T17,1)	-@ROUND(0 .34*U17,1)
19	"------	"------	"------	"------	"------	"------	"------
20	+O17+O18	+P17+P18	+Q17+Q18	+R17+R18	+S17+S18	+T17+T18	+U17+U18
21							
22	-O15	-P15	-Q15	-R15	-S15	-T15	-U15

PROBLEM 1   *(continued)*

	-O-	-P-	-Q-	-R-	-S-	-T-	-U-
23							
24							
25	"------	"------	"------	"------	"------	"------	"------
26	+O20+O22+ O24	+P20+P22+ P24	+Q20+Q22+ Q24	+R20+R22+ R24	+S20+S22+ S24	+T20+T22+ T24	+U20+U22+ U24
27							
28							
29							
30							
31							
32							
33							
34							
35	@DDB(800, 0,20,O6)	@DDB(800, 0,20,P6)	@DDB(800, 0,20,Q6)	@DDB(800, 0,20,R6)	@DDB(800, 0,20,S6)	@DDB(800, 0,20,T6)	@DDB(800, 0,20,U6)
36	+N36-O35	+O36-P35	+P36-Q35	+Q36-R35	+R36-S35	+S36-T35	+T36-U35
37	@IF(N35>N 37,(N36/(20-N6)),N 37)	@IF(O35>O 37,(O36/(20-O6)),O 37)	@IF(P35>P 37,(P36/(20-P6)),P 37)	@IF(Q35>Q 37,(Q36/(20-Q6)),Q 37)	@IF(R35>R 37,(R36/(20-R6)),R 37)	@IF(S35>S 37,(S36/(20-S6)),S 37)	@IF(T35>T 37,(T36/(20-T6)),T 37)
38	@IF(O35>O 37,O35,O3 7)	@IF(P35>P 37,P35,P3 7)	@IF(Q35>Q 37,Q35,Q3 7)	@IF(R35>R 37,R35,R3 7)	@IF(S35>S 37,S35,S3 7)	@IF(T35>T 37,T35,T3 7)	@IF(U35>U 37,U35,U3 7)
39							

PROBLEM 1 (*concluded*)

	-V-	-W-
1		
2		
3		
4		
5		
6	[19]	[20]
7		
8		
9	[1,250.0]	[1,250.0]
10	-@ROUND(0.37*V9,1)	-@ROUND(0.37*W9,1)
11	[(10.0)]	[(10.0)]
12	[(450.0)]	[(450.0)]
13	"------	"------
14	@SUM(V9..V12)	@SUM(W9..W12)
15	-V38	-W38
16	"------	"------
17	+V14+V15	+W14+W15
18	-@ROUND(0.34*V17,1)	-@ROUND(0.34*W17,1)
19	"------	"------
20	+V17+V18	+W17+W18
21		
22	-V15	-W15

	-V-	-W-
23		
24		
25	"------	"------
26	+V20+V22+V24	+W20+W22+W24
27		
28		
29		
30		
31		
32		
33		
34		
35	@DDB(800,0,20,V6)	@DDB(800,0,20,W6)
36	+U36-V35	+V36-W35
37	@IF(U35>U37,(U36/(20-U6)),U37)	@IF(V35>V37,(V36/(20-V6)),V37)
38	@IF(V35>V37,V35,V37)	@IF(W35>W37,W35,W37)
39		

Problem 2.

The net present value for the SUN Company investment is $60,750 and the investment should be made. The major component of the cash flows are the high depreciation allowances. The analysis is done as follows.

	-A-	-B-	-C-	-D-	-E-	-F-	-G-
1	'4-2						
2							
3				'SUN Comp any			
4							
5				'Years			
6							
7							
8		[0]	[1]	[2]	[3]	[4]	[5]
9							
10							
11	'Sales		[120.0]	1.15*C11	1.15*D11	1.15*E11	1.15*F11
12	'Op Cost		-0.39*C11	-0.39*D11	-0.39*E11	-0.39*F11	-0.39*G11
13			"-----	"-----	"-----	"-----	"-----
14	'Gross		+C11+C12	+D11+D12	+E11+E12	+F11+F12	+G11+G12
15	'Depr 1		@IF(C37>C 39,-C37,- C39)	@IF(D37>D 39,-D37,- D39)	@IF(E37>E 39,-E37,- E39)	@IF(F37>F 39,-F37,- F39)	@IF(G37>G 39,-G37,- G39)
16	'Depr 2				@IF(E42>E 44,-E42,- E44)	@IF(F42>F 44,-F42,- F44)	@IF(G42>G 44,-G42,- G44)
17			"-----	"-----	"-----	"-----	"-----
18	'PBT		+C14+C15+ C16	+D14+D15+ D16	+E14+E15+ E16	+F14+F15+ F16	+G14+G15+ G16
19	'Taxes		-@ROUND(0 .34*C18,1)	-@ROUND(0 .34*D18,1)	-@ROUND(0 .34*E18,1)	-@ROUND(0 .34*F18,1)	-@ROUND(0 .34*G18,1)
20			"-----	"-----	"-----	"-----	"-----

PROBLEM 2 *(concluded)*

	-A-	-B-	-C-	-D-	-E-	-F-	-G-
21	'PAT		+C18+C19	+D18+D19	+E18+E19	+F18+F19	+G18+G19
22							
23	'Noncash						
24	'Depr 1		-C15	-D15	-E15	-F15	-G15
25	'Depr 2		-C16	-D16	-E16	-F16	-G16
26							
27	'Cap Inv	[(200.0)]		[(60.0)]			
28		"-----	"-----	"-----	"-----	"-----	"-----
29	'Net CF	+B21+B24+B27	@ROUND(+C21+C24+C25+C27,1)	@ROUND(+D21+D24+D25+D27,1)	@ROUND(+E21+E24+E25+E27,1)	@ROUND(+F21+F24+F25+F27,1)	@ROUND(+G21+G24+G25+G27,1)
30							
31	'NPV	+B29+@NPV(0.1,C29..G29)					
32							
33							
34							
35	'Depr. Analysis						
36	'Investment 1						
37	'DDB		+B38*0.4	+C38*0.4	+D38*0.4	+E38*0.4	+F38*0.4
38	'Undepr	[200.0]	+B38-C37	+C38-D37	+D38-E37	+E38-F37	+F38-G37
39	'ST Line		+B38/5	@IF(C37>C39,(C38/(5-C8)),C39)	@IF(D37>D39,(D38/(5-D8)),D39)	@IF(E37>E39,(E38/(5-E8)),E39)	@IF(F37>F39,(F38/(5-F8)),F39)
40							
41	'Investment 2						
42	'DDB				+D43*2/3	+E43*2/3	+F43*2/3
43	'Undepr			[60.0]	+D43-E42	+E43-F42	+F43-G42
44	'ST Line				+D43/3	@IF(E42>E44,(E43/2),E44)	@IF(F42>F44,(F43),F44)

Problem 3.
Kertin Company

Of the two projects Kertin management is considering, project 1 is better if payback or net present value is used. However, if benefit/cost ratio is the criterion, they are equal. Since net present value is the best criterion, project 1 should be accepted.

	-A-	-B-	-C-	-D-	-E-	-F-	-G-
1	'4-3						
2							
3					'Kertin C ompany		
4							
5	'Project 1						
6			[0]	[1]	[2]	[3]	[4]
7							
8	'Sales			[500]	[500]	[500]	[500]
9	'Op Cost			@ROUND(-0 .49*D8,0)	@ROUND(-0 .49*E8,0)	@ROUND(-0 .49*F8,0)	@ROUND(-0 .49*G8,0)
10				"----	"----	"----	"----
11	'Gross			+D8+D9	+E8+E9	+F8+F9	+G8+G9
12	'Adver			[(50)]	[(50)]	[(50)]	[(50)]
13	'Depr			@IF(D59>D 61,-D59,- D61)	@IF(E59>E 61,-E59,- E61)	@IF(F59>F 61,-F59,- F61)	@IF(G59>G 61,-G59,- G61)
14				"----	"----	"----	"----
15	'PBT			+D11+D12+ D13	+E11+E12+ E13	+F11+F12+ F13	+G11+G12+ G13
16	'Taxes			-@ROUND(0 .34*D15,0)	-@ROUND(0 .34*E15,0)	-@ROUND(0 .34*F15,0)	-@ROUND(0 .34*G15,0)
17				"----	"----	"----	"----
18	'PAT			+D15+D16	+E15+E16	+F15+F16	+G15+G16
19	'Noncash						
20	'Depr			-D13	-E13	-F13	-G13

PROBLEM 3   (continued)

	-A-	-B-	-C-	-D-	-E-	-F-	-G-
21							
22	'Cap Inv		[(800.0)]				
23			"------	"----	"----	"----	"----
24	'Net CF		+C18+C20+C22	@ROUND(+D18+D20+D22,1)	@ROUND(+E18+E20+E22,1)	@ROUND(+F18+F20+F22,1)	@ROUND(+G18+G20+G22,1)
25							
26	'NPV		+C24+@NPV(0.1,D24..M24)				
27	'B/C		@SUM(D24..M24)/C60				
28							
29							
30	'Project 2						
31			[0]	[1]	[2]	[3]	[4]
32							
33	'Sales			[350]	+D33*1.1	+E33*1.1	+F33*1.1
34	'Op Cost			@ROUND(-0.5*D33,0)	@ROUND(-0.5*E33,0)	@ROUND(-0.5*F33,0)	@ROUND(-0.5*G33,0)
35				"----	"----	"----	"----
36	'Gross			+D33+D34	+E33+E34	+F33+F34	+G33+G34
37	'Adver			-0.25*D33	-0.25*E33	-0.25*F33	[(100)]
38	'Depr			@ROUND((@IF(D67>D69,-D67,-D69)),0)	@ROUND((@IF(E67>E69,-E67,-E69)),0)	@ROUND((@IF(F67>F69,-F67,-F69)),0)	@ROUND((@IF(G67>G69,-G67,-G69)),0)
39	'Train		[(200)]				

PROBLEM 3 *(continued)*

	-A-	-B-	-C-	-D-	-E-	-F-	-G-
40			"------	"----	"----	"----	"----
41	'PBT		+C39	+D36+D37+D38	+E36+E37+E38	+F36+F37+F38	+G36+G37+G38
42	'Taxes		-@ROUND(0.34*C41,0)	-@ROUND(0.34*D41,0)	-@ROUND(0.34*E41,0)	-@ROUND(0.34*F41,0)	-@ROUND(0.34*G41,0)
43			"------	"----	"----	"----	"----
44	'PAT		+C41+C42	@ROUND(+D41+D42,0)	@ROUND(+E41+E42,0)	@ROUND(+F41+F42,0)	@ROUND(+G41+G42,0)
45	'Noncash						
46	'Depr			-D38	-E38	-F38	-G38
47							
48	'Cap Inv		[(600)]				
49			"------	"----	"----	"----	"----
50	'Net CF		+C44+C46+C48	@ROUND(+D44+D46+D48,1)	@ROUND(+E44+E46+E48,1)	@ROUND(+F44+F46+F48,1)	@ROUND(+G44+G46+G48,1)
51							
52	'NPV		+C50+@NPV(0.1,D50..M50)				
53	'B/C		@SUM(D50..M50)/-C50				
54							
55							
56							
57							
58	'Depr. An						

PROBLEM 3   *(continued)*

	-A-	-B-	-C-	-D-	-E-	-F-	-G-
	alysis Pr oject 1						
59	'DDB			+C60*0.2	+D60*0.2	+E60*0.2	+F60*0.2
60	'Undepr A mt		-C22	+C60-D59	+D60-E59	+E60-F59	+F60-G59
61	'ST Line			+C60/10	@IF(D59>D 61,(D60/(10-D6)),D 61)	@IF(E59>E 61,(E60/(10-E6)),E 61)	@IF(F59>F 61,(F60/(10-F6)),F 61)
62							
63							
64							
65							
66	'Depr. An alysis Pr oject 2						
67	'DDB			+C68*0.2	+D68*0.2	+E68*0.2	+F68*0.2
68	'Undepr A mt		[600.0]	+C68-D67	+D68-E67	+E68-F67	+F68-G67
69	'ST Line			+C68/10	@IF(D67>D 69,(D68/(10-D6)),D 69)	@IF(E67>E 69,(E68/(10-E6)),E 69)	@IF(F67>F 69,(F68/(10-F6)),F 69)

PROBLEM 3   *(continued)*

	-H-	-I-	-J-	-K-	-L-	-M-
1						
2						
3						
4						
5						
6	[5]	[6]	[7]	[8]	[9]	[10]
7						
8	[500]	[500]	[500]	[500]	[500]	[500]
9	@ROUND(-0 .49*H8,0)	@ROUND(-0 .49*I8,0)	@ROUND(-0 .49*J8,0)	@ROUND(-0 .49*K8,0)	@ROUND(-0 .49*L8,0)	@ROUND(-0 .49*M8,0)
10	"----	"----	"----	"----	"----	"----
11	+H8+H9	+I8+I9	+J8+J9	+K8+K9	+L8+L9	+M8+M9
12	[(50)]	[(50)]	[(50)]	[(50)]	[(50)]	[(50)]
13	@IF(H59>H 61,-H59,- H61)	@IF(I59>I 61,-I59,- I61)	@IF(J59>J 61,-J59,- J61)	@IF(K59>K 61,-K59,- K61)	@IF(L59>L 61,-L59,- L61)	@IF(M59>M 61,-M59,- M61)
14	"----	"----	"----	"----	"----	"----
15	+H11+H12+ H13	+I11+I12+ I13	+J11+J12+ J13	+K11+K12+ K13	+L11+L12+ L13	+M11+M12+ M13
16	-@ROUND(0 .34*H15,0)	-@ROUND(0 .34*I15,0)	-@ROUND(0 .34*J15,0)	-@ROUND(0 .34*K15,0)	-@ROUND(0 .34*L15,0)	-@ROUND(0 .34*M15,0)
17	"----	"----	"----	"----	"----	"----
18	+H15+H16	+I15+I16	+J15+J16	+K15+K16	+L15+L16	+M15+M16
19						
20	-H13	-I13	-J13	-K13	-L13	-M13
21						

PROBLEM 3 *(continued)*

	-H-	-I-	-J-	-K-	-L-	-M-
22						
23	"----	"----	"----	"----	"----	"----
24	@ROUND(+H 18+H20+H2 2,1)	@ROUND(+I 18+I20+I2 2,1)	@ROUND(+J 18+J20+J2 2,1)	@ROUND(+K 18+K20+K2 2,1)	@ROUND(+L 18+L20+L2 2,1)	@ROUND(+M 18+M20+M2 2,1)
25						
26						
27						
28						
29						
30						
31	[5]	[6]	[7]	[8]	[9]	[10]
32						
33	+G33*1.15	+H33*1.15	+I33*1.15	+J33*1.1	+K33*1.1	+L33*1.1
34	@ROUND(-0 .5*H33,0)	@ROUND(-0 .5*I33,0)	@ROUND(-0 .5*J33,0)	@ROUND(-0 .5*K33,0)	@ROUND(-0 .5*L33,0)	@ROUND(-0 .5*M33,0)
35	"----	"----	"----	"----	"----	"----
36	+H33+H34	+I33+I34	+J33+J34	@ROUND(K3 3+K34,0)	+L33+L34	+M33+M34
37	[(100)]	[(100)]	[(100)]	[(100)]	[(100)]	[(100)]
38	@ROUND((@ IF(H67>H6 9,-H67,-H 69)),0)	@ROUND((@ IF(I67>I6 9,-I67,-I 69)),0)	@ROUND((@ IF(J67>J6 9,-J67,-J 69)),0)	@ROUND((@ IF(K67>K6 9,-K67,-K 69)),0)	@ROUND((@ IF(L67>L6 9,-L67,-L 69)),0)	@ROUND((@ IF(M67>M6 9,-M67,-M 69)),0)
39						
40	"----	"----	"----	"----	"----	"----
41	+H36+H37+ H38	+I36+I37+ I38	+J36+J37+ J38	+K36+K37+ K38	+L36+L37+ L38	+M36+M37+ M38

PROBLEM 3   *(continued)*

	-H-	-I-	-J-	-K-	-L-	-M-
42	-@ROUND(0 .34*H41,0)	-@ROUND(0 .34*I41,0)	-@ROUND(0 .34*J41,0)	-@ROUND(0 .34*K41,0)	-@ROUND(0 .34*L41,0)	-@ROUND(0 .34*M41,0)
43	"----	"----	"----	"----	"----	"----
44	@ROUND(+H 41+H42,0)	@ROUND(+I 41+I42,0)	@ROUND(+J 41+J42,0)	@ROUND(+K 41+K42,0)	@ROUND(+L 41+L42,0)	@ROUND(+M 41+M42,0)
45						
46	-H38	-I38	-J38	-K38	-L38	-M38
47						
48						
49	"----	"----	"----	"----	"----	"----
50	@ROUND(+H 44+H46+H4 8,1)	@ROUND(+I 44+I46+I4 8,1)	@ROUND(+J 44+J46+J4 8,1)	@ROUND(+K 44+K46+K4 8,1)	@ROUND(+L 44+L46+L4 8,1)	@ROUND(+M 44+M46+M4 8,1)
51						
52						
53						
54						
55						
56						
57						
58						
59	+G60*0.2	+H60*0.2	+I60*0.2	+J60*0.2	+K60*0.2	+L60*0.2
60	+G60-H59	+H60-I59	+I60-J59	+J60-K59	+K60-L59	+L60-M59
61	@IF(G59>G 61,(G60/(10-G6)),G 61)	@IF(H59>H 61,(H60/(10-H6)),H 61)	@IF(I59>I 61,(I60/(10-I6)),I 61)	@IF(J59>J 61,(J60/(10-J6)),J 61)	@IF(K59>K 61,(K60/(10-K6)),K 61)	@IF(L59>L 61,(L60/(10-L6)),L 61)

PROBLEM 3   *(concluded)*

	-H-	-I-	-J-	-K-	-L-	-M-
62						
63						
64						
65						
66						
67	+G68*0.2	+H68*0.2	+I68*0.2	+J68*0.2	+K68*0.2	+L68*0.2
68	+G68-H67	+H68-I67	+I68-J67	+J68-K67	+K68-L67	+L68-M67
69	@IF(G67>G 69,(G68/(10-G6)),G 69)	@IF(H67>H 69,(H68/(10-H6)),H 69)	@IF(I67>I 69,(I68/(10-I6)),I 69)	@IF(J67>J 69,(J68/(10-J6)),J 69)	@IF(K67>K 69,(K68/(10-K6)),K 69)	@IF(L67>L 69,(L68/(10-L6)),L 69)

CHAPTER 5—SOLUTIONS

Solving these problems is not enhanced through the use of Lotus 1-2-3.

CHAPTER 6—SOLUTIONS

Problems 1–3.

Not appropriate for Lotus modeling.

Problem 4.

To maximize the shareholders' returns, Mr. Santiago should sell for a price not less than $301 million. At any price below that the shareholders' value will be destroyed.

	-A-	-B-	-C-	-D-	-E-	-F-	-G-
1	'6-4						
2							
3					'Action Corporation		
4							
5					'Projected Cash Flows		
6							
7							
8			[1988]	[1989]	[1990]	[1991]	[1992]
9							
10	'Sales		250*1.03	+C10*1.03	+D10*1.03	+E10*1.03	+F10*1.03
11	'COGS		-C10*0.75	-D10*0.75	-E10*0.75	-F10*0.75	-G10*0.75
12	'SGA		-C10*0.1	-D10*0.1	-E10*0.1	-F10*0.1	-G10*0.1
13	'Depr		[(7.0)]	[(7.0)]	[(7.0)]	[(7.0)]	[(7.0)]
14			"-----	"-----	"-----	"-----	"-----
15	'Profit BT		@ROUND(@SUM(C10..C13),1)	@ROUND(@SUM(D10..D13),1)	@ROUND(@SUM(E10..E13),1)	@ROUND(@SUM(F10..F13),1)	@ROUND(@SUM(G10..G13),1)
16	'Taxes		@ROUND(-C15*0.34,1)	@ROUND(-D15*0.34,1)	@ROUND(-E15*0.34,1)	@ROUND(-F15*0.34,1)	@ROUND(-G15*0.34,1)
17			"-----	"-----	"-----	"-----	"-----
18	'Profit AT		+C15+C16	+D15+D16	+E15+E16	+F15+F16	+G15+G16
19	'Depr		-C13	-D13	-E13	-F13	-G13

PROBLEM 4   *(continued)*

	-A-	-B-	-C-	-D-	-E-	-F-	-G-
20	'Terminal Value						
21			"-----	"-----	"-----	"-----	"-----
22	'Tot Cash Flow		+C18+C19+ C20	+D18+D19+ D20	+E18+E19+ E20	+F18+F19+ F20	+G18+G19+ G20
23							
24	'PV		@NPV(C29, C22..J22)				
25							
26							
27	'COD		0.101*(1- 0.34)				
28	'COE		[0.12]				
29	'WACC		(0.15*C27)+(0.85*C 28)				
30	'Terminal Value		(J18+J19) /(C29-0.0 3)				

PROBLEM 4 *(concluded)*

	-H-	-I-	-J-
1			
2			
3			
4			
5			
6			
7			
8	[1993]	[1994]	[1995]
9			
10	+G10*1.03	+H10*1.03	+I10*1.03
11	-H10*0.75	-I10*0.75	-J10*0.75
12	-H10*0.1	-I10*0.1	-J10*0.1
13	[(7.0)]	[(7.0)]	[(7.0)]
14	"-----	"-----	"-----
15	@ROUND(@SUM(H10..H13),1)	@ROUND(@SUM(I10..I13),1)	@ROUND(@SUM(J10..J13),1)
16	@ROUND(-H15*0.34,1)	@ROUND(-I15*0.34,1)	@ROUND(-J15*0.34,1)
17	"-----	"-----	"-----
18	+H15+H16	+I15+I16	+J15+J16
19	-H13	-I13	-J13
20			+C30
21	"-----	"-----	"-----
22	+H18+H19+	+I18+I19+	+J18+J19+

	-H-	-I-	-J-
1	H20	I20	J20
23			
24			
25			
26			
27			
28			
29			
30			

CHAPTER 7—SOLUTIONS

Problem 1.

If Zumar can gain more than $8.1 million in earnings before interest and taxes, the debt alternative will result in larger EPS.

	-A-	-B-	-C-	-D-	-E-	-F-
1	'7-1					
2						
3			'Zumar, Inc.			
4						
5		'Debt Financing			'Equity Financing	
6		"Old	"New		"Old	"New
7						
8	'Rev	[100.0]	[120.0]		+B8	+C8
9	'EBIT	0.13*B8	0.13*C8		@ROUND(0.13*E8,1)	@ROUND(0.13*F8,1)
10		"-----	"-----		"-----	"-----
11	'Int - Old	[(2.8)]	[(2.8)]		[(2.8)]	[(2.8)]
12	' - New	[(1.5)]	[(1.5)]			
13		"-----	"-----		"-----	"-----
14	'PBT	+B9+B11+B12	+C9+C11+C12		+E9+E11+E12	+F9+F11+F12
15	'Tax	-0.34*B14	-0.34*C14		@ROUND(-0.34*E14,1)	@ROUND(-0.34*F14,1)
16		"-----	"-----		"-----	"-----
17	'PAT	@ROUND(+B14+B15,1)	@ROUND(+C14+C15,1)		@ROUND(+E14+E15,1)	@ROUND(+F14+F15,1)
18	'# shares	[2.0]	[2.0]		@ROUND(2.75,1)	@ROUND(2.75,1)
19	'EPS	+B17/B18	+C17/C18		+E17/E18	+F17/F18
20						
21						
22	'Equivalency EBIT			((C18*-C11)-(F18*-F11)-(F18*-C12))/(C18-F18)		

Problem 2.

	-A-	-B-	-C-	-D-	-E-	-F-
25	'7-2					
26						
27			'Zumar, Inc.			
28						
29						
30		'Debt Financing			'Equity Financing	
31		"Old	"New		"Old	"New
32						
33	'Rev	[100.0]	[120.0]		+B33	+C33
34	'EBIT	0.13*B33	0.13*C33		0.13*E33	0.13*F33
35		"-----	"-----		"-----	"-----
36	'Int - Old	[(2.8)]	[(2.8)]		[(2.8)]	[(2.8)]
37	' - New	[(1.5)]	[(1.5)]			
38		"-----	"-----		"-----	"-----
39	'PBT	+B34+B36+B37	+C34+C36+C37		+E34+E36+E37	+F34+F36+F37
40	'Tax	-0.34*B39	-0.34*C39		-0.34*E39	-0.34*F39
41		"-----	"-----		"-----	"-----
42	'PAT	@ROUND(+B39+B40,1)	@ROUND(+C39+C40,1)		@ROUND(+E39+E40,1)	@ROUND(+F39+F40,1)
43	'# shares	[2.0]	[2.0]		@ROUND(2.75,1)	@ROUND(2.75,1)
44	'DPS	[$0.75]	+B44		+C44	+E44
45						
46	'Div Cov	(+B42/B43)/B44	(+C42/C43)/C44		(+E42/E43)/E44	(+F42/F43)/F44

Problem 3.

Not appropriate for Lotus modeling.

Problem 4.

	-A-	-B-	-C-	-D-	-E-
49	'7-4				
50			'Zumar, Inc.		
51					
52			'Debt Financ ing		
53					
54	'Rev		[120.0]	+C54*1.02	+D54*1.02
55	'EBIT		@ROUND(0.13* C54,1)	@ROUND(0.13* D54,1)	@ROUND(0.13* E54,1)
56					
57	'Int - Old		[(2.8)]	[(2.8)]	[(2.8)]
58	' - New		[(1.5)]	[(1.5)]	[(1.5)]
59			"----	"----	"----
60	'PBT		+C55+C57+C58	+D55+D57+D58	+E55+E57+E58
61	'Tax		-0.34*C60	-0.34*D60	-0.34*E60
62			"----	"----	"----
63	'PAT		+C60+C61	+D60+D61	+E60+E61
64					
65	'CF		+C63	+D63	+E63
66	'TV		[0.0]	[0.0]	+E65/(0.169- 0.02)
67			"----	"----	"----
68	'Net CF		+C65+C66	+D65+D66	+E65+E66
69	'NPV	@NPV(C45,C68 ..E68)			
70	'NPV/share	+B69/2			

PROBLEM 4   *(concluded)*

	-A-	-B-	-C-	-D-	-E-
71					
72					
73			'Equity Financing		
74					
75					
76	'Rev		+C54	+D54	+E54
77	'EBIT		@ROUND(0.13*C76,1)	@ROUND(0.13*D76,1)	@ROUND(0.13*E76,1)
78					
79	'Int O		[(2.8)]	[(2.8)]	[(2.8)]
80	' N				
81			"----	"----	"----
82	'PBT		+C77+C79+C80	+D77+D79+D80	+E77+E79+E80
83	'Tax		-0.34*C82	-0.34*D82	-0.34*E82
84			"----	"----	"----
85	'PAT		+C82+C83	+D82+D83	+E82+E83
86					
87	'CF		+C85	+D85	+E85
88	'TV		[0.0]	[0.0]	+E87/(0.154-0.02)
89			"----	"----	"----
90	'Net CF		+C87+C88	+D87+D88	+E87+E88
91	'NPV	@NPV(F45,C90..E90)			
92	'NPV/share	+B91/2.8			

Index

Accelerated Cost Recovery System, 75–77, 97
Accounts payable to cost of sales ratio, 14
Accounts receivable aging, 44
Accounts receivable to net sales ratio, 13–14
Acid-test ratio, 18–19
Acquisitions and divestitures
  book value valuation technique, 151
  earnings valuation method, cash flows, 148–51
  liquidation value, 151–52
  market value, 152
  present value analysis, cash flows, 140–48
  reasons for discussing, 139–40
  replacement cost, 152
After-tax cost of debt, 118–19
American Stock Exchange, 107
Asset to equity ratio, 16
Asset utilization ratios
  accounts payable to cost of sales, 14
  accounts receivable to net sales, 13
  days' sales outstanding, 13–14
  efficiency, 11–15
  inventory turnover, 12–13
  return on assets, 12
  total asset turnover, 11–12, 21

Balance account management, 42
Benefit/cost ratio, 82
Bond rating, 110
Bonds, 108–11, 119, 164
Book value, 24–25, 151
Book-value capital structure, 132
Breakeven point, 173
Business cycles, and risk, 170

Calling, bonds, 110
Call protection, bonds, 110
Capital appreciation, 111

Capital asset pricing model, capital-market estimations, 126–30, 176
Capital budgeting
  cost-benefit analysis, investments, 73–76
  defined, 72
  incremental costs and benefits evaluation, 76–82
  investment choices, 82–94
  miscellaneous considerations, value creation, 99–102
Capital investments, 72, 78
Capitalization ratios
  acid-test, 18
  asset to equity, 16
  coverage, 19–20
  current, 18
  leverage, 15–16
  liquidity, 18
  long-term debt to equity, 17
  long-term debt to total assets, 17
  return on equity, 16–17
  total liabilities to assets, 18
Capital-market estimations, risk-premium methods, 124–30
Capital markets
  debt markets, 108–11
  equity markets, 111–16
  types of, 106–7
Capital structure, 113, 163
Cash balances investment, 42–43
Cash benefits, investments, 74
Cash budgets, 51, 52–54, 57
Cash flow coverage ratio, 19–20
Cash flow/debt-service coverage ratio, 169
Cash flow/interest coverage ratio, 168–69
Cash flow maximization, 112
Cash flows, affordability of debt and, 167–68
Cash flows analysis
  book value, 151
  earnings valuation method, 148–51

Cash flows analysis—*Cont.*
  liquidation value, 151
  present value method, 140–48
  replacement cost and market value, 152
Cash flow timing, discounting techniques,
    84–87
Cash flow valuation, dividend discount
    method, 120–24
Cash management, 40–43
Cash payments, investments, 74–76
Certainty equivalent, 92–93
Commercial paper, 46
Common stock, 111, 164
Comparative ratio analysis
  historical, 26–28
  with industry, 29–30
  with other companies, 29–30
Complex models, Lotus 1–2–3, 209–13
Component percentage analysis, 14–15, 18
Constant growth model, 123–24
Control, outside capital acquisition, 179–81
Construction, financial model, 195
Corporate value, leverage and, 185, 187
Cost-benefit analysis, investments, 73–76
Cost of capital
  capital markets, 106–16
  debt cost determination, 116–19
  debt markets, 108–11
  equity cost determination, 120–32
  equity markets, 111–16
  required return determinants, 106
  weighted-average calculation, 132–34
Cost of retained earnings, 131
Covenants, bonds, 110
Coverage ratios
  cash flow coverage, 19–20
  Cash flow/debt service coverage, 169
  Cash flow/interest coverage, 168–69
  debt service, 19
  earnings before interest and taxes, 10,
    19–20, 168–69, 173–75
Current ratio, 18
Cycles
  business, 170
  working capital, 35–40

Data tables creation, Lotus 1–2–3, 221–25
Days' sales outstanding ratio, 13–14
Debt capacity, 168
Debt cost determination, 116–19
Debt financing, 180–81
Debt markets, 108–11
Debt policy, 168

Debt-service coverage ratio, 20
Debt-service ratios, 19, 20
Deposit concentration, and cash
    management, 42
Depreciation
  Accelerated Cost Recovery System, 75–77,
    97
  and acquisition valuation, 145
  double-declining balance, 75–76, 77, 96,
    98
  straight-line, 75–77, 96
  and tax shield, 97
Disbursements management, 42
Disclosure regulations, financial statements,
    1–2
Discounting, 84
Discounting techniques, cash flow timing,
    84–87
Discount rate, 90, 105
Dividend discount, 122
Dividend discount method, cash flow
    valuation, 120–24
Dividend growth model, 122
Dividend income, 111
Dividend payout ratio, 7, 20
Dividend yield ratio, 25–26
Documentation, financial model, 195–96
Double-declining balance depreciation, 75–
    76, 77, 96, 98

Earnings, 2
Earnings before interest and taxes, 10, 19–
    20, 168–69, 173–75
Earnings before interest and taxes/sales
    ratio, 10
Earnings/interest coverage ratio, 168
Earnings per share, 22, 24, 172–79
Earnings retention ratio, 21
Earnings valuation method, acquisition
    valuation, 148–51
Efficiency ratio, 11–15
Efficient market, 112
Electronic funds transfer, and cash
    management, 41–42
Enable, 224
ENCORE!, 225
Entering model, Lotus 1–2–3, 201–9
Equity cost determination
  capital-market estimations, risk-premium
    methods, 124–30
  cash flow valuation, dividend discount
    method, 120–24
  miscellaneous concerns in, 130–32

Equity financing, and outside capital
    acquisition, 179–80
Equity markets, 111–16
Excel, 224
Expected value, 95

Factoring, 46
Financial modeling
    introduction to, 192–93
    model construction, validation, and
        documentation, 195–96
    modeling process, 193–96
    objectives determination, 193–94
    relationships definition, 194
    sensitivity analysis, 196–98
    variables specification, 194
Financial statement analysis
    asset utilization ratios, 10–15
    capitalization ratios, 15–20
    comparative ratio analysis, 26–30
    market ratios, 22, 23–26
    points of analysis, 6, 8
    profitability ratios, 8–10
    sustainable growth rate, 20–23
Financial statements
    changes in financial position, 3–4
    disclosure regulations regarding, 1–2
    earnings, 2
    financial position, 2–3
    projected, 51, 54, 57–60
    shareholders' equity, 4–6
Finished goods inventory, 40
Fixed-coupon bonds, 108
Float, 42
Floating interest rates, 108
Forecasting
    assumptions and methods involved in, 51–
        52, 60–68
    cash budgets, 51, 52–54, 57
    historical comparisons, 60, 63–64
    probability analysis, 68–69
    projected financial statements, 51, 54, 57,
        57–60
    sensitivity analysis, 64, 68
Framework, 224
Funds flow statement, 3
Futures market, 107
Future value, 84

Gearing, 16
Graphics, Lotus 1–2–3, 217–21
Gross margin, 9
Growth, sustainable, 20–23

Hedging/speculating, outside capital
    acquisition, 181–84
High-yield bonds, 110
Historical comparisons
    comparative ratio analysis, 26–28
    forecasting, 60, 63–64
Hurdle race, 90–91

Idle cash balances, 43
IFPS/Personal, 225
Illiquidity, 156
Illiquidity premium, 106
Implied price/earnings ratio, 150–51
Income, and outside capital acquisition,
    172–79
Income statement, 2
Incremental costs and benefits evaluation,
    76–82
Indenture agreement, bonds, 108
Independent investments, 77
Inflation
    and acquisition valuation, 145
    return for, 156
    and value of investments and revenues,
        100–102
    and working-capital management, 37–38
Insurance companies, 107
Internal rate of return, 85, 87–88
Internal Revenue Service, 113
Inventory turnover ratio, 12–13
Investment choices
    cash flow timing, discounting techniques,
        84–87
    ranking projects, 89–90
    risk and, 90–95
    simple valuation method, 82–83

Javelin, 225
Junk bonds, 110

Leasing, 185
Leverage
    and corporate value, 185, 187
    and cost of debt, 113–14
    defined, 15–16, 112
    and shareholders' risk, 176
    value of, outside capital, 157–63
Leverage ratios, 15–20
Line of credit, 45–46
Liquidation value, acquisition assets, 151–
    52

Lockboxes, and cash management, 41
London Interbank Offering Rate (LIBOR),
    108
Long-term debt to equity ratio, 17–18
Long-term debt to total assets ratio, 17–18
Lotus 1–2–3
    changing worksheet, 213–17
    complex models, 209–13
    data tables creation, 221–25
    entering model, 201–9
    getting started, 199–201
    graphics, 217–21
    worksheet changes, 213–17

Marginal debt cost, 119
Marginal value of acquisition
    without synergy, 140–42
    with synergy, 142–48
Market ratios
    dividend yield, 25–26
    earnings per share, 22, 24
    price/earnings, 24, 25
Market-to-book value ratio, 24–25
Market value, acquisition assets, 152
Market-value capital structure, 132
Maturity, bonds, 108
Merger activity, United States, 139–40
Monte Carlo simulation, 198
Moody's, 110, 111
Mortgage debt, 110
Multiplan, 224
Multiple-scenario analysis, 93–95
Mutual funds, 107
Mutually exclusive investments, 77

NASDAQ, 107
National Association of Securities Dealer
    107
Negative balance, 42
Net income and loss, 2
Net present value, 85–86, 98, 105
Net present value profile, 87–89
Net profit, 9
Net working capital, 3, 48
New equity issues, 130
New York Stock Exchange, 107
Nominal return, 106

Objectives, financial model, 193–94
Operating margin, 10
Optimal capital structure, 114, 163

Options market, 107
Outside capital acquisition
    leverage, value of, 157–63
    RICHS analysis, 163–64, 167–89
Over-the-counter market, 107

Par value, bonds, 108
Payables payment period, 14
Payback period, investment choices, 82–8:
Pension funds, 107
Percentage change analysis, 27–28
Preauthorized checks, and cash
    management, 42
Preferred stock, 111, 131–32
Present value, 84–87
Present value analysis, cash flows
    marginal benefit of acquisition with
        synergy, 142–48
    marginal value of acquisition without
        synergy, 140–42
Present value index, 86–87
Present value payback, 85
Pre-tax cost of debt, 117–18
Price/earnings ratio, 24, 25
Primary capital market, 106, 108
Private placements, capital, 107
Probability analysis, 68–69
Production-sales cycle, 35–40
Profitability ratios
    earnings before interest and taxes, 10,
        19–20
    earnings before interest and taxes/sales,
        10
    gross margin, 9–10
    operating margin, 10
    return on sales, 8–10, 16, 21
Profit and loss statement, 2
Profit margin, 9
Profits, 2
Projected financial statements, 51, 54, 57–
    60

Quattro, 224
Quick ratio, 18–19

Ranking investment projects, 89–90
Rate of return, 8
Ratios
    accounts payable to cost of sales, 14
    accounts receivable to net sales, 13
    acid-test, 18–19

Ratios—*Cont.*
  asset to equity, 16
  asset utilization, 10–15
  benefit/cost, 82
  capitalization, 15–20
  cash flow/interest coverage, 168–69
  coverage, 19–20
  current, 18
  days' sales outstanding, 13–14
  debt-service, 19, 20
  debt-service coverage, 20
  dividend yield, 25–26
  earnings before interest and taxes, 10
  earnings before interest and taxes
      coverage, 19–20
  earnings/interest coverage, 168
  earnings per share, 22, 24, 172–79
  earnings retention, 21
  efficiency, 11–15
  gross profit, 9–10
  implied price/earnings, 150–51
  inventory turnover, 12–13
  leverage, 15–20
  liquidity, 18
  long-term debt to equity, 17–18
  long-term debt to total assets, 17–18
  market, 22, 23–26
  market-to-book value, 24–25
  net profit, 9
  operating margin, 10
  price/earnings, 24, 25
  profitability, 8–10
  profit margin, 9
  quick, 18–19
  receivables collection period, 13–14
  return on assets, 12
  return on equity, 16–17
  return on sales, 8–10, 16, 24
  sustainable growth rate, 20–22
  total asset turnover, 11–12, 21
  total liability to assets, 18
  turnover, 11–15
Real return, 106
Receipts management, 41–42
Receivables collection period, 13–14
Refunding, bonds, 110
Relationships definition, financial model,
    194–95
Replacement cost, acquisition assets, 152
Replacement investment, 95–100
Retained earnings, 131
Return on assets ratio, 12
Return on equity ratio, 16–17
Return on investment, 122, 159

Return on sales ratio, 8–10, 16, 21
RICHS analysis
  control, 179–81
  defined, 163
  financing decision, 184
  hedging/speculating, 181–84
  income, 172–79
  leasing, 185
  leverage and corporate value, 185, 187
  risk to lenders, 167–72
Risk
  and business cycles, 170
  and investment choices, 90–95
  to lenders, 167–72
  return for, 156
  to shareholders, outside capital
      acquisition, 175–79
Risk-premium methods, capital-market
    estimations, 124–30

Sales growth, and working-capital
    management, 38–39
Secondary capital market, 106–7
Securities and Exchange Commission (SEC),
    107
Sensitivity analysis, 64, 68, 196–98
Shareholders' risk, outside capital
    acquisition, 175–79
Short-term debt, 17–18, 119
Simple valuation methods, investment
    choices, 82–83
Simulation, 68–69, 95, 98, 196
Sinking fund, 20, 109–10
Sources and uses of funds statement, 3–4
Spontaneous investments, 72
Standard & Poor's, 110, 111
Standard & Poor's 500 Index, 125
Statement of changes in financial position,
    3–4
Statement of changes in shareholders'
    equity, 4–6
Statement of earnings, 1
Statement of financial position, 2–3
Statement of retained earnings, 4–6
Stock, 111, 131–32, 164
Stock-bond yield-spread method, capital
    market estimations, 125–26
Straight-line depreciation, 75–77, 96
Subordinated debt, 111
Sunk cost, 75
SuperCalc, 4, 224
Sustainable growth rate, 20–23

Sustainable growth rate ratios
   dividend payout, 20
   earnings retention, 21
Symphony, 224

Tax shield, 97
Time value of money, 106
Total asset turnover ratio, 11–12, 21
Total liabilities to assets ratio, 18
Treasury bills, 43, 156, 181
Turnover ratio, 11–15
Twin, 224

Validation, financial model, 195
Variable sales demand, and working-capital
   management, 39–40
Variables specification, financial model, 194
VP-Planner, 224

Weighted-average cost of capital, 114, 132–
   34, 132–34
Working capital management
   cash balances investment, 42–43
   cash management, 40–43
   cycle defined, 35–36
   disbursement management, 42
   financing working-capital needs, 44–47
   inflation and, 37–38
   receipts management, 41–42
   sales growth and, 38–39
   variable sales demand and, 39–40
   work-capital needs minimization, 43–44
   working-capital cycle, 35–40
Worksheet changes, Lotus, 1–2–3, 213–17

Yield to maturity, bonds, 108

Zero-coupon bonds, 109

NOTES

NOTES

NOTES